Five Ways Patricia Can
Kill Her Husband

Five Ways Patricia Can Kill Her Husband

A Theory of Intentionality and Blame

LEO ZAIBERT

OPEN COURT
Chicago and La Salle, Illinois

To order books from Open Court, call 1-800-815-2280 or visit
www.opencourtbooks.com.

Open Court Publishing Company is a division of Carus Publishing Company.

Library of Congress Cataloging-in-Publication Data

Zaibert, Leo, 1966-
    Five ways Patricia can kill her husband : a theory of intentionality and blame
  / Leo Zaibert.
      p. cm.
    Includes bibliographical references and index.
    ISBN-13: 978-0-8126-9576-2 (trade paper : alk. paper)
    ISBN-10: 0-8126-9576-3 (trade paper : alk. paper)
    1. Blame. 2. Intention—Moral and ethical aspects. I. Title.

BJ1471.5.Z35 2005
170'.42—dc22   2005015102

For Elizabeth

Contents

Acknowledgments

This book is a distant descendant of my 1997 doctoral dissertation in the Department of Philosophy at the State University of New York–Buffalo. In the intervening years, the dissertation underwent major modifications, and during these years I have become indebted to many people. I cannot possibly mention by name all of those who have helped me to refine my views. Thanks are due to my students at the University of Wisconsin–Parkside and the Universidad Simón Bolívar, to the various audiences who commented as I presented parts of this book in talks, and to those referees who, like anonymous donors, give without expecting any public praise, and who have considerably improved the present book. I would also like to expressly thank at least the following colleagues: Ken Alpern, Guyora Binder, James Brady, Rafael Tomás Caldera, Pablo DeGreiff, Markus Dubber, Antony Duff, George Fletcher, Newton Garver, Douglas Husak, Ingvar Johansson, John Longeway, Elizabeth Millán-Zaibert, Fabio Morales, John Searle, Barry Smith, and Aaron Snyder. While some of these people have been more closely connected with my project than others, the obligatory caveat applies equally to everyone: I alone deserve the blame for the infelicities and errors herein. I wish to thank Open Court, and in particular David Ramsay Steele and Cindy Pineo. Amongst those who have been more closely connected to the evolution of my views, I owe a special debt of gratitude to Elizabeth, to Barry, and to Aaron, for their enthusiastic support and for their many suggestions, both of which have shaped this book in innumerable ways. By and large, the book in its current form was written in Leipzig, Germany, as I enjoyed a research fellowship funded by the Alexander von Humboldt Foundation; I gratefully acknowledge its generous support.

Parts of chapter 2 have been previously published in my "Intentionality, Voluntariness, and Criminal Liability: A Historical-Philosophical Analysis," *Buffalo Criminal Law Review* 1, vol. 2 (1998): 459–500 (reprinted in *Aristotle and Modern Law*, ed. James Bernard Murphy and Richard O.

Brooks, 263–304 [London: Ashgate/Dartmouth, 2003]). Parts of chapter 6 have been previously published in my "Intentions, Promises, and Obligations," in *John Searle*, ed. Barry Smith, Contemporary Philosophy in Focus, 53–84 (Cambridge: Cambridge University Press, 2003).

Introduction

This book is about the relationship between mental states—that is, things like desires, beliefs, emotions, and, above all, intentions—and the normative assessment of wrongdoing. These mental states allow us to pass judgment regarding the blameworthiness of these instances of wrongdoing; I shall refer to the theory that articulates the blameworthiness of instances of wrongdoing by attending to the mental states people have when they do wrong as a theory of culpability.

Piecemeal treatments of isolated aspects of theories of culpability are, in many contexts, almost inescapable, and indeed abound in the philosophical literature. But in chapter 1 I try to show the conceptual unity of culpability, and the usefulness of treating it comprehensively and, to the extent that it is possible, independently of related issues having to do rather with responsibility, accountability, liability, and so forth, with which culpability is commonly confused. The crucial feature of culpability is that it is concerned exclusively with the *intentional* (in a sense to be explained in chapter 1) mental states that we have *at the time* we act. Also in chapter 1 I put forth what I take to be the central principle of any theory of culpability, a principle attuned to some fundamental aspects of our common-sense psychology. The reactions I have witnessed to this principle range from the claim that it is so obviously false that it is absurd, to the claim that it is so obviously true that it is trivial. At any rate, I shall show that something resembling this principle has been the object of major controversy throughout history, and that the exact ways in which mental states affect the degree of blameworthiness of our actions remain controversial.

In chapters 2 and 3, I seek to present an analysis of intentionality and blame situated in a historical context. While this historical approach is not, strictly speaking, absolutely necessary for the deployment of the analysis of mental states and their relationship to the blameworthiness of our actions, it surely is at least valuable. The history of theories of culpability

1

that I present in what follows has not been told; some of the sources, and all too frequently some of the very passages upon which I focus, have been discussed by others without their bearings upon theories of culpability having received much-deserved attention.

I begin this historical investigation at the times when *lex talionis* held sway, a period in which many believe mental states were of no importance in determining the blameworthiness of action. Canvassing some key developments in Greek, Roman, medieval, and modern thinkers, I conclude the historical investigation with an analysis of contemporary theories of culpability. My historical account does not seek to be comprehensive, but rather to call attention to a common thread in the history of culpability in the West. The study of problems regarding theories of culpability with which past scholars grappled is a valuable means for understanding contemporary problems. As we shall see, there are connections between Aristotle's definition of *akousios* actions, for example, and the contemporary concept of recklessness; Bentham's concept of oblique intention is related to the doctrine of double effect and to the contemporary "felony murder rule"; Paulus's aphorism *Magna negligentia culpa est: magna culpa dolus est* can be seen as a forerunner to contemporary debates about the normativity of mental states and the blameworthiness of negligent behavior, and so on.

Although even the historical aspects of my project are undergirded by analytical concerns, it is in chapter 4 where I begin to develop the most conspicuously analytical account of culpability. As shall become clear in what follows, the discussion of intentional action has been historically tied up with the discussion of voluntary action, so in chapter 4 I argue that it is important to separate the two discussions and suggest a way of doing so. One influential philosophical theory, the volitional theory of action, defines action by attending to the presence of a special intentional mental state: a volition. Although the most promising accounts of the volitional theory of action assert that volitions are a species of intentions, volitions remain rather mysterious intentional states in that they are exclusively concerned with bodily movements, and thus I reject volitional theories of action. In chapter 4, then, I undertake to explain the way in which intentions figure in the definition of action, and the descriptive and normative implications of the distinctions between (1) action and nonaction, (2) voluntary action and involuntary movements, (3) intended and unintended action, and (4) intentional and unintentional action.

The relationship between having intentions and doing things intentionally is particularly subtle and complicated. In chapter 5 I try to clarify this relationship. I defend the view that intending to *X* is not necessary in order to do *X* intentionally. And I furthermore argue that while the distinction between intentional and unintentional action does not map exactly unto the distinction between intended and unintended action, it shares with the latter a certain exhaustiveness regarding its way of breaking down the realm of action. Since the distinction between intentional and unintentional action serves normative purposes, then, theories which postulate the existence of additional ways of acting which are not subtypes of these two general ways, but fail to explain what are the normative implications of those additional ways of acting, are problematic.

In chapter 6 I present an analysis of intentions, and argue that the very logical structure of intentions gives rise to nontrivial normative claims. It is not a coincidence that throughout history theories of culpability have focused upon intentions, for, among all intentional states, intentions have the closest relationship to actions. Moreover, intentions are also very closely related to rationality. These two connections combine together in explaining why intentions have such important normative force that they properly constitute the skeleton of theories of culpability. Intentions commit us, and although these are by no means the only commitments that we have, they nevertheless speak about who we are, and specifically as to how much blame we deserve for our wrongdoing.

Finally, in chapter 7 I present an analysis of blaming. While of course we can blame people "to their face," I focus upon the purely mental, private phenomenon of blaming people for their wrongdoing. The overwhelming tendency in the specialized literature is to run together the phenomenon of blaming with its communication, and with punishing, insofar as it is typically believed that studying purely mental blame is not by itself useful. This tendency is so powerful that even authors who claim to be exclusively interested in the mental phenomenon of blaming conflate private blaming with its communication and with punishment. In contrast, I shall argue that analyzing the mental phenomenon of blaming is extremely valuable, insofar as such analysis reveals what exactly it is to blame someone, independently of whether or not one does something about the fact that one believes that someone is blameworthy. In this last chapter I offer an analysis of blame. I try to answer the question: What happens "inside someone's mind" when she blames someone else's wrongdoing? I argue that blaming entails endorsing a set of beliefs and also that blaming entails experiencing an irreducible emotion. I conclude by discussing the theoretical and practical implications of my account of blame.

[1]

On Culpability:
The Logic of Blame

The central question that this book seeks to answer is how it is possible to apportion different degrees of blame to agents who bring about identical evil outcomes. In the course of answering this question I shall make explicit some fundamental aspects of the moral psychology of wrongdoing that seem to have escaped those who have attempted to answer this question. The way in which I pose the question attests to the fact that I assume that it is indeed possible to blame agents who bring about identical evil outcomes more or less severely. This assumption coheres nicely with many deep-seated intuitions. While throughout the book I shall stress that there are important differences between blaming and punishing, taking a look, at the outset, at the institution of punishment is helpful for my purposes, since such a look lends strength and plausibility to my assumption. After all, criminal legislation based on precisely this assumption exists all around the globe and has so existed throughout history. The central distinction between *actus reus* (roughly: guilty act) and *mens rea* (roughly: guilty mind) allows for punishing differently, say, one and the same homicide depending on considerations regarding the mental states that the defendant had at the time she acted. These differences in the severity of punishment are the result, to a great extent, of the more fundamental distinctions of blameworthiness with which I am here concerned. My goal in what follows, then, is to explain how and why these differences in blameworthiness come about.

In order to make this daunting enterprise manageable, I shall at the outset attempt to specify the exact scope of my project. First, I would like to say a couple of things about the expression "evil outcome." I do not wish to discuss which specific outcomes should be considered evil in the first place. I use "evil outcome," and similar expressions like "bad thing," "wrongdoing," "bad act," and so forth, in as naturalistic and neutral a way as I possibly can. I wish to refer to those actions that are considered either immoral, illegal, prohibited, unfortunate, unbecoming, infelicitous, or in any way viewed negatively *within a given context*, even if within other con-

5

texts they would be viewed positively. We can blame people for things that we consider bad in this very neutral and general sense and not only for things that are immoral or sinful or vicious in a full-blown sense. Though the notions of "evil outcome" or "bad thing" I use here are clearly normative, they are not thick normative notions, in the sense that they do not commit me to any comprehensive moral doctrine whatsoever. I shall discuss these notions again in the last chapter of the book, but now I would like to echo Bernard Williams, who has expressed this idea eloquently: "People can be blamed for missing their opportunities or making mistakes, and they can be blamed by non-moralizing people. For example, one partner to a bank-robbery may ruin it by an idiotic mistake and be blamed by his companion for the fact that they are in jail."[1]

The sense of blame with which Williams is concerned, just like the sense of blame with which I am concerned in this book, is not the purely "diagnostic" sense of blame as "when we blame the valve for the failure of the rocket"; it is a normative sense of blame. Yet, the companion of the idiotic bank robber "does not think that [his companion's mistake] was an offence against moral canons." There clearly is "something in the idea that the failure . . . has some kind of ethical dimension to it."[2] After all, "when the failure is explained, it seems that for blame to be appropriate, there must be some generally reprehensible characteristic involved in the explanation: the agent must have been careless, or lazy, or self-serving, or something of the sort."[3] Williams's reference to "reprehensible characteristics," followed by an open-ended list of such characteristics, is sufficient to suggest how diverse and multifarious these characteristics are. Indeed, there are innumerable factors affecting the judgments of blame that we pass upon people for the bad things they do. I shall concentrate upon one cluster of factors: the mental states that the agent has at the time that the act occurs. A theory of culpability, as I shall here understand the expression, is concerned with the ways in which the mental states a person has when she brings about an evil outcome allow for blaming her more or less severely for bringing it about. By "blame" or "blaming" I mean the *mental* phenomenon of *judging* that someone who acts in this or that way deserves condemnation. As we shall see, most studies of blame focus on its communication or on its relationship with punishment, not on the mental phenomenon of blaming itself.

A theory of culpability, as I understand it, is part and parcel of a larger philosophical enterprise: the study of the *Intentionality* of mental phe-

---

1. Bernard Williams, *Making Sense of Humanity and Other Philosophical Papers 1982–1993* (Cambridge: Cambridge University Press, 2003), 40.
2. Bernard Williams, *Making Sense of Humanity*, 40.
3. Bernard Williams, *Making Sense of Humanity*, 40.

nomena. By uppercase Intentionality I refer to that feature of *mental* phenomena whereby they represent states of affairs, that is, to that feature whereby mental phenomena are "about" or "directed at" or "of" states of affairs. By lowercase intentionality I shall refer to a very complex feature of *actions* (rather than of mental phenomena) whereby they are related (in ways which will become clear in due course) to intentions.[4] Intentions, it should be clear, are just one Intentional state among many: desires, hopes, fears, and many other mental phenomena are also Intentional; but, for my purposes, the relationship between Intentionality and intentionality shall prove to be crucial.

Although I shall come back to these issues later on, I would like to present a brief outline of the basic structure of the analysis of Intentional states that I seek to carry out. Many Intentional states have "conditions of satisfaction"; these are the events that would need to obtain in order for the Intentional state to "succeed." For example, my desire that it should rain has as conditions of satisfaction that it rain; my fear that it is too late is satisfied if it is too late, my believing that there is a bird in front of me is satisfied if there is a bird in front of me, my hoping to write a good book is satisfied if I write a good book, and so on. Many Intentional states thus exhibit what is known in the specialized literature as "direction of fit." There are mainly two directions of fit: mind-to-world, or world-to-mind.

G. E. M. Anscombe, famously, illustrated these two directions of fit by distinguishing between a list made by someone who goes to the store to buy groceries, and the list made by someone whose job it is to spy on the first one and compose a list of everything he buys. If there are discrepancies between the shopper's list and what he bought, it is the shopper's mistake, namely, he failed to get some of the items listed, but if there are discrepancies between the spy's list and what the shopper bought, then the mistake is in the list he composed, namely, he failed to list items that the shopper had bought.[5] Similarly, Searle has usefully evoked the story of Cinderella in order to explain the notion of direction of fit: "If Cinderella goes into a shoe store to buy a new pair of shoes, she takes her foot size as a given and seeks shoes to fit (shoe-to-foot direction of fit). But when the prince seeks the owner of the shoe, he takes the shoe as given and seeks a foot to fit in the shoe (foot-to-shoe direction of fit)."[6]

In order for my belief that there is a bird in front of me to be satisfied, it needs to be the case that there is a bird in front of me; my belief needs

---

4. I borrow the distinction between uppercase Intentionality and lowercase intentionality from John Searle. See John R. Searle, *Intentionality: An Essay in the Philosophy of Mind* (Cambridge: Cambridge University Press, 1983), 3ff. and passim.
5. See G. E. M. Anscombe, *Intention* (Oxford: Basil Blackwell, 1957). See also I. L. Humberstone, "Direction of Fit," *Mind* 101 (1992): 59–83.
6. Searle, *Intentionality*, 8, n. 2.

to fit the world that exists independently of my beliefs: beliefs thus have a mind-to-world direction of fit. In contrast, however, in order for my intention to write a book to be satisfied I need to carry out my intention, making the world conform to what I intend: intentions have a world-to-mind direction of fit. Other Intentional states, such as regretting and admiring, have no clear direction of fit (although these are complex Intentional states whose parts might themselves have direction of fit). The explanatory potential of this seemingly simple framework for analyzing Intentional states is considerable, as will become clear later in the book.

Two main elements in my account of a theory of culpability stand out: the concern with *degrees* of blameworthiness and the concern with Intentionality. These two elements serve to conceptually distinguish theories of culpability from related theories with which theories of culpability are commonly confused, such as theories of responsibility, theories of accountability, theories of appraisability, and the like.

Although theories of culpability rarely receive comprehensive, systematic attention, moral and legal philosophers pervasively discuss them, albeit partially and in passing. Works dealing with punishment or with responsibility or with desert or with liability almost necessarily have to deal with some aspect or another of a theory of culpability.[7] For example, the classical debate regarding the justification of punishment, that is, the debate between retributivists and consequentialists, is actually inseparable from the discussion of culpability in ways that I shall discuss in due course. Yet, though specific aspects of theories of culpability are virtually unanimously admitted to be of utmost importance, most authors tend to skip the discussion of theories of culpability proper, as they simply discuss some aspects of culpability in piecemeal fashion. The very existence of a theory of culpability is not typically acknowledged—even by authors who discuss some of its central aspects rather extensively. For example, Joel Feinberg in his influential *Doing and Deserving* tells us: "There should be a conventional name for that branch of philosophy which straddles ethics, philoso-

---

7. Works that discuss (issues pertaining to) culpability in sophisticated ways are: R. A. Duff, *Intention, Agency and Criminal Liability* (Oxford: Oxford University Press, 1990); Joel Feinberg, *Doing and Deserving: Essays in the Theory of Responsibility* (Princeton: Princeton University Press, 1970); George P. Fletcher, *Rethinking Criminal Law* (Boston: Little, Brown and Company, 1978); Douglas Husak, *Philosophy of Criminal Law* (Totowa, NJ: Rowman and Littlefield, 1987); Leo Katz, *Bad Acts and Guilty Minds* (Chicago: University of Chicago Press, 1987); Michael Moore, *Placing Blame* (Oxford: Clarendon Press, 1997); Jeffrie G. Murphy and Jean Hampton, *Forgiveness and Mercy* (Cambridge: Cambridge University Press, 1988); and George Sher, *Desert* (Princeton, Princeton University Press, 1987). For all the many merits of these books, they do not seek to put forth a systematic theory of culpability like the one presented here.

phy of mind, and philosophy of law and concerns itself with such concepts as 'act,' 'cause,' 'harm,' 'blame,' and the like. On the model of 'the theory of knowledge' and 'the theory of value' (which studies problems which are no more well defined), I suggest 'the theory of responsibility.'"[8]

Feinberg does not tell us *exactly* what the concepts are with which his "theory of responsibility" must deal, but judging from those concepts he does mention, I think that there is either another good name for this indeed important branch of philosophy, or there is an important sub-branch of his theory of responsibility: namely, "theory of culpability." After all, theories of culpability are concerned with the degrees of blame that we pass upon agents for their wrongdoing and which stem from considerations having to do with the connections between (some of) their mental states and their actions. Theories of culpability, at least as much as theories of responsibility, "straddle" ethics, the philosophy of mind, and the philosophy of law; and these three branches of philosophy are the focus of this book. (I shall come back to the distinction between responsibility and culpability shortly.)

Similarly, in an epoch-making article, J. L. Austin, referring to this discipline that partakes of ethics, psychology, and legal theory, tentatively termed it a "theory of excuses." In the first lines of *A Plea for Excuses*, Austin tells us:

> The subject of this paper, *Excuses*, . . . is, or might be, the name of a whole branch, even a ramiculated branch, of philosophy . . . I am here using the word 'excuses' *for a title*, but it would be unwise to freeze too fast to this one noun and its partner verb: indeed for some time I used to use 'extenuation' instead. Still, on the whole 'excuses' is probably the most central and embracing term in the field, although this includes others of importance—'plea', 'defence', 'justification', and so on.[9]

Both from the perspective of the legal and ordinary uses of these terms, Austin's view seems inappropriate in that "excuse" is not the most general term. As a matter of fact, it is "defenses" that can be divided into justifications and excuses, and so the term "defenses" stands out as a better candidate for the name of that branch of philosophy which Austin is analyzing. And though Austin is one of the emblematic figures of ordinary language philosophy, it is not clear that even within ordinary language "excuse" is a more general term than "defense"; thus, a "theory of defenses" would

---

8. Feinberg, *Doing and Deserving*, vii.
9. J. L. Austin, "A Plea for Excuses," *Proceedings of the Aristotelian Society* (1957): 1. This piece has been reprinted many times, among others, in J. L. Austin, *Philosophical Papers* (London: Oxford University Press, 1970), 175–204.

have fit Austin's bill more nicely (though, as we shall see, a theory of culpability is much more narrow than a theory of defenses).

Surely Feinberg and Austin are after an important subject, a subject still in need of a great deal of clarification and analysis. In calling this subject "culpability," I am taking a cue from criminal law theory and history. The term itself is not as well known in the Anglo-American context (where the favored term is *mens rea*) as it is in the rest of the world. Unless otherwise noted, I shall use "*mens rea*" and "culpability" interchangeably, in spite of the fact that the standard use of *mens rea* is rather loose, failing to emphasize culpability's concern for degrees of blameworthiness. I do not wish to claim that Feinberg, or Austin, or for that matter anyone else, is wrong in choosing this or that name to refer to what I call a theory of culpability. What I wish to show is that theories of culpability are conceptually distinct from theories of responsibility, of justifications, or of excuses, and that this difference is not typically acknowledged.

Terms such as "responsibility" and "culpability" are frequently assumed to be synonymous; but I shall argue that they are not. The main difference between these two notions is roughly the following: a person is *responsible* whenever she is a moral agent and is therefore accountable for what she does. In standard cases no one can be more or less responsible. A given person is either responsible or is not responsible, in the sense that she is a moral agent or she is not, and the change of status occurs pretty much all at once. To claim that agency allows no degrees is not an uncommon move; *loci classici* of this sort of view are neo-Kantian ethical theories. Consider, for example, what Alan Gewirth says about this in his *Reason and Morality*: "there are degrees of approach to being prospective purposive agents, but there are not degrees of actually being such agents . . . agency is an absolute or noncomparative condition."[10] There might be complicated cases in which we might want to say that there is something like diminished capacity, say, regarding children: though children are not full-blown agents, neither are they nonagents. But in standard cases, involving adult human beings, issues of responsibility are typically nongradational.

A theory of responsibility, then, aims at showing how it is at all possible to pass judgments of blame (or of praise) upon people. In contrast, a theory of culpability assumes that there is an agent, that she has done

---

10. Alan Gewirth, *Reason and Morality* (Chicago: University of Chicago Press, 1978), 122, 141, and passim. Now, these approaches are not free from difficulties, of course. For a discussion of some of the problems with this view, particularly concerning the interplay between "potential," "prospective," and "full-blown" agency in Gewirth's work, see my "Normative Insufficiency of Gewirth's Principle of Generic Consistency," *Apuntes Filosoficos* 4 (1994): 195–210 (in Spanish).

something bad (in the sense of bad sketched above), and then explains the relationships between certain Intentional states of the agent and what she brought about, which allow us to pass a *more or less* stern judgment of blame upon her. Notice that it is culpability and not responsibility that explains how it is possible to have different degrees of blame attached to identical bad acts, and this is the main difference between the two notions: responsibility is concerned with the very possibility of blaming, whereas culpability is concerned with *degrees* of blame.

In highlighting the contours of the sorts of cases with which a theory of culpability is concerned, I wish to start by showing how these cases differ from related sets of phenomena. I shall distinguish the elements of a theory of culpability from excuses, from justifications, from mitigating circumstances, that is, from variegated forms of "extenuations" in the Austinian sense.[11] In so doing, the distinction between theories of culpability and other sorts of theories, such as theories of responsibility, theories of punishment, and normative ethical theories will emerge.

In developing these distinctions, the appeal to Intentional states is inevitable. The main Intentional state that shall occupy my attention, as noted, is intending. While my analysis of this and other Intentional phenomena is entrenched in contemporary philosophy of mind, I would like to state at the outset that I will ignore the debate about the ultimate ontological status of these phenomena: whether they can be reduced to cerebral states, or whether they are identical to those cerebral states, and so forth. I can altogether avoid the thorny discussion of the relationship between the mental and the cerebral. The comparative merits and demerits of behaviorism, functionalism, identity theories, monism, reductionism, and so on, do not affect my theory. From my perspective, if John wishes to kill Kim, for example, the ultimate ontological status of his relevant mental phenomena, that is, whether they can be reduced to neural firings, or whether they are identical to neural firings, and so forth, is not important. Quite simply, we believe certain things, we wish certain things, and we have certain intentions, and these phenomena are, from my perspective, unproblematic, indisputable aspects of our everyday experience; as Franz Brentano, one of the most important theorists of Intentionality, would have it, "no one can really doubt that a mental state which he perceives in himself exists, and that it exists just as he perceives it."[12] Consequently, my

---

11. As is clear from the passage quoted above, Austin was opposed to petty terminological discussions. I am too. But, though admittedly a small a point, given the technical meaning that the term "excuse" has within criminal law theory, Austin would have done better using "extenuations" instead of "excuses."

12. Franz Brentano, *Psychology from an Empirical Standpoint* (London: Routledge, 1995), 10.

avoidance of the discussion regarding the ultimate ontological status of these mental phenomena is justified (and innocuous) insofar as it allows me to focus on the analysis of the structures according to which we blame each other. The incorrigibility and other features of the Intentional phenomena that shall be the focus of my attention will also allow me to avoid other momentous debates in the philosophy of mind, such as the free will/determinism debate: whether or not we are really free to really choose, sometimes it seems to us as if we are really choosing, and we behave as if we really choose.

General Defenses and Modes of Culpability

Not all cases in which two identical actions that nevertheless yield different degrees of blame fall within the scope of a theory of culpability. Rather, a theory of culpability zeroes in on differences in blameworthiness that directly follow from considerations having to do with Intentionality. Theories of culpability identify sets of Intentional phenomena that could accompany the bringing about of an evil outcome and that give rise to more or less severe judgments of blame. These sets of Intentional phenomena are called modes of culpability.

Before presenting the sorts of situations covered by theories of culpability, that is, those situations in which the different degrees of blame are the result of the analysis of specific sets of Intentional phenomena, I will mention the types of cases that, although displaying differences in blameworthiness, are not relevant to a theory of culpability.

(1) Think of Susan, a doctor, who, while performing an operation and aiming at saving the life of a child, kills the child. Contrast her with Paul, a doctor, who kills his neighbor's child not in the course of practicing medicine, but because the child's crying at night bothers him. It is obvious that Paul deserves a much sterner condemnation than does Susan (in fact, Susan may perhaps not be blamed at all). Yet, the reason why this sort of case does not belong to a theory of culpability is that the rationale for a lesser degree of blame to Susan is not comprised exclusively of *Intentional states*. Rather, it is an external state of affairs: *the fact* that a child was dying and that Susan was attempting to save the child. Of course, "attempting to save" involves several mental states,[13] but we blame Susan leniently due to

---

13. On the importance of "attempting" and "trying" for the definition of action, see Brian O'Shaughnessy, "Trying (As the Mental 'Pineal Gland')," *Journal of Philosophy* 70: 365–86, and more generally his *The Will* (Oxford: Oxford University Press, 1980); and Jennifer Hornsby, *Actions* (London/Boston: Routledge & Kegan Paul, 1980), especially pp. 33–46.

a complex set of factors that includes mental states *and* states of affairs that are external to her mind.[14] To the extent that this type of case requires the analysis of these external states of affairs it does not really belong in a theory of culpability.

(2) Consider now Sarah, who kills a human being for sport. Contrast her with Daniel, who kills a human being in self-defense, that is, in order to prevent imminent and unjustifiable harm to himself that was not preventable in any other reasonable way. Again, Sarah's action is more blameworthy than Daniel's. And what explains why we apportion less blame to Daniel for his action (assuming we would blame him for his action at all), is *the fact* that he acted in self-defense.

Both cases, Susan's and Daniel's, can be seen as cases of justified behavior. But justifications of behavior are based on considerations about the states of affairs that surround a given act. To act in order to protect someone's life, including one's own, is a paradigmatic example of a justification. Typically, cases of justification admit of no degrees, in the sense that a given act is either justified or it is not justified. There could be degrees of imminence regarding the danger being averted, degrees of proportionality in the response, or degrees in many of the evidentiary aspects surrounding justifications, but not, in principle, regarding the justification of the act itself. Insofar as theories of justification require analyses of states of affairs (in addition to some analyses of mental states) and insofar as they are not inherently gradational, they differ from theories of culpability.

(3) Consider now Hannah, who wrongly (but somewhat reasonably) believes she is being attacked and then proceeds to kill her "attacker," assuming that she is acting in self-defense. Contrast her with Peter, a serial killer who kills for fun. Surely we would blame Hannah much more leniently than we would Peter, who just kills for pleasure. Yet, and unlike the previous example, it appears as if it is no longer *the fact* that she is acting in self-defense (for, technically speaking, she is not) which allows us to diminish (or perhaps to do away with) the condemnation for Hannah's act. But, here again what mitigates our blame is something partially outside the agent's mind (a state of affairs that she erroneously, though reasonably, believes to give rise to a justification).[15] Though cases of this sort—like

---

14. The talk of "external to the mind" has a Cartesian dualist ring to it, but since I am avoiding the discussion of the ontology of mental phenomena in general, I hope that it is clear that I embrace this talk simply for clarity of exposition.

15. For interesting discussions of the problem of distinguishing between excuses and justifications, and also that of distinguishing between putative justification and putative defense, see Fletcher, *Rethinking Criminal Law*, 759–875, especially pp. 762–74; and Albin Eser and George P. Fletcher, eds., *Justification and Excuse: Comparative Criminal Law Theory* (Freiburg: Max Planck Institute), 1987.

cases that are the concern of a theory of culpability—exhibit a clearly gradational normative nature, they also include relevant aspects that are not mental: namely, the state of affairs whereby there exists an intruder who is wrongly, though reasonably, believed to be an attacker. Thus, cases of this sort also fall beyond the scope of a theory of culpability.

(4) Albert, a thirty-five-year-old lawyer, commits a murder; and so does Lisa, a thirteen-year-old schoolgirl. In all likelihood, we would blame Albert more severely than we would Lisa. But this is another type of variation in the severity of the judgment of blame that falls beyond the scope of a theory of culpability. The rationale for blaming Lisa less severely than we blame Albert is that Lisa has not developed the psychological capacities that would allow her to fully understand the distinction between right and wrong. Lisa would receive such a treatment regardless of whether or not she enjoyed, intended, or foresaw what she did, that is, regardless of many mental states she might have had at the time she acted. The more lenient condemnation for Lisa is not the result of an analysis of her mental states at the time she acted, but of an analysis of her mental capacities. The distinction between mental states and mental capacities should be clear and unproblematic. The logical relations between states and capacities in general obviously hold here as well. Having this or that mental capacity might be a necessary condition for having this or that mental state, but it is never a sufficient condition: having this or that mental state is a sufficient indication of the presence of this or that mental capacity, but it might not be a necessary indication.

(5) Contrast now Mary and Joan. Mary kills her husband because she finds him engaged in lascivious acts with their daughter. Joan kills her husband because she grew bored of him. It is obvious that the pain that Mary experienced as a result of the behavior of her husband affects how severely we blame her for behaving in the way she did—if we blame her at all. But, mitigating circumstances, such as Mary's reasonable indignation, fall, almost by definition, beyond the scope of a theory of culpability: circumstances and states of affairs that are external to the agent's mind are not important for a theory of culpability. Mitigating circumstances sometimes include mental states (experiencing pain is a good example of this) but they are invariably linked to some external states of affairs that cause that mental state.[16]

---

16. Difficult cases can arise. Modify this example so that Mary is misperceiving the situation; there is nothing strange going on between her husband and daughter. Here, it might be argued, there is just the pain, a mental state, and so it might be argued that this sort of case is of concern for a theory of culpability. But this is not true, because for any sort of extenuation to be successful either a state of affairs external to the agent's mind, the one which is misperceived, is necessary, or the extenuation is the result of the agent not having the mental capacity of distinguishing reality from illusion. Either way, this sort of case falls beyond the scope of culpability.

While the *reasons* that the characters in the examples above have for acting are radically and significantly different, reasons are not themselves Intentional states. From the perspective of a theory of culpability, whatever considerations distinguish these cases are not important. Considerations having to do with reasons are extremely important in other respects. But, for reasons that shall become clearer as we move along, and for general considerations regarding conceptual clarity, I wish to focus only on Intentional phenomena.

There is an Intentional phenomenon in relation to which all these cases are similar, and it is precisely this similarity which best explains why they fall beyond the scope of a theory of culpability. The characters in these examples have all acted with the *intention* of bringing about more or less exactly what they in fact brought about. When Mary, consumed by anger, decides to kill her husband, she acts with the intention of killing him, just as Joan, Albert, and the rest of the main characters in the previous examples do. So, with respect to this crucial mental state accompanying the agents' actions, these cases are hard to distinguish.

Some authors distinguish between different types of intentions attending to temporal considerations. John R. Searle, for example, distinguishes between "prior intentions" and "intentions-in-action"; Michael Bratman distinguishes between present-directed intentions and future-directed intentions; R. A. Duff calls prior intentions "bare intentions" and adds a third type of intention called "further intentions," which functions analogously to reasons for action or motives.[17] Although prior or bare intentions and intentions-in-action are clearly Intentional states (future intentions might be more complicated cases), the theory of culpability I seek to develop focuses on intentions-in-action (as shall become clear immediately, other Intentional states are relevant to my theory, but not other types of intentions).[18] And, then, since in the preceding cases the structures of the intentions-in-action are not relevantly different, these cases do not fall within the scope of my theory of culpability.

I have no principled objection to the broadening of the scope of theories of culpability; I am not interested either in suggesting that the sorts of problems with which my theory of culpability is concerned are more important than those other problems that I avoid. I restrict the scope of my project simply in order to make it manageable. Let me illustrate, then,

---

17. See Michael Bratman, *Intention, Plans, and Practical Reason* (Cambridge, MA.: Harvard University Press, 1987), passim; Duff, *Intention, Agency, and Criminal Liability*, 38ff.; Searle, *Intentionality*, 83ff.

18. I argue against temporally distinguishing between different types of intention in chapter 6 and in my exchange with John R. Searle, Barry Smith, and Josef Moural. See John R. Searle et al., "Rationality in Action: An Exchange," *Philosophical Explorations* 4, no. 2 (2001): 66–94.

the cases that are the focus of my theory of culpability. Consider the following five additional cases, exemplifying five different ways in which Patricia can bring about the death of her husband.

(6) She sets fire to her apartment because she intends to kill her husband.

(7) She sets fire to her apartment, not intending to kill her husband, but intending to destroy the apartment (for whatever reason) but knowing that her husband is inside the apartment and will in all likelihood die in the fire.

(8) She sets fire to her apartment not intending to kill her husband, just intending to destroy the apartment (again for whatever reason) though this time she is not certain that her husband is inside; she suspects that it is likely that he is inside, and this suspicion is not enough to dissuade her from carrying out her intention.

(9) She forgets to turn off the stove, and as a result the apartment is set on fire and her husband is killed. She intends neither to kill her husband nor to set a fire, and she is unaware that she is actually killing him or even creating a fire.

(10) She turns on her TV set because she intends to watch the news; the TV set subsequently malfunctions, it explodes, and it causes a fire. As in (9), she has the intention neither to kill her husband nor to cause a fire.

Assuming that the outcome is identical in each case (the husband dies in the fire), we still blame Patricia differently in each case, in spite of the fact that there are no justifications, excuses, or mitigating circumstances in any of these cases. Why? Because Patricia's Intentional states in each case are relevantly different. In (6) she intends to kill her husband; in (7) she does not intend to kill him, but she is pretty much certain that she will kill him; in (8) she does not intend to kill him, though she is risking killing him; and in (9) and (10) she does not intend to kill him and is unaware that she is doing so.

Case 10 seems to be a case in which the set of Intentional states accompanying Patricia's action seems not to warrant any blame whatsoever. Her bringing about the death of her husband was a mere accident, and thus this specific set of Intentional states yields no blameworthiness: (10) exemplifies a mere accident for which she is not to blame. Cases 6, 7, 8, and 9 roughly map onto the modes of culpability of the Anglo-American legal tradition. They correspond to what the Model Penal Code calls "purpose," "knowledge," "recklessness," and "negligence," respectively.[19] A mode of

---

19. American Law Institute, *The Model Penal Code and Commentaries* (Philadelphia: American Law Institute, 1985), vol. 1, pp. 225–27 (MPC § 2.02). The appeal to the Model Penal Code is merely expository; I am not committed to the view that the Model Penal Code is the last word on these matters.

culpability, a crucial concept for my purposes, is a description of a set of Intentional states a person has when she acts that corresponds to a certain degree of blameworthiness in the way in which the bad action is done. Modes of culpability are not, strictly speaking, extenuations in the same sense that justifications, excuses, and mitigating circumstances are extenuations. Independently of any other factors, these modes of culpability give us clues as to the blameworthiness of Patricia's involvement in the death of her husband. Referring to "five ways" in the title of this book is not to be interpreted as a suggestion that there are only five modes of culpability, but merely that these five (the four which map onto the Anglo-American legal tradition together with the case of a pure accident) are perhaps the most conspicuous, belonging to any plausible theory of culpability. Ceteris paribus, from top to bottom, the degree of blame we attach to Patricia in each of these examples decreases (we shall study subtle and interesting exceptions to this hierarchy below). Why? This is the question I am interested in answering.

The Basic Structure of a Theory of Culpability

As stated below, a theory of culpability is concerned with the Intentionality of some mental states, above all that of intentions. At the outset of his groundbreaking *Intentionality*, a book that, as shall be clear in the later chapters of this book, greatly influences my own work, Searle warns us not to be misled by the obvious connection between Intentionality and intentions: "intendings and intentions are just one form of Intentionality among others, they have no special status."[20] Searle is right in that intentions are no more Intentional than any other Intentional states: perceptions, beliefs, and desires are as Intentional as intentions. But there is a different sense in which intentions are indeed special: they are the most important Intentional state in a theory of culpability. This is so because, as we shall see in due course, intentions are the Intentional state most directly connected to action, and theories of culpability tell us how severely to blame people for their evil actions.[21]

---

20. Searle, *Intentionality*, 3.
21. Indeed, so linked are intentions to actions that even the most sophisticated analyses of, say, certain types of intentions actually confuse them with certain types of actions. See, for example, my "Collective Intentions and Collective Intentionality," *American Journal of Sociology and Economics* 60, no. 1 (2003): 209–32, reprinted in *Searle and the Institutions of Social Reality*, ed. Lawrence Moss and David Koepsell, 209–32 (Oxford: Blackwell, 2003), where I suggest that Searle himself might have confused intentions and actions.

Ceteris paribus, to bring about a certain evil outcome with the intention to bring it about is, prima facie, never less blameworthy than to bring it about without such intention. It may appear more natural to express this idea using the adverbs "intentionally" and "unintentionally" rather than the perhaps cumbersome locution "with the intention of." But I wish to resist this natural inclination. The ordinary usage of the distinction between acting intentionally and acting unintentionally is hopelessly confused. In saying that someone did *X* intentionally (or unintentionally) we typically conflate two different enterprises: (1) the description of the way in which an agent did it, and (2) some sort of indication of the way in which the agent should be blamed for this (assuming of course that *X* is a bad thing in the sense explained at the outset). I think that it is sufficiently clear that saying "He broke the vase intentionally" could in some contexts have either descriptive or normative connotations (or, perhaps most commonly, both).

I shall make use of Duff's important distinction between the "intended" and the "[lowercase] intentional" in order to avoid the muddled talk of (lowercase) intentionality.[22] I am not sure that Duff and I agree entirely on the nature of the distinction between the intended and the intentional, for Duff believes that "intended agency reveals the core meaning of the concept of intention; the idea of intentional agency involves an extension of that core meaning."[23] I do not believe that, in general, the talk of intentional action (or agency) simply expands the core meaning of "intention," which is captured more fully by intended action (or agency). What I shall claim is that the notion of intended action is purely descriptive (though it has normative implications), whereas the notion of intentional action is frequently *simultaneously* descriptive and normative. To say that someone intended to bring about *X* is purely to describe the way in which she did it; it is to say that she had the intention of bringing it about. To say that someone's bringing about an evil outcome was unintended would be to say that she did not intend to bring it about. To say that someone brought about an evil outcome intentionally is a muddled way of both describing and pronouncing judgment as to the blameworthiness of her action. I shall, for these reasons, sometimes talk about intendedness, about intended action, and about doing things intendedly, meaning something quite specific, and quite different from intentional action and doing things intentionally. Moreover, since I will argue that it is possible to do *X* intentionally-and-unintendedly, and perhaps also to do *X* intendedly-and-unintentionally, it is clear to me that "intentional" is not part of the core meaning of "intention."

---

22. Duff, *Intention, Agency and Criminal Liability*, 43ff.
23. Duff, *Intention, Agency and Criminal Liability*, 43ff.

Typically, then, the distinction between intentional and unintentional conflates two distinctions: (1) the distinction between the intended and the unintended; and (2) some loose (and clumsy, as we shall see immediately) variant of the distinction between the more blameworthy and the less blameworthy. There is a sense in which we could all gain from simply abandoning the distinction between intentional and unintentional; when we wished to merely describe we would use the talk of intended action, when we wished to indicate blameworthiness we would just talk about blameworthiness (or culpability). I am not interested in linguistic diatribes. I do need, however, to clarify the exact scope of the operative terms of the theory of culpability advanced herein.

Contemporary philosophers have shown great interest regarding the naturalistic fallacy, that is, the fallacy of invalidly "deriving" normative statements from merely descriptive statements, or, as the famous slogan has it, deriving "ought" from "is."[24] Here I am interested in another aspect of the relationship between normativity and description: some expressions are not wholly descriptive or wholly normative. The context in which the expression is used of course has a lot to do with its exact import. Hilary Putnam, notoriously, has encapsulated the interplay between normativity and description as follows: "every fact is value loaded and every one of our values loads some fact."[25] While I suspect that it is an exaggeration to claim that every fact is value loaded (think of "squares have four sides"), Putnam offers some enlightening examples of what he has in mind: "'Jealous' may be a term of blame and may be used without any intention to blame at all. . . . The use of the word 'inconsiderate' seems to me a very fine example of the way in which the fact/value distinction is hopelessly fuzzy in the real world and in the real language."[26] To claim that an agent did *X* intentionally typically contains, in a fuzzy way, descriptive and normative elements. Sometimes, as I shall argue is the case of intentional action, the failure to recognize the fuzzy boundaries between normativity and description gives rise to difficulties.

I take the distinction between intended and unintended action, in contrast, to be purely descriptive, though it has crucially important normative consequences. Whether someone is, say, eighteen years old, is just an empirical, descriptive issue, though this empirical issue has obvious normative implications (having the right to vote, to run for office, to drive,

---

24. For an excellent compilation of articles dealing with the is/ought question, see: W. D. Hudson, ed., *The Is/Ought Question: A Collection of Papers on the Central Problem of Moral Philosophy* (London: MacMillan, 1963).
25. Hilary Putnam, *Reason, Truth and History* (Cambridge: Cambridge University Press, 1981), 201.
26. Putnam, *Reason, Truth and History*, 138–39.

etc.). To say that intentional wrongdoing is more blameworthy than unintentional wrongdoing is, in a sense, tautological and to that extent uninformative. But to say that intended wrongdoing is more blameworthy than unintended wrongdoing is not tautological, and precisely why this is so is what I shall explain in this book.

One further problem with the standard way in which the normative elements found in the sloppy talk of intentional action play out is that the nature of the distinction between the intentional and unintentional is frequently assumed to be nongradational. Yet, to say that "she did it intentionally" is not simply to say that she is blameworthy, but to say that she should be blamed *more* severely than otherwise; to say that "she did it unintentionally" is not simply to say that she is not to be blamed, but to say that she should be blamed *less* severely than otherwise.

For all the intuitive appeal of the obvious gradational normativity contained in the talk of intentional and unintentional action, this normativity has nonetheless been systematically misunderstood. Frequently, intentional action is understood in nongradational terms as something along the lines of "action for which one is accountable," or "action for which one is responsible." A corollary of sorts then naturally flows from this flawed view according to which it is *only* for intentional actions that one can be punished. Consider Socrates' reply to Melitus's charge of corrupting the youth in *The Apology*: "Either I have not a bad influence [on Athenian youth], or it is unintentional, so that in either case your accusation is false. And if I unintentionally have a bad influence, the correct procedure in cases of such involuntary misdemeanors is not to summon the culprit before this court, but to take him aside for instruction and reproof, because obviously if my eyes are opened, I shall stop doing what I do not intend to do."[27]

Another famous trial has elicited reactions from well-known philosophers that are grounded on the same erroneous assumption that only intentional actions are punishable. Consider Hannah Arendt's dictum as she reported Adolf Eichmann's trial for *The New Yorker*: "Foremost among the larger issues at stake in the Eichmann trial was the assumption current in all modern legal systems that *intent* to do wrong is *necessary* for the commission of a crime. On nothing, perhaps, has civilized jurisprudence prided itself more than on this taking into account of the

---

27. Plato, *Apology*, 26a, in *Plato: The Collected Dialogues*, trans. Hugh Tredennick (Princeton: Princeton University Press, 1961), 12. Note that this passage conflates intentionality and voluntariness, a distinction that shall occupy my attention in chapter 2. See also my "Intentionality, Voluntariness, and Culpability: A Historical-Philosophical Analysis," *Buffalo Criminal Law Review* 1, no. 2: 459–501, and in the same issue see A. P. Simester, "On the So-Called Requirement for Voluntary Action," 403–31.

subjective factor. Where this intent is absent . . . we feel that no crime has been committed."[28]

Arendt is wrong in suggesting that where there is no intention there is no crime. What is true is that where the crime is committed intendedly, then, ceteris paribus, it in principle gives rise to a more severe judgment of blame than if committed unintendedly. (There is a complicated issue regarding the ways in which these passages seem to conflate blame and punishment, which I will discuss in the next section.)

There is a passage in *The Metaphysics of Morals* in which Kant appears to be making a similar mistake: "An *unintentional* transgression which can still be imputed to an agent is called a mere *fault* (*culpa*). An *intentional* transgression (i.e., one accompanied by consciousness of its being a transgression) is called a *crime* (*dolus*)."[29] It is of course false that crimes can only be committed intendedly; the concomitant and widespread view that we ought to be punished only for those acts which we intend to do is also false.

The confusion regarding punishment stems from a more fundamental confusion regarding blame, namely, that one ought only to be blamed for what one does intendedly. Whether an action is intended or not is indeed crucially important for establishing how sternly it should be blamed. The normative force of the distinction is extraordinarily appealing; it is the sort of bedrock intuition that unbiased rational beings, say, deliberating behind a Rawlsian veil of ignorance, or ideal observers endowed with impartiality, would endorse.[30] A typical response of children when they are reprimanded for having done something wrong is to say, "I did not mean to do it," which I think can be translated (though not by the children themselves) as saying something along the lines of "I did not have the intention to do it." In addition, evidence can also be gathered from the theories of culpability tacitly assumed in many different legal systems, where the distinction between intended and unintended action is of paramount importance.[31]

In spite of the fact that in the Anglo-American legal tradition the pre-eminent role of the distinction between intended action and unintended action is not overtly exhibited, the distinction is present and *used* similarly to the way in which it is used elsewhere. Many Anglo-American scholars

---

28. Hannah Arendt, *Eichmann in Jerusalem: A Report on the Banality of Evil* (New York: Penguin Books, 1977), 275 (my emphasis).
29. Immanuel Kant, *The Metaphysics of Morals*, trans. Mary McGregor (Cambridge: Cambridge University Press, 1991), 50.
30. For more on the veil of ignorance see John Rawls, *A Theory of Justice*, 2nd ed. (Cambridge, MA.: Harvard University Press, 1999), 102–70. For more on the ideal observer see Roderick Firth, "Ethical Absolutism and the Ideal Observer," *Philosophy and Phenomenological Research* 12 (1952): 317–45.
31. American Law Institute, *Model Penal Code*, vol. 1, 225–27 (MPC § 2.02).

celebrate, for example, that the Model Penal Code avoids talking about intentions, yet I shall show that the modes of culpability of the Model Penal Code appeal to intentions and intended action as much as modes of culpability elsewhere do.

For example, as he comments on Alan White's *Misleading Cases*, Douglas Husak, one of the leading contemporary criminal law theorists, tells us:

> Almost all of the criminal cases discussed by White are English and, thus, are likely to be unfamiliar to American readers. Moreover, some of the concepts he analyzes are more central to British than to American law. For example, White spends much of a chapter deciding whether a person intends whatever consequences he knows will result from his conduct. The difficulty of answering this question is one reason the Model Penal Code (and those jurisdictions that have adopted it) have abandoned the word "intention" in favor of "knowledge" and "purpose."[32]

Rather than emphasizing the differences between this and that code, I shall try to show what different legal systems have in common, at least regarding their theories of culpability. My strategy will be to present the history of theories of culpability and to argue that theories of culpability are not merely part of the criminal law—they transcend the criminal law. Drafters of penal codes, whether consciously or not, cope with the central philosophical problems of theories of culpability for pragmatic considerations, because the problems associated with culpability are more pressing within the criminal law than in other disciplines. Criminal codes try to capture and to articulate the way human beings blame other human beings for the evil outcomes that they bring about. Regardless of the terminological diatribes, the underlying facts remain the same: the Model Penal Code merely avoids *the talk* of "intended actions" though it does not avoid intended actions themselves at all.

As I have mentioned already, intentions are the cornerstone of a theory of culpability, yet, a full-blown theory of culpability has to take other Intentional states into account as well. We also need a distinction that focuses on the cognitive Intentional state of being aware or knowing, rather than on the conative Intentional state of intending. This is the second operative distinction in the theory of culpability defended here. To a great extent, it is the interplay between these two types of Intentional states that explains how there could be intentional actions that are not intended. It is the interplay between these two types of Intentional states that allows for a fourfold map of modes of culpability (such as the one containing 6,

---

32. Douglas Husak, "Review of White's *Misleading Cases*," *Ethics* (1993): 418.

7, 8, and 9 sketched above—I focus now on only the four cases that give rise to blame, ignoring the fifth case of pure accidents) rather than the coarse twofold map that arises from looking at intentions alone.

It is extremely difficult to establish which acts are intentional and which are not, and though we know that such a distinction marks an important normative difference, we do not know exactly in what that difference consists. We know that intentional actions are, in principle, more blameworthy than unintentional actions, typically insofar as in principle intentional actions are intended and unintentional actions are unintended. This discussion has been at the core of theories of culpability for several millennia. (In the next chapter I shall show how important these issues were for Plato and for Aristotle.) Let me refer now to the opinions of two leading contemporary criminal law theorists who comment on the distinction between intentional and unintentional action. Hans Welzel states that "distinguishing between *dolus eventualis* and *culpa* (with representation) [*bewusste Fahrlässigkeit*] is one of the most difficult and more discussed problems of the criminal law."[33]

As shall become clear later, in the continental legal tradition *dolus* means "intentional criminal action" and *culpa* means "unintentional criminal action," and thus Welzel's suggestion translates into the claim that the distinction between the intentional and the unintentional "is one of the most difficult and more discussed problems of the criminal law." In a similar vein, George P. Fletcher acknowledges the importance of this problem:

> The basic cleavage in the states of mind used in criminal legislation is between those that focus on the actor's goal (willfulness, intention, purposefulness) and those that focus on the risk that the actor creates in acting (recklessness and negligence). The difficult problem confronted in all legal systems is working out the precise boundary between these two clusters of mental states—or, more precisely, between these two ways of committing offenses.[34]

These "two ways of committing offenses," or "two clusters of mental states," are marked by the distinction between intentional and unintentional action, and this distinction is in turn (loosely) based on the distinction between intended and unintended actions.

The realms of the intentional and the unintentional can be further subdivided, as we saw in the examples above, by adding the distinction between acting while being aware that one is bringing about the evil outcome and acting while being unaware that it is likely that one will bring about the evil outcome. Each mode of culpability describes one way in

---

33. Hans Welzel, *Das Deutsche Strafrecht*, 11th ed. (Berlin: Gruyter, 1988), 101.
34. Fletcher, *Rethinking Criminal Law*, 442.

which an agent's Intentional states can be related to her action, which gives rise to a certain judgment of blame. It should by now be obvious that a clear definition of intentions, and a clear grasp of what is involved in fixing the boundary, first between the intended and the unintended, and second, between the intentional and the unintentional, are crucial for understanding the essential features of the theory of culpability defended herein.

The distinction between intended action and unintended action gives us a robust, albeit coarse, distinction between judgments of blame. A more fine-grained map of culpability emerges once we take into account our other deep-seated moral intuitions. Ceteris paribus, and in typical cases, to do evil with the awareness that one is doing it is never less blameworthy than to do it without such awareness. And though I have neither invented nor discovered these intuitions, I here attempt to present a comprehensive and systematic analysis of them which does dispel common misconceptions.

It is of singular importance to show how what has counted as intentional action has changed throughout time, and continues to change from place to place. Actions that in ancient Rome, or in medieval Europe, as a matter of course, were considered intentional, nowadays would not be so considered: actions that counted as intentional in the past do not count as such today, and conversely. What is more interesting, perhaps, is that actions that nowadays are considered to be unintentional, say in Germany, might be nowadays considered intentional, say in England, and vice versa. I would like to argue, however, that the "counts as" formula does not apply to intended and unintended action, that whatever is intended now would have been intended in ancient times, and would be intended everywhere. The intendedness of action is a wholly empirical affair, a fact which might be obscured by the epistemological problems related to knowing the contents of other people's minds; the (lowercase) intentionality of action is loosely linked to the empirical distinction regarding intendedness, but it also contains a major normative implication: intended action is never less blameworthy than unintended action.

Let me conclude this section by discussing a certain skepticism that surrounds the very possibility of developing a comprehensive, "general" theory of culpability. I would like to preempt an objection to my project. Jeremy Horder has undertaken to show how attempts to find one single all-encompassing concept that can by itself be sufficient for supporting a theory of culpability have failed.[35] By no means, then, do I wish to add to that long list of theories with names such as "the defiance theory," "the capacities theory," "the choice theory," my own, "the intentionality the-

---

35. Jeremy Horder, "Criminal Culpability: The Possibility of a General Theory," *Law and Philosophy* 12: 193–215.

ory." As stated already, in the context of a theory of culpability, we frequently have to make distinctions between different types of unintentional actions, and different types of intentional actions. So, it must be remembered that my claim is that the distinction between intended action and unintended action is the most basic distinction in culpability, and not that it is the only one.

But, more importantly, Horder fails to notice in an otherwise illuminating article that the theories that he attacks under the rubric of "theories of culpability" are actually partially theories of culpability, partially theories of punishment, partially theories of responsibility, and so on. The models put forward by the authors whom Horder attacks all have something in common: *one single element* is purported to be a sufficient condition for a person to be an agent, such as: the person's uncoerced choice, her capacities, her defiance of the law, among others. As a matter of fact, I share a great deal of Horder's skepticism regarding these attempts, but I still think that such skepticism does not affect the theory of culpability that I defend here.

The theory of culpability defended here differs from those Horder criticizes, because this theory of culpability is not concerned with grounding or justifying responsibility or accountability in the first place. Whatever the ultimate grounds for imputing responsibility might turn out to be, the question as to the rationale for different degrees of blame remains a sufficiently independent issue. The theory of culpability defended here is an extension of the recent work (most notably Searle's) on the Intentionality of mental phenomena to the analysis of the ways in which we blame each other. It does not seek to show what makes us agents, but rather, how, assuming we are agents, there can be principled differences in the condemnation that some of our acts deserve, and which stem directly from facts about our Intentional states.

Culpability and Moral Theory

The theory of culpability defended here, insofar as it is an extension of the theory of Intentionality, is an unusually good candidate for a far-reaching theory in the realm of human values. By "far-reaching" I mean that it is likely to hold across different cultures and in different eras. I do not wish to systematically argue that my theory of culpability is far-reaching in this sense. Yet, this theory of culpability is much more likely to be far-reaching than other substantive moral theories. Different cultures have different views regarding which acts are considered wrong. For example, incest is condemned in some cultures and accepted in others, cannibalism is accepted in some cultures and not in others, and female circumcision/

castration is accepted in some cultures and abhorred in others. Though I am sympathetic to moral realism in general, I wish to steer clear of meta-ethical discussions regarding ultimate values in morality.[36] Yet, suggesting that the theory of culpability that I defend here is far-reaching is, on its face, easier than suggesting that this or that behavior is universally good or evil. Regardless of which specific actions any given culture condemns or prohibits, the theory of culpability sketched above is likely to obtain.

Those cultures that, for example, find incest reprehensible are likely to blame more severely someone who engaged in intended incestuous behavior than someone who engaged in unintended incestuous behavior, and so on. A theory of culpability does not say much about substantive morality, focusing instead on a formula that many different substantive moral codes are likely to endorse. Whatever a society considers to be wrong in the first place, be it incest, polygamy, shaving one's head, or speaking loudly, the theory of culpability based on the distinction between intended and unintended action is likely to hold. If speaking loudly were an evil in our society, we would more sternly blame those who speak loudly intendedly than we would those who speak loudly unintendedly. Similarly, the conditions for agency, that is, the conditions that make a person responsible in the first place, can vary between cultures and even within one and the same culture between different political entities. Some cultures might consider a thirteen-year-old boy to be a fully responsible agent, whereas in other cultures twenty-one years are required. Some cultures have denied agency to foreigners, heretics, members of racial or ethnic minorities, and so on; others restrict full agency only to the possessors of certain statuses, for example being a *pater familias* (recall the Roman distinction between *sui iuris* and *alieni iuris*) or being a landowner. Quite pathetically, some cultures still today deny full agency to females. Yet, in any of these cultures, and whenever we are dealing with a responsible agent, the theory of culpability sketched above is likely to obtain—it is after all a matter that is *rationally* justified.

This proto-universal appeal constitutes a further difference between culpability and the other extenuations discussed above. What counts as an excuse, a justification, or a mitigation varies, sometimes quite dramatically, between different cultures and different eras. But the moral distinctions that arise from attending to whether the agent acted with an intention to

---

36. On moral realism, see: David O. Brink, *Moral Realism and the Foundations of Ethics* (Cambridge: Cambridge University Press, 1989), both for its strong defense of moral realism and for its excellent bibliography; Michael Moore, "Moral Reality," *University of Wisconsin Law Review* (1982): 1061–156, and "Moral Reality Revisited," *Michigan Law Review* 90 (1992): 2424–533; and for an excellent collection of essays see George Sayre-McCord, ed., *Essays on Moral Realism* (Ithaca, NY: Cornell University Press, 1988).

bring about the evil outcome or without such an intention do not vary through cultures or through time. To kill while engaged in a gladiator match, for example, was justified in ancient Rome but is not today; to kill while avenging one's honor might have been an excuse or a justification in some eras, but is not generally today, and so on.

Both the specific actions that different societies condemn in the first place and the punishments that are meted out for those who engage in those actions can be dramatically diverse. Homicide, adultery, and many other types of action, for example, are punished differently in different cultures and in different eras. Institutional punishment carried out by the state is a political, public phenomenon, which stands in need of a special political justification. But blaming (understood as a mental phenomenon) a human being for something bad she has done is not public, and it does not call for a political justification. Blame, as I understand it here, is never *inflicted*. Justification in blaming is quite different from the way justification affects thickly institutional punishment. To justify blaming someone this or that severely could also be a private affair, and it is closely linked to one's own view of rationality. Very roughly, it is irrational to blame more severely the unintended doing of X than the intended doing of X (when X has an evil outcome in the sense already explained, of course). Theories of culpability are susceptible to rational justifications, similar in many respects to epistemological justifications, and quite unlike the sort of political justifications that embed appeals to thick conceptions of rights, citizenship, and the like.

Searle's *Intentionality* begins with an important claim to the effect that "the philosophy of language is a branch of the philosophy of mind."[37] Aside from the particularities of this or that language that allow for this or that speech act or for this or that utterance, the capacity of the mind to relate to states of affairs is more stable, and "more fundamental"—one can think about, say, a question, before engaging in the speech act of asking the question. Something similar happens with the relationship between a theory of culpability, concerned mainly with Intentional states, and theories of punishment, which presumably draw from theories of culpability considerably, but which also have to deal with all sorts of phenomena that are not as fundamental as Intentional mental states.

For example, consider the normative debate between retributivists and consequentialists regarding the justification of punishment. This debate concerns itself exclusively with the justification of punishment, but has little currency regarding a theory of culpability. There are, strictly speaking, no retributive or consequentialist theories of culpability, there is just

---

37. Searle, *Intentionality*, vii.

blaming (when one understands blaming as I do here, as a private mental phenomenon). Blaming is something humans do, similar to admiring, fearing, liking, and so forth. Though any of these phenomena can be both externalized and influenced by external considerations, these phenomena can also be entirely internal to the agent.

Perhaps (this is a deceivingly simple question), it would be a wonderful world if, whenever punishments were administered, their severity coincided with the amount of blame that the agent deserved. Yet the world in which we live is such that there are agents whom we blame but do not punish, and agents whom we punish but do not blame, and some whom we punish less than we blame, and so on. Although some radical differences between the blameworthiness of certain actions and the severity of the punishment that we inflict upon agents who carry them out might be criticizable, there are good reasons justifying some differences between these two realms.

When dealing with responsibility, normative ethics, or theories of punishment we can hardly escape considerations pertaining to political philosophy, but we can more easily deal with culpability without getting tangled up in political issues. Once the seemingly innocuous point that to blame people in accordance with the theory of culpability sketched above is something we can do privately (like admiring or fearing) is granted, it becomes harder to argue in favor of sharp theoretical distinctions between moral and legal culpability. Nowhere, perhaps, have theories of culpability gained more in sophistication than in the criminal law, but culpability is first and foremost part of the philosophy of mind and action, however much the criminal law might have incorporated it into its core. Culpability is both a part of the criminal law and an independent subject which transcends the criminal law. This book presents a theory of culpability that accounts for the degrees of blame that arise from any sort of evil action, criminal and noncriminal alike. The fact that some laws proscribe punishments which deviate from the blameworthiness of the action is not an objection to my claim that the blameworthiness of actions is determined independently of whatever legal systems proscribe. The theory of culpability defended here is based on facts about the ways in which some mental states are connected to human action.

Many blameworthy acts are not punished (legally or otherwise). Invidious or selfish acts, for example, may spawn widespread feelings of condemnation or blame, but that does not entail that such blameworthy acts should also be punished (legally or otherwise). Although punishment policies are the result of human conventions, they are closely linked to Intentional states regarding blameworthiness, which are not entirely conventional. Indeed, as criminal law theory has evolved, the ties between blame and punishment have tightened. This claim might erroneously be taken to suggest that I am embracing a radically retributivist stance. I am not. There need not be a conflict between accepting my way of linking blame and punishment and accepting deterrence or other consequentialist policies. Even Mill, surely not a retributivist, acknowledged this intimate relation between blame and punishment, and to a greater degree than I do. In *Utilitarianism*, he tells us that some wrongdoers "we do not blame," and that this "not blaming them" entails that "we do not think that they are proper objects of punishment."[38] It follows from this passage that for Mill blame is actually a necessary condition for punishment. Moreover, Mill further tells us that "how we come by these ideas of deserving and not deserving punishment [blaming, for my purposes] will appear, perhaps, in the sequel."[39] Such a sequel Mill never wrote, and, in part, my theory of culpability should be understood precisely as an answer to the question "How do we do it?"

I am not suggesting that with the passing of time societies have tended to punish more and more of those actions that those societies happen to find blameworthy. Rather, I suggest that *whenever* societies do punish an agent for the evil outcomes she has brought about, they increasingly tend to demand that the punishment be proportionate to the blameworthiness of the act. The relation between blame and punishment does not seem to be symmetrical; if some evil outcome is punished, it tends to be because it is blameworthy, but that an evil outcome is blameworthy tells us less about its punishability. There are many blameworthy evil outcomes for which it does not seem just, expedient, or convenient to punish (legally or otherwise) those agents who bring them about.

Moreover, there are cases in which we punish wrongdoers regardless of whether or not they are blameworthy. Having thus sketched a theory of culpability, having shown how it straddles certain mental states with certain normative judgments of blame, I would like to end this chapter by considering these cases, insofar as on first approximation, they seem to pose a threat to theories of culpability in general. These cases are known as strict liability offenses. The kernel of strict liability, though not always made explicit, is quite simple: some actions should have a fixed punishment, regardless of fault, and since the notion of fault involves reference to Intentional states, strict liability offenses render theories of culpability useless. As Duff would have it: "liability is strict if it does not require proof of fault or *mens rea* as to *an* aspect of the offence."[40] Paradigmatic cases of

---

38. John Stuart Mill, *Utilitarianism* (Indianapolis, IN: Hackett Publishing Company, 1979), 48.
39. Mill, *Utilitarianism*, 48.
40. R. A. Duff, "Strict Liability, Legal Presumptions, and the Presumption of Innocence" in *Appraising Strict Liability*, ed. Andrew P. Simester (Oxford: Oxford University Press, 2005, forthcoming).

strict liability offenses include: selling alcohol to minors, speeding, parking violations, and the like.

To the extent that some societies attach strict liability to certain actions in the legal realm, such societies would be driving a perhaps reasonable wedge between culpability and legal punishment, but this would not affect the nature of the theory of culpability itself. To suggest that this or that conduct be made into a strict liability crime says nothing about how severely it is blamed, it is merely to say that the state will punish it. It could be compellingly argued that in spite of the fact that it might be a good *policy* to punish the liquor shop attendant who intendedly sells vodka to minors to the same degree as we punish the one who does so unintendedly, we would still blame her differently. It seems to me rather clear that we in fact blame more leniently, for example, a person who parks in a prohibited parking space unintendedly than we do one who parks there intendedly (just as we are more lenient with the driver who parks there in order to save a child from drowning than we are with the driver who parks there just out of laziness) although we might endorse having this sort of behavior fall outside the scope of actions regulated by theories of culpability. Again, here we see the usefulness of distinguishing between blame and punishment.

Emphasizing the distinction between blame and legal punishment helps us to see that nothing in the hypothetical proliferation of strict liability legal offenses would affect the truth of the more fundamental and general theory of culpability. Of course, the proliferation of strict liability offenses can indeed cast doubt as to the *importance* of a theory of culpability. Yet, the analysis of the ways in which human beings blame each other, the logic of blame, would remain an important subject—at least insofar as no society has turned all the actions it punishes or prohibits into strict liability offenses, and no society seems likely to do so. As a matter of fact, a sure sign of progress in political philosophy and in criminal law is to make the punishment "fit" the crime, and this fit probably requires a close connection between blame and punishment. At most, the proliferation of strict liability offenses might pose a threat to the thesis that blame and punishment should always go together, but this thesis is not defended here, nor indeed is it a thesis any theory of culpability needs to address.

There is one final reason why it is important for me to address strict liability. The way in which I formulated the central thesis of my theory of culpability, that intended evil is *never less* blameworthy than unintended evil, allows for the possibility that in truly *exceptional* cases the blameworthiness of intended evil (even in its prima facie most blameworthy manifestation) is identical to the blameworthiness of unintended evil (even in its prima facie least blameworthy manifestation). That is, in these exceptional cases the blameworthiness of bringing about this or that evil outcome would be the same no matter what was the mode of culpability of the agent. While this might suggest that I am endorsing strict liability at least in these exceptional cases, I am not. For the typical rationale of proponents of strict liability offenses is based on cost-benefit analysis regarding the functioning of an efficient criminal justice system, whereas my rationale is based on a principled account of the impact that Intentional states have in the apportioning of blame. My admission that in some exceptional cases the distinction between some or all the modes of culpability could be, in part or in whole, diminished has nothing to do with pragmatic considerations relating to the smooth operation of the criminal justice system.

Imagine, for example, someone who is trying to learn to juggle, and who enters a room filled with children while attempting to juggle half a dozen live grenades. Imagine that one of the grenades falls and explodes. It is of course *possible* that the wannabe juggler was really unaware of the risks involved in her behavior—that is, that she was merely negligent—or that she was aware that there was some risk but did not want the risk to come to happen and was in no way certain that it would come to happen— that is, that she was merely reckless. It is likely that her Intentional states in cases like these do not really give rise to significant differences regarding the blameworthiness of what she did.

The existence of cases of this sort constitutes no problem for my theory. First and foremost because, as I already stated, the basic normative implication of the distinction between intended and unintended action is that, ceteris paribus, the former is *never less* blameworthy than the latter. Thus, logically speaking, the possibility of cases in which the distinction between intended and unintended action would be immaterial is of no significance—the case of the juggler conforms to the principle. Furthermore, the existence of cases of this sort is the exception that confirms the rule. Most cases are not like the juggler's case.

Focusing on Intentional states themselves, rather than on the externalization or communication of those Intentional states, shall thus allow me to avoid the thorny political issues having to do with punishment and its justifications, with what to criminalize in the first place, with what are the limits of the State's power, and many more issues of this sort. But the focus on the structure of Intentional states has the additional advantage of allowing me to bracket, as I noted above, several famous debates in contemporary philosophy such as the free will–determinism debate and the debates dealing with the ultimate relationship between the mind and the brain. As Searle discusses the advantages of his approach to Intentionality, he starts by saying: "One advantage of this approach, by no means a minor one, is that it enables us to distinguish clearly between the logical properties of Intentional states and their ontological status; indeed, on this account, the question concerning the logical nature of Intentionality is not an ontological problem at all."[41] What I shall attempt to do here is to show that among the logical properties of intentions is that they are more intimately linked to actions than any other Intentional states, and that this tight connection explains why they have the normative force that I shall claim that they have.

As popular debates in contemporary philosophy show, the constitutive rules of practices have normative implications. For example, when someone promises to do X, assuming a host of conditions obtain (she is a moral agent, is not telling a joke or performing a role in a play, etc.) she undertakes an obligation to do X, that is, she, in a sense, ought to do X. I have elsewhere written about the complexity of this sense of ought (and about the fact that it can be overridden),[42] and I will have more to say about these issues in the later chapters of the book, but what seems to me undeniable is that there exists at least one sense in which she indeed ought to do X. There is, then, a sense in which the logical structure of Intentional states has normative implications.

---

41. Searle, *Intentionality*, 14ff.
42. Leo Zaibert, "Intentions, Promises and Obligations," in *John Searle,* ed. Barry Smith, 53–84 (Cambridge: Cambridge University Press, 2003).

[2]

Intentionality and the Apportioning of Blame: A Historical Analysis

In this chapter I offer a critical analysis of a handful of important moments in the history of culpability regarding the distinctions between (1) intended and unintended action, between (2) more culpable and less culpable actions, and of course, that complicated distinction between (3) intentional and unintentional action. Antiquity is a period in which the importance of these distinctions in shaping theories of culpability has been systematically underestimated. My strategy here is not to present an exhaustive map of the history or the ethnography of culpability or to discuss many variegated theories of culpability advanced in different cultures. I shall simply break down the ancient history of culpability in the West into four periods that I find particularly illuminating.

The most ancient period can be viewed as the prehistory of culpability; the assertion that considerations pertaining to culpability were important in this period continues to be typically met with skepticism, insofar as the paradigm principle of blame and punishment was the allegedly rigid and crude biblical *lex talionis*: an eye for an eye, a tooth for a tooth. The second and third periods belong to the era of Greek philosophical fervor, in which we witness the earliest systematic advancements of a theory of culpability informed by concerns regarding the interplay between the Intentionality of mental states and the intentionality of human action. In this period we witness the first coherent division of action into intended and unintended (Plato), as well as incipient definitions of each type of action (Aristotle). Finally, I wish to discuss Roman criminal law, insofar as it draws considerably from Greek philosophers, and because it constitutes the forerunner of many contemporary theories of culpability. There is a common conceptual thread linking contemporary theories of culpability not only to Roman law, but to Aristotle and Plato. Regrettably, this thread, by and large, has not hitherto received the attention it deserves. This neglect is of interest both in terms of the history of ideas and of the concrete analytical lessons which its study provides.

33

Perhaps a somewhat daring thought experiment can allow us to conceive of a time in human history in which there were no differences in the blameworthiness of actions stemming from the set of Intentional states accompanying them, but that such a scenario ever materialized seems unlikely. It seems natural to suppose that among the first types of rules to arise in any society some would have included some prohibitions: things that, for society's sake, should not be done. This would be a subset of those rules which, famously, H. L. A Hart called "primary rules," that is, rules that are duty- (or obligation- or punishment-) imposing, which he contrasts to more sophisticated rules that are power-conferring, and which he called "secondary rules."[1] According to Hart, the conjunction of these two types of rules constitutes the essence of a legal system, but it is perhaps possible to imagine an extraordinarily primitive society that might have had only primary rules. Hart, rightly, thinks that a real society without any secondary rules is very unlikely to have ever existed. I think that a society without *any* rules whatsoever is virtually impossible to even imagine.

It is equally natural to suppose that violation of some of these rules would give rise, in such a society, to some sort of sanction; simply prohibiting *X* without imposing a sanction upon those who do *X* surely would be ineffective. For example, to stipulate that the killing of a human being is prohibited without also stipulating what is supposed to happen to someone who kills another human being seems unlikely. Now, I wish to advance the thesis that these sanctions have been shaped by considerations having to do with the Intentional states (mainly intentions) of the killers. I strongly believe that, barring limit cases such as the grenade juggler's (in chapter 1), it seems intuitively appealing that people would be blamed (and eventually punished) differently based on Intentional states that they have when they act. This intuition strikes me as a primitive of human psychology if ever there was one, to be found, too, in some nonhuman animals: recall Oliver Wendell Holmes's famous remark that "even a dog knows the difference between being kicked and being stumbled upon."[2] Naturally, the dog would react differently when it thinks that it has been kicked than when it thinks that it has been merely stumbled upon, just as humans would blame (and eventually punish) those who kick and those who stumble differently. Yet, conventional wisdom has it that not only is this intuition not a primitive of human psychology at all, but also that there was at least one specific period in human history during which Intentional states were utterly irrelevant in the apportioning of blame and in the punishment

---

1. See H. L. A. Hart, *The Concept of Law*, 2nd ed. (Oxford: Oxford University Press, 1997), 79ff.
2. Oliver Wendell Holmes, *The Common Law* (Boston: Little, Brown, 1881), 7.

of wrongdoers: the period when the (in)famous "an eye for an eye, a tooth for a tooth" held sway.

Biblical Culpability and *Lex Talionis*

Lex talionis finds its clearest and most straightforward formulations in *Exodus* 21:

> If men who are fighting hit a pregnant woman and she gives birth prematurely but there is no serious injury, the offender must be fined whatever the woman's husband demands and court allows. But if there is serious injury, you are to take life for life, eye for eye, tooth for tooth, hand for hand, burn for burn, wound for wound, bruise for bruise.[3]

The second sentence in this passage contains the eloquent and famous motto characteristic of biblical policies of punishment. It appears as if the biblical account of retaliation is mainly, if not exclusively, concerned with the evil outcomes brought about, regardless of the agents' intentions. It also appears as if the biblical account of retaliation has much to do with establishing appropriate punishment (or compensation) and little to do with apportioning blame. Indeed, the traditional interpretation of *lex talionis* is that it is a stern, unexceptionable, and rigid principle of punishment, keyed exclusively to the outcomes of actions. "An eye for an eye, a tooth for a tooth" is a slogan commonly utilized—by laymen as well as by scholars—in order to solve more or less petty disputes in an expediently just way; for example, "You took my candy, I take yours," "You stood me up, so I stand you up." Indisputably, this is the common, widespread interpretation of *lex talionis*. And there is little doubt that this interpretation is common in academic circles as well. Consider, for example, Mill's dictum: "No rule on the subject [of the legitimacy of inflicting punishment] recommends itself so strongly to the primitive and spontaneous sentiment of justice as the *lex talionis*, an eye for an eye and a tooth for a tooth. Though this principle of the Jewish law and the Mohammedan law has been generally abandoned in Europe as a practical maxim, there is, I suspect, in most minds, a secret hankering after it."[4]

Here, Mill is obviously suggesting that this "primitive" sentiment of justice is indeed too coarse and that its abandonment is justified. But other scholars are much more direct about their dissatisfaction with *lex talionis*.

---

3. C. I. Schofield, ed., *Oxford New International Version Schofield Study Bible* (New York: Oxford University Press, 1984), 89.
4. Mill, *Utilitarianism*, 55–56.

Nicola Lacey, for example, has stated that "the crudest yet the most fundamental attempt [to justify punishment] is represented by the ancient lex talionis: an eye for an eye, a life for a life, and so on."[5] For Lacey, *lex talionis* is not merely crude and ancient, for she continues: "this principle, if it merits the name, certainly has the attraction of simplicity: unfortunately this is all that can be said for it."[6]

Bucking the trend, I would like to suggest that *lex talionis* is not as crude or as empty as the widespread view has it, and that it relates to theories of culpability in meaningful, yet typically ignored ways. Although an emphasis on evil outcomes and punishment, at the expense of intentions and blame, is clearly visible in the biblical account of retaliation, I wish to show that the discussion of intending and blaming, though admittedly incipient, was also of importance then. The discussion of biblical culpability is difficult, in part, precisely because the realms of blame and of punishment were not clearly distinguished. But that the distinction between these realms was not clearly drawn in no way entails that it did not exist—in our own day it continues to be difficult, at times, to distinguish between these two realms.

First, as a general word of caution, rabbinical interpretations always understood *lex talionis* in terms of compensation and not in the stern literal sense in which the slogan is expressed.[7] But, more importantly for my purposes, at least as frequently as we find passages in the Old Testament containing formulations of ancient retaliatory policies in stern and rigid fashion, we encounter passages where more sophisticated and less rigid policies are put forth, policies which do indeed take into account the Intentional states of the agents. Consider the following passages:

> Anyone who strikes a man and kills him shall surely be put to death. However, if he does not do it intentionally, but God lets it happen, he is to flee to a place I will designate. But if a man *schemes* and kills another man deliberately, take him away from my altar and put him to death.[8]

> If anyone with *malice aforethought* shoves another or throws something at him intentionally so that he dies or if in hostility he hits him with his fist so that he dies, that person shall be put to death; he is a murderer. . . . But if *without hostility* someone *suddenly* shoves another or throws something at him unintentionally or, *without seeing him*, drops a stone on him that could kill him, and he

---

5. Nicola Lacey, *State Punishment: Political Principles and Community Values* (London: Routledge, 1988), 17.
6. Lacey, *State Punishment*, 17.
7. See the classical commentaries compiled in A. Cohen, ed., *The Soncino Chumash: The Five Books of Moses with Haphtaroth* (London: Soncino, 1956), 475ff., 759ff.
8. Exodus 21:12–14 (Schofield, Oxford New International Bible, 89; emphasis added).

dies, then since he was not his enemy and he did not intend to kill him . . . the assembly must protect the accused of murder and send him back to the city of refuge to which he fled.[9]

When you cross the Jordan into Canaan, select some towns to be your cities of refuge, to which a person who has killed someone accidentally may flee. They will be places of refuge from the avenger, so that a person accused of murder may not die before he stands trial before the assembly.[10]

This is the rule concerning the man who kills another and flees there to save his life—one who kills unintentionally, without malice aforethought. For instance, a man may go into the forest with his neighbor to cut wood, and as he swings his ax to fell a tree, the head may fly off and hit his neighbor and kill him. That man may flee to one of these cities and save his life. Otherwise, the avenger of blood might pursue him in a rage, overtake him if the distance is too great, and kill him even though he is not deserving of death, since he did it to his neighbor without malice aforethought. . . . But if a man hates his neighbor and *lies in wait* for him, assaults and kills him, and then flees to one of these cities, the elders of his town shall send him over the avenger of blood to die. . . . Show no pity: life for life, eye for eye, tooth for tooth, hand for hand, foot for foot.[11]

Reference to policies regarding designated havens or refuges for those who have unintentionally caused the death of other human beings is pervasive in the Old Testament. This fact alone should make it clear that this was an important issue at the time. The raison d'être of refuge cities seems to have been none other than to give practical significance and applicability to the otherwise merely theoretical distinction between intended and unintended homicides. These passages, I think, suffice to disprove the widespread, uncritical view that the biblical *lex talionis* accurately captures the spirit of an era in which Intentionality was insignificant.

I have emphasized some expressions in the preceding passages, such as "malice aforethought," "suddenly [and] without hostility," and others. These expressions are clear, albeit naive, attempts to explain why some actions are intentional and others are unintentional. An act done with "malice aforethought" would be considered intentional; one done "suddenly and without hostility" would be unintentional. Of course, the assumption probably current during those times was that if the act was intentional it was also intended and if it was unintentional it was unin-

---

9. Numbers 35:10–25 (Schofield, Oxford New International Bible, 187–88; emphasis added).

10. Numbers 35:9–12 (Schofield, Oxford New International Bible, 187).

11. Deuteronomy 19:4–13 (Schofield, Oxford New International Bible, 207; emphasis added).

tended. It is not until very recent times that the distinction between the intended and the intentional—that some intentional actions need not be intended—came to be recognized, and even now this is not *widely* recognized.[12] (This confusion between the intended and the intentional renders some passages of this book rather carping. Remembering that, historically, it has been traditionally assumed that a necessary condition for an action to be intentional is that it also be intended, should help clarify things. So, when Plato, or Aristotle, for example, are translated as referring to this or that action as "intentional," in many cases that would correspond to what I here call "intended," and I shall so note it.)

In addition to these eloquent passages showing the inadequacies of the prevailing watered-down view of ancient policies of punishment that still hold sway, more sophisticated philological analyses also help to support my thesis. David Daube, in his thorough and illuminating *Studies in Biblical Law,* carries out some such analyses.[13] For example, Daube concludes that some classical passages where biblical retaliation is put forth make sense only if we accept that the writers of the Old Testament were limiting the application of *lex talionis* to the intended bringing about of certain outcomes, even if this is not expressly stated, or where it is obscured by translational difficulties. "At all events," Daube points out, "there is no doubt that the crime of Deuteronomy xxv. 11 f. is committed intentionally, and I think that of Exodus xxi. 22 ff., too, must be regarded as a deliberate, malicious attack."[14] Daube considers the case of killing someone else's animal, a case in which the Intentional states of the killer are of no importance, to be an exception to the general rule applicable for homicides: that the *lex talionis* only applies in cases where agents acted intendedly. He writes: "As for Leviticus xxiv. 18 ff., the position is as complicated as it is interesting. I very much doubt whether in this section retaliation is restricted to intentional wrongdoing . . . [in contrast to restitution in the case of human deaths] restitution for a beast has presumably to be made whether he who killed it did so intentionally or by accident."[15]

Daube indicates that this difference in the role accorded to intentions in the case of human deaths and other animal deaths is the traditional rabbinical interpretation of the passage.[16] Causing the death of a nonhuman animal, was in biblical times, a bona fide case of what we would nowadays call a strict liability offense, that is, an offense for which a certain sanction

---

12. I shall discuss the relationship between intentions and intentional action in chapter 5 below.
13. David Daube, *Studies in Biblical Law* (New York: Ktav Publishing House, 1969).
14. Daube, *Studies in Biblical Law,* 108. (These are the crimes I have cited above.)
15. Daube, *Studies in Biblical Law,* 110.
16. Daube, *Studies in Biblical Law,* 149, n. 16.

is imposed independently of fault, and thus independently of any concern for the Intentional states of the agent. But of course the widespread view that I am trying to refute here is that the application of *lex talionis* treated *all* offenses as if they were strict liability offenses.

Anachronistic as it is, the talk of refuge cities, avengers of blood, and town elders should not obscure other issues at stake in biblical times: the distinction between intended and unintended action, and its relationship to the apportioning of blame. These issues are of utmost contemporary relevance. Ancient theories of culpability that ground ancient theories of punishment are less outrageous than they have commonly been held to be and have much in common with contemporary ones.

Is going to a refuge city a punishment? If we answer this question affirmatively, then it is clear that even in biblical times, actions done unintendedly were, ceteris paribus, never blamed more severely than if they were done intendedly, although they were blamed nevertheless. But if we answer this question negatively, that is, if we conclude that being forced to go to a refuge city in order to save one's life is not a punishment, then it turns out that unintended wrongdoing was not punishable and presumably not blameworthy either. This all-or-nothing policy whereby an intention to do wrong is a necessary condition for the blaming and for the punishment of wrongdoing is mistaken. The gradational nature of the central distinction of culpability which I presented above (to be further supplemented later) shows that the intention to do wrong entails, ceteris paribus, that the blameworthiness of the wrongdoing is at least as high as (and typically higher than) the blameworthiness of the wrongdoing had it been brought about unintendedly.

Formality of *Lex Talionis*

If, then, *lex talionis* is not a strict principle only concerned with evil outcomes and punishments, impervious to analyses of Intentional states, how are we to understand it? The essence of the answer is that the principle contained in *lex talionis* is that the punishment should fit the gravity of the wrongdoing.[17] Yet, the exact meaning of "fitting the crime" remains elusive. Michael Davies presents a thorough account of two general ways to interpret *lex talionis*:

---

17. In relation to the philosophical implications of *lex talionis* see Igor Primorac, "On Retributivism and the Lex Talionis," *Rivista Internazionale di Filosofia del Diritto* 61 (1984): 83–94, and Michael Mitias, "Is Retributivism Inconsistent with Lex Talionis?" *Rivista Internazionale di Filosofia del Diritto* 60 (1983): 211–30.

> *Lex talionis* (or *jus talionis*) may once have referred unequivocally to a certain principle defining or limiting the right of retaliation, but it has long since become equivocal. *Lex talionis* may now refer to [1] a general principle of corrective justice or to [2] a particular principle of criminal law. As a general principle of corrective justice, *lex* requires the wrongdoer to suffer as much as (but no more than) he has wrongfully made others suffer. This principle is more at home in the mountains of Corsica or in a schoolyard fight than in the criminal law.[18]

Before I discuss Davies's views on *lex talionis* as a principle of criminal law, I shall discuss his view on *lex talionis* as a general principle of corrective justice. I take it that in opposing principles of corrective justice to principles of the criminal law, Davies is distinguishing the moral and legal realms, given that the realm of corrective justice is broader than the realm of criminal law. I further take it that Davies's suggestion to the effect that Corsica and schoolyards are proper *loci* of *lex talionis* understood as a principle of corrective justice is meant to indicate that such interpretation of retaliation is primitive and coarse. And such a view coincides with the general view mostly everybody espouses in relation to the meaning and alleged rigidity of *lex talionis* in ancient times that I have just presented. Though I have also presented evidence showing that even when *lex talionis* supposedly held sway, its allegedly unexceptionable character was curbed by provisos pertaining to a theory of culpability. Not even in ancient times was a person who unintentionally (and thus supposedly unintendedly) caused the death of his neighbor forced to suffer as much as her victim (or her victim's family) had suffered. As a matter of fact, the unintended wrongdoer was sent to a refuge city, and while it is open to discussion whether or not this constitutes punishment, even if it does, it is a lesser punishment, probably stemming from the fact that the unintended wrongdoer is less blameworthy.

Davies, however, talks about "suffering as much as the wrongdoer has wrongfully made others suffer," and the use he makes of the word "wrongfully" must be analyzed carefully. If his wording of *lex talionis* as a general principle of corrective justice includes the notion of "wrongful" evil outcomes, then even the most primitive forms of *lex talionis* must be read as "an eye for a wrongfully severed eye, a tooth for a wrongfully severed tooth," and so on. Fleshing out just what "wrongfulness" is, and how we are to measure it, are of course crucial issues.

Since an essential aim of my project to show that the distinction between intended and unintended action provides a neat framework for our schemes of apportioning blame both in the legal and in the moral

---

18. Michael Davies, "Harm and Retribution," *Philosophy and Public Affairs* (1986): 239.

realms, that is, both within the criminal law and in the more general realm of corrective justice (of which the criminal law is but a sub-part), I wish to argue against any sharp distinctions between legal and moral culpability. In light of the passages of the Old Testament discussed above, it seems to me that Davies's account of *lex talionis* as a general principle of corrective justice merely repeats the old shibboleth according to which *lex talionis* is crude, rigid, and so forth, without really arguing for this position.

Let me now, then, turn to Davies's accounts of *lex talionis* as a *principle of criminal law*. He claims that there are two ways of understanding *lex talionis* as a principle of criminal law: materially and formally. "[*Lex talionis*] understood formally . . . is the principle that punishment should be proportioned to the gravity of the offense or otherwise made 'to fit the crime'. *Lex talionis* may also be understood 'materially,' that is, requiring punishment to be proportioned (in part at least) to harm done (or, perhaps, to be limited by the harm done)."[19]

If we substitute "crime" and "harm done" for "evil outcome," it is difficult to see how Davies's formal interpretation of *lex talionis* differs from its mainstream interpretation or from Davies's own corrective justice interpretation, discussed above. This would further support my goal of undermining sharp distinctions regarding culpability—such as the one Davies proposes—between moral and legal culpability. Moreover, except for the emphasis put on harm in the material interpretation of *lex talionis*, it is also difficult to see how the material and the formal interpretations of *lex talionis* differ from each other. But, a further question arises: is Davies justified in emphasizing harm so much in the material interpretation of *lex talionis*? I think not.

Davies equates his two accounts of *lex talionis* understood as a principle of criminal law with two general principles of retribution put forth by Hugo Bedau. Bedau's principles read as follows: (1) the severity of the punishment must be proportional to the gravity of the offense, and (2) the gravity of the offense must be a function of fault in the offender and harm caused in the victim.[20] Davies maintains that his formal interpretation of *lex talionis* maps onto Bedau's first principle and his material interpretation maps onto Bedau's second principle. Now, although Davies leaves open the possibility of something other than mere harm to be included in the formula for calculating proportionate punishment, the fact that, unlike Bedau, he does not include "fault" in his formula speaks volumes about

---

19. Davies, "Harm and Retribution," 238–39.
20. H. A. Bedau, "Classification-Based Sentencing: Some Conceptual and Ethical Problems," in *Criminal Justice*, ed. J. Roland Pennock, Nomos: Yearbook of the American Society for Political and Legal Philosophy XXVII (New York: NYU Press, 1985), 102.

the flaws inherent in Davies's allegedly crisp boundary dividing the legal and moral realms in relation to *lex talionis*. Davies's failure to mention fault shows that his material *lex talionis* is but a modified rendering of the mainstream view that *lex talionis* is not concerned with blaming, but only with punishing, not concerned with Intentional states, but only with outcomes. Unless one is willing to expand the meaning of "criminal law" so as to include most of moral philosophy, it is clear that the comparisons between harm-plus-fault on the one hand and blame and punishment on the other are not the parochial monopoly of the criminal law. Moreover, to the extent that Davies expands the meaning of criminal law so much, he also obliterates the distinction between the legal and moral realms.

At any rate, what is clear from Bedau's principles is that the crucial unresolved issue of *lex talionis*, in any of its formulations, always boils down to this: how to make the punishment fit the crime, that is, how do we determine when the punishment is proportionate to the evil act? If our response is that we know that it is so when it corresponds to some formula whose variables include at least harm and fault, then we have what appears to be—and indeed is—an eminently formalistic answer.

Like other biblical principles, quite notoriously like the golden rule (i.e., "do unto others as you wish done unto you"), *lex talionis* exhibits an eminently formalistic character. Just as the golden rule does not provide concrete guidance for action, so *lex talionis* does not provide concrete guidance for making the punishment (or the blame) fit the crime (or the wrongdoing). One way in which *lex talionis* is rendered less formalistic, or at least one way in which its formalities are laid bare, is by introducing specific modes of culpability, and the most fundamental distinction giving rise to these different modes of culpability is, as we have seen, the distinction between intended and unintended action.

The history of culpability is, broadly conceived, the history of the attempts to fill the gaps in *lex talionis*. Clearly, it is not enough merely to stipulate that the punishment should fit the crime, without explaining when and why it so fits the crime. *Lex talionis* is among the first attempts in recorded history to provide a method for inflicting fitting punishments. I have argued that even this pristine attempt rested, to no small extent, upon issues related to Intentionality. What makes ancient policies governing blame and punishment inadequate is not that they exhibit indifference to the Intentional states of the wrongdoers. Rather, it is the fact that these policies were not accompanied by much-needed definitions of intended and unintended actions, and by ways of articulating the relationship between the intended/unintended pair and the intentional/unintentional pair.

On the Transition from Biblical to
Greco-Roman Culpability

In Greco-Roman philosophy and legislation, we witness a refinement of biblical theories of culpability. Ancient institutions of blood avengers, refuge cities, and the like steadily lose relevance in Greek philosophy. More importantly, for the first time in history, we see deep theoretical discussions concerning the definitions of—and the criteria that allow us to distinguish between—intended and unintended action. Some of the Greek contributions are so sophisticated and insightful that they cause many to minimize contributions made earlier, particularly those contributions contained in *lex talionis*. For example, J. M. Kelly, in his *A Short History of Western Legal Thought*, claims: "The administering of punishment in the most primitive age was probably instinctive and unreflecting, the product of a victim's feelings and those of his kin. . . . It is an important step when calm reflection is applied to the infliction of punishment, and objective reasons of policy are found to justify it. This stage in Western thought is recorded first in Plato."[21]

Plato did inaugurate a new era in the history of culpability, but not because previous theories were instinctive or unreflecting. What I have already said regarding culpability in biblical times contradicts this view. Kelly's own rather simple view should also be met with skepticism given that many of Plato's own views on culpability can be traced to earlier Athenian orators and legislators, such as Demosthenes and Drakon.[22] Moreover, Plato himself admits that the normative content of the distinction between intended and unintended action has always been present in human history. In book 9 of *The Laws*, Plato expresses this thesis as follows: "We have never extricated ourselves from our perplexity about this matter; we have never achieved any clear demarcation between these two types of wrongs, the voluntary [*hekousion*] and the involuntary [*akousion*], which are recognized as distinct by every legislator who has ever existed in any society and regarded as distinct by all law."[23] That these two types of wrongdoing, voluntary and involuntary, correspond, in this context, to intended and unintended shall become clear immediately. Plato, in any event, does not think of himself as introducing this distinction to the

---

21. J. M. Kelly, *A Short History of Western Legal Thought* (Oxford: Clarendon Press, 1992), 31.
22. Cf. Michael Gagarin, *Drakon and Early Athenian Homicide Law* (New Haven: Yale University Press, 1981); Stephen Usher, trans., *On the Crown*, by Demosthenes (Warminster: Aris & Phillips, 1993); Douglas M. MacDowell, trans., *Against Meidias*, by Demosthenes (Oxford: Clarendon Press, 1990).
23. A. E. Taylor, trans., *The Laws of Plato* (London: J. M. Dent and Sons, 1934), 249.

world; instead he sees himself as trying to make this difficult distinction intelligible. Several millennia later this remains an unfinished task, as philosophers continue to grapple with this excruciatingly difficult issue. But the mainstream view, so neatly patent in Kelly's writings, has it differently: "The Greek mind addressed also the relation of punishment to the wrongdoer's state of intent. The notion which seems elementary in the modern world, that guilt and liability to punishment depend on the state of mind which accompanied the injurious act—expressed in the criminal law of the common law world by the maxim '*actus non facit reum nisi mens sit rea*'—was by no means axiomatic in the ancient world."[24] Thus, Kelly both understates and overstates the value of Plato's project: he understates it insofar as Plato's aim is one of the most ambitious and yet unresolved tasks facing any theory of culpability, not merely an attempt "to apply calm reflection to the infliction of punishment." Kelly overstates the project because grounding culpability and punishment on Intentionality was not Plato's—or even Greece's—creation.

Plato on Culpability: *Hekousion* and *Akousion*

Regrettably, Plato did not offer much in the way of a conceptual clarification regarding the notions of intended and unintended action in themselves; for that we must wait until Aristotle. Although, as I intend to show, Plato's importance in the history of culpability is colossal, the relevance of Plato's major contributions lies elsewhere. First, Plato's work on culpability is of great importance as he seems to have been the first philosopher to discuss vexing problems associated to the distinction between intended and unintended action. Second, Plato can also be seen as a forerunner of later refinements in culpability which opened up the spectrum of modes of culpability. Finally, the provisions of the Magnesian penal code that Plato puts forth in *The Laws* (particularly those found in book 9 of this extraordinary though somewhat neglected work, which occupied Plato's later days) bring welcome organization to a theory of culpability unequivocally based on the Intentional states of the wrongdoer.

I will address the first issue, then, by explaining the relationship between "voluntary" and "intended" in Plato. This analysis of the relationship between these terms, incidentally, holds for other Greek authors as well. The Greek terms that Taylor translates as "voluntary" and "involuntary" actions are *hekousios* and *akousios* actions, respectively. Taylor, however, translates these same Greek terms in other contexts as "intentional"

---

24. Kelly, *A Short History*, 32.

and "unintentional." This problem is pervasive in translations of *hekousios* and *akousios* into English, and extends beyond Taylor's Plato. Authoritative works in the area are multifarious in that they sometimes translate these terms as "intentional" and "unintentional" exclusively, sometimes as "voluntary" and "involuntary" exclusively, some treat "voluntary" and "intentional" as synonyms, and some even use other terms such as "willing," "unwilling," and the like.[25]

I want to avoid, as much as possible, a purely philological discussion regarding how these terms should be translated into English, but I still need to say a few words about these translational issues. The crucial issue that I want to address is not how to *translate* these terms, but, rather, how to *understand* them. Plato, as noted, does not provide much-needed definitions of *hekousios* and *akousios* actions; neither did his predecessors. Several clues regarding these definitions, however, are available; most of these clues relate to the broad definition of intending to which I have already alluded: Someone brings about an outcome intendedly if she desires it and her conduct is aimed at bringing it about. In light of the absence of conceptual clarifications of this matter in pre-Aristotelian works, one must turn to Plato's examples of *hekousios* and *akousios*. Plato analyzes these examples within the context of his discussion of homicide.

Plato's classification of homicides is highly sophisticated; there are thirteen types of unintentional homicide and nine types of intentional homicide.[26] Some of these are cases that Plato is not comfortable classifying as either intended or unintended. Many of these types of homicide are unimportant for my purposes here, insofar as they turn on considerations not related to Intentionality. For example, many of the distinctions between types of homicide are based on whether the perpetrators or the victims were slaves, foreigners, relatives, and so on. Some other types are perhaps

---

25. For authors who, in this context, consider these terms synonyms, cf. Taylor, *The Laws of Plato*; Usher, *On the Crown*, 147 and 264; and perhaps also Terence Irwin, trans., *Nicomachean Ethics*, by Aristotle (Indianapolis: Hackett, 1985), 53–70 and especially 431–32. For those who translate the terms as intentional and unintentional, cf. Sir Paul Vinogradoff, *Outlines of Historical Jurisprudence*, vol. 2 (Oxford: Oxford University Press,1922), 182–85; MacDowell, *Against Meidias*, 113 and 257–63; Gagarin, *Drakon and Early Athenian Homicide Law*, passim; and Kelly, *A Short History*, 31–35. For translations that use voluntary and involuntary exclusively, cf. R. G. Bury, trans., *The Laws*, by Plato, vol. 11 (Cambridge, MA: Harvard University Press, 1926), 273–96; R. F. Stalley, *An Introduction to Plato's Laws* (Oxford: Basil Blackwell, 1983), 160–65; Leo Strauss, *The Argument and the Action of Plato's Laws* (Chicago: University of Chicago Press, 1975), 126–39. Finally for someone who considers all these translations flawed, see A. D. Woozley, "Plato on Killing in Anger," *Philosophical Quarterly* (1972): 303–17.
26. Trevor Saunders's *Plato's Penal Code: Tradition, Controversy, and Reform in Greek Penology* (Oxford: Oxford University Press, 1994) contains an excellent analysis of Plato's writings on criminal law theory.

laughable nowadays, such as homicides committed by beasts or inanimate objects.[27]

What is crucial for my purposes is to show that, according to my definitions, Plato's *hekousios* homicides correspond to intended homicides and *akousios* homicides to unintended homicides. I shall therefore limit my analysis of Plato's treatment of homicide only to those relevant cases whose differences stem from Intentional states, leaving aside those cases that merely differ in relation to the characteristics of the agents involved.

The first case of *akousios* homicide that Plato discusses reads as follows: "if a man unintentionally [*akousios*] causes the death of a person with whom he is on friendly terms, in competition or at the public sports. . . ."[28] An initial indication that in these contexts the most accurate rendering of *akousios* is "unintended" and not "involuntary" is that, by and large, when we practice a sport, our actions are not involuntary but (at times) unintended (many among our unintended actions, but perhaps also some of our intended actions, are also unintentional). For example, if while playing baseball I accidentally break a window, the breaking of the window is unintended, it would probably be unintentional as well, but, quite clearly, it will not be involuntary. Although not too eloquently put, Plato's point here seems to be that the wrongdoer in this case did not desire and did not act in order to bring about the death of his victim, thus that the death was not intended, not *akousios*. And this interpretation of Plato's point is sufficiently supported by Athenian law and by legal commentators of the time. Demosthenes, for example, praising an ancient Athenian law that held the killing of a human being in athletic contests to be an *akousios* action, observes the following: "Mark how righteously and admirably these distinctions are severally defined by the lawgiver who defined them originally. 'If a man kills another in athletic contest,' he declared him not to be guilty, for this reason, that he had regard not to the event but to the intention of the agent. The intention is not to kill his man, but to vanquish him unslain."[29]

Another example that Plato gives of *akousios* homicide is the following: "In the case of all medical practitioners, if the patient meets his end by an

----

27. Plato even provides guidelines for the trial that the inanimate thing must stand. "If an inanimate thing causes the loss of a human life—an exception being made for lightning or other such visitations of God—any object which causes death by its falling upon a man or his falling against it shall be sat upon judgment by the nearest neighbor, at the invitation of the next of kin, who shall hereby acquit himself and the whole family of their obligation; on conviction the guilty object to be cast beyond the frontier, as was directed in the case of a beast." Taylor, *The Laws of Plato*, 264.

28. Taylor, *The Laws of Plato*, 254.

29. J. H. Vince, trans., *Against Aristocrates*, in *Demosthenes* (Cambridge, MA: Harvard University Press, 1935), 23.54.

unintentional [*akousios*] act of the physician, the law should hold the physician clear."[30] This is an interesting case in that it seems to conflate the analysis of Intentional states with the analysis of justifications. What renders the physician's actions blameless is in part that it was not his desire to bring about the death of the patient. But what is beyond dispute is that the medical practitioner did not act involuntarily (as we shall see more clearly below and in chapter 4). All other cases of *akousios* homicide that Plato discusses lack one of the two requirements (either the desire or the planning) that I lay down in my sketch of a definition of intended action.

Let us now turn to Plato's discussion of *hekousios* homicide. Plato's preamble to this section is eloquent: "We are next to deal with the case of acts in this kind done with intent, [*hekousios* acts] in downright wickedness, and of deliberate design, at the dictation of overmastering pleasures, cupidities, and jealousies."[31] This is all Plato offers by way of conceptual clarification of the nature of *hekousios* homicide, and such meager treatment of the theoretical foundations of this type of homicide is surely in keeping with his treatment of *akousios* homicide (so we had to appeal to examples). But here, too, it is difficult to interpret the absence of wickedness, or cupidities, jealousies, and the like, to be involuntary. There is, however, an interesting difference between Plato's treatment of these two types of homicide, for now Plato is mainly interested in the psychological outlook of agents who commit *hekousios* homicides. Plato thus focuses on what he deems to be typical motivational factors behind this type of homicide. Concupiscence, guilt, fear, rivalry, envy, and other familiar vices are gathered together in a lengthy list. Now, what is important to point out is that in actions where an agent is driven by any of these motives, her actions exhibit, undoubtedly, both the desire and the planning required by my definition of intended action. These are my reasons, then, for claiming that Plato's distinction between *akousios* and *hekousios* maps, in hitherto unnoticed ways, onto the distinction between intended and unintended action.[32]

As he discussed homicides done in anger or passion, Plato confessed his inability to know whether they were *hekousios* or *akousios* actions, or in my terms, intended or unintended actions. Now, what is it to commit an act in anger or passion? Plato answers this question by giving two examples:

---

30. Taylor, *The Laws of Plato*, 254.
31. Taylor, *The Laws of Plato*, 259.
32. It should be clear, then, that if someone disagrees with my definitions of intentional and unintentional action, then she can refute this later claim, but not otherwise. The definition of intentional and unintentional action is, as stated, an extremely difficult enterprise, one to which I shall devote full consideration in chapter 5. Yet, I think that the broad definition I am using should encounter little resistance.

[1] [An act] is an act of passion when a man is done away with on the impulse of the moment, by blows or the like, suddenly and without any previous purpose to kill and remorse instantly follows on the act; [2] it is also an act of passion when a man is roused by insult in words or dishonouring gestures, pursues his revenge, and ends by taking a life with purpose to slay and without subsequent remorse for the deed.[33]

Both these acts have their origin in decisions made on the spur of the moment. Under this light it is easier to understand Plato's inability to decide whether or not these sorts of actions are intended or unintended, insofar as it is difficult to tell whether they were planned or desired. And thus it is also difficult to say how severely they should be blamed. After all, on first approximation, they seem to be less blameworthy than if they would have been carried out without anger, but not as leniently blamed as if they would have been clearly unintended. Plato's treatment of this sort of case represents an early attempt to show that distinctions other than the one between intended and unintended, such as the distinction between intending and foreseeing, shed much needed light on these sorts of cases, and are probably required by more comprehensive theories of culpability.[34]

It must be remembered that Plato is unable to *know* whether killing in anger is intended or unintended; thus, his problem here is strictly epistemological. This is an important point, because I wish to argue that Plato cannot simply, willy-nilly as it were, propose a third category of actions side by side with the categories of intended and unintended action without at the same time proposing a correlative category in the normative realm. But Plato expresses contrasting views in this regard: "It should seem that boundary is not in all cases immediately adjacent to boundary; where there is a border-land, this interposing belt touches either region first and it is common ground to both. In particular we have said that the deeds of passion form such a border-land between the intentional and the unintentional."[35] It appears then that in this passage Plato expresses a straightforward thesis concerning the existence of a third ontological category of action (deeds of passion), which I wish to deny. I shall echo A. D. Woozley's insightful remarks, as my first step in showing that Plato is not really presenting a third ontological category of action. Woozley observes:

In 878b [the passage of *The Laws* I have just quoted] comes the most important sentence in the whole section, where we meet (possibly for the first time in Western philosophy) a formulation of the concept of *vagueness*. Plato does

---

33. Taylor, *The Laws of Plato*, 256.
34. The distinction between intention and foresight, and also the distinction between foresight and inadvertence, shall occupy my attention in the next chapter.
35. Taylor, *The Laws of Plato*, 269.

not have quite the right model. Each of a pair of contrasting terms is vague, *not*, as he represents it, when each has a boundary line, but there is a border area between the boundary lines [Plato's border-land], *but* when neither has a fixed boundary line and there is a border area such as there is no decision procedure for determining, with regard to something falling within that area, that it falls within the extension of one term rather than within that of the other.[36]

This vagueness to which Woozley alludes is precisely what I have been insisting upon here: that Plato did not offer clear definitions of *akousios* and *hekousios* actions. (It is worth noticing that, if Woozley is correct, such a crucial concept, vagueness, appeared for the first time in the West in the context of a theory of culpability.) Woozley is certainly right, however, in suggesting that our passage is not so clear after all. After fastidious philological analyses, Woozley further tells us that "Plato is maintaining . . . that *hekousios* and *akousios* are contradictory terms, but also that they are vague, so that there are some acts, specifically those done in anger, that are not indubitably one rather than the other. Whether Plato realized what a fatal blow his admission of vagueness dealt to his doctrine of real kinds we do not know: and that does not matter here."[37]

Analyzing whether Plato in fact dealt a fatal blow to his metaphysical doctrines does matter for my purposes. I think that Woozley commits an error similar to Plato's, as he fails to fully distinguish epistemology from ontology. After all, the vagueness to which Woozley refers can best be understood as an epistemological notion (doubtfulness surely is an epistemological notion). A pair of concepts (or, better, a pair of propositions) are contradictory when they *are* mutually exclusive and jointly exhaustive. Then, if *hekousios* and *akousios* are contradictory in Plato, then there is no way in which an action can fail to be one or the other. So, an action done in anger cannot fail to be *hekousios* or *akousios*, even when Plato or anyone else may ignore which kind of action we are in the presence of in any given case. If Plato's border-land were an ontological category, not only would he be dealing a fatal blow to some of his cherished metaphysical doctrines, but he would be inflicting a similar mortal wound to the very cogency of his arguments too. Plato's border-land is best understood as a region of epistemological uncertainty, not as an ontological region.

Consider the following two contradictory propositions: (1) it is raining, and (2) it is not raining. This pair of propositions constitutes a classical example of contradictoriness, for (a) it is either raining or not raining,

---

36. Woozley, "Plato on Killing in Anger," 312.
37. Woozley, "Plato on Killing in Anger," 312–13. (Incidentally, Plato's discussion of crimes committed in anger is also relevant when analyzing the contemporary notion of provocation—say, that found in the Model Penal Code, for example.)

and (b) it cannot be true both that it is raining and that it is not raining. But suppose that the following proposition, (3) it is drizzling, is true. In light of (3)'s truth, we are not sure whether proposition (1) is true or whether proposition (2) is true. Formally, this set of propositions is fully analogous to Plato's set of propositions describing intended, unintended, and anger-motivated homicides. But if (1) and (2) are contradictory, then (3) must fall within the extension of only one of them. The way to solve this difficulty is simple; we need to properly define rain and drizzle, in such a way that either drizzle would be rain or not be rain. Just the same must be done for killing in anger; we need to define anger and passion in such a way that actions done in anger are either intended or unintended. This Plato did not do.

Yet, Plato deserves credit, for he was the first to expand the number of distinctions that a sound theory of culpability requires. He saw that merely dividing actions into *hekousios* and *akousios* would not do justice to our rational considerations concerning blame. He sought to develop a more fine-grained theory of culpability by introducing acts done in anger. For it seems clear that cases of evil outcomes brought in anger give rise to less blame than if they would have been brought about intendedly, but more than if they would have been brought about unintendedly. As noted, Plato was unclear about the distinction between the intended and the unintended, on the one hand, and the distinction between the intentional and the unintentional, on the other, and of course he was unclear regarding the correct status of acts done in anger within each of these distinctions.

Nonetheless, expanding the spectrum of distinctions needed in a theory of culpability is an insight that remains valuable. The very same types of problems arising from "middle categories" abound in contemporary theories of culpability, where discussions concerning actions done, say, recklessly, are often inconclusive. Plato's distinction between acts committed in anger and those not committed in anger plays a similar role in his theory of culpability to the role played by modern distinctions based on awareness or foresight, which are central to contemporary theories of culpability. Plato's Magnesian penal code is the first place where, albeit unclearly, a theory of culpability is refined by *adding* other important distinctions to the fundamental distinction between intended and unintended action.

Plato's work on culpability is also valuable because it is the first attempt to create a *general* theory of culpability. By "general" I mean that the theory can be applied to all types of evil outcomes, whether they are harms, offenses, or any specific crimes. The mere fact that there is in *The Laws* a whole section devoted to the analysis of all types of homicide is a major development, especially when one contrasts this with the predominantly piecemeal approach of the Old Testament. Moreover, the same principles that Plato lays down for homicides apply as well, in his view, to injuries and perhaps even to other types of evil outcomes. Plato's theory, however, is still incipient with respect to its general applicability, for in spite of the possibility of inferring some fundamentals of a theory of culpability from Plato's discussion of specific crimes, nowhere does he explicitly make those claims. In light of the importance Plato gave to the social or familial status of wrongdoers or victims, that is, whether they were citizens, slaves, relatives, and so on, an alleged general principle of apportioning blame tacitly expressed by Plato would be vulnerable to too many exceptions.

In the preamble to this section of *The Laws*, Plato expresses his interest in accomplishing a "clear demarcation between these two types of wrongs, the voluntary and the involuntary [*hekousios* and *akousios*]," and so he seems to be interested in a general theory of culpability, and not one merely aimed at clarifying homicide.[38] Later, too, when Plato introduces what Woozley has termed the first formulation of vagueness in the West, Plato appears to be talking in general terms. Many, if not most, of Plato's claims regarding, say, homicide or injuries, can be seen as useful principles for the generality of evil outcomes.

A relevant reason that might explain the general thrust of Plato's theory of culpability is that he seems to have been relatively indifferent to distinctions between the legal and moral realms, at least regarding culpability itself. For Plato's initial interest in shedding light on the nature of the distinction between intentional and unintentional action was to explain an apparent paradox, which is in no way restricted to any of these two realms. This paradox applies to all wrongdoing.

With penetrating Socratic flavor, the paradox obtains when we struggle to reconcile the view that humans can only do wrong unwillingly (a cornerstone of Socratic ethics) with the view that there are two types of wrongs, *hekousios* and *akousios*, which Plato, adding insult to injury, considers to be "recognized as distinct by every legislator who has ever existed."[39] So, as it turns out, in all cases in which someone desires and plots to do wrong, she does this unwillingly. And this "unwillingly willing something," naturally, appears paradoxical to Plato. It is not important or possible for me to resolve the paradox of Socratic ethics here, it is sufficient to observe that the Platonic sense of "willing," which perplexed Gorgias, Polus, and Callicles in Ancient times and continues to perplex philosophers today, is drastically different from contemporary accounts of what willing is (as we shall see, some authors, plausibly, deny that there is any willing at all).[40]

---

38. Taylor, *The Laws of Plato*, 249.
39. Taylor, *The Laws of Plato*, 249.
40. This sense, although present in practically every related dialogue, was immortalized by Socrates in *Gorgias*, 466e, when Socrates, referring to Archelaus and other tyrants,

In spite of the fact that Plato's work is perhaps the greatest single improvement from one period to the next in the history of culpability, many issues remained unresolved. Beyond the numerous faults resulting from anachronistic views, some of them perhaps traceable to the biblical tradition of *lex talionis,* and some probably the offspring of the Homeric heritage, Plato's theory of culpability fails at the conceptual level. Much-needed definitions of intended and unintended actions are wanting, as is a set of criteria for distinguishing one type of action from the other, but above all what is lacking is a way of correlating the purely descriptive level of discussion concerned with the distinction between the intended and the unintended and the normative level of discussion concerned with the distinction between the (more) culpable and the (less) culpable. Some of these themes are improved upon in Aristotle's discussion of culpability, to which we now turn.

Aristotle on Culpability: The Birth of Action Theory

In spite of the fact that Plato's incipient theory of culpability is found in his most important legal work, I have suggested that it applies both to the legal and moral realms. Insofar as Aristotle's discussion of *hekousios* and *akousios* is found in his ethical writings, it is perhaps easier to see that he was not narrowly focused on legal issues either. Aristotle's ethical doctrine is known as virtue ethics, and it suggests that the goal of our existence is to develop certain "virtuous" character traits. Yet, for an action to be considered virtuous, it must be *hekousios* action, and thus the distinction between the intended and the unintended plays a much more visible role in Aristotle's ethical theory than it does in Plato's. The issue of the necessity of an action being *hekousios* in order to be a candidate for virtuous action is discussed at length in all of Aristotle's major ethical works: I shall focus on the *Nicomachean Ethics,* where Aristotle presents his views in a most refined and clear manner. But, as shall become clear, Aristotle's theory of culpability, just like Plato's and that of *lex talionis,* is applicable both in the legal and moral realms.

Aristotle is commonly viewed as the founding father of what we now know as the "theory of action," and his contributions to this area corrected previous theories. David Charles describes the importance of Aristotle's contribution thus: "In the philosophy of action, Aristotle occupies a central position analogous to that of Frege in the philosophy of language. He

---

claims that "they do just about nothing they want [will] to, though they certainly do whatever they see most fit to do." Cf. Donald J. Zeyl, trans., *Plato's Gorgias* (Indianapolis, IN: Hackett 1987), 28ff.

initiated the philosophical discussion of issues concerning the ontology, analysis and explanation of intentional action, and his questions, assumptions and arguments yield a framework within which much contemporary work can be located and better understood."[41] It is possible, however, to read translations of any of Aristotle's ethical works from cover to cover without finding words relating to intentions, thus casting skeptical shadows over Charles's thesis (which I endorse) regarding Aristotle's important analyses of intentional action. There is an explanation which, by now, should be straightforward: the words *hekousion* and *akousion* that Aristotle uses are the same that Plato, Demosthenes, Drakon, and others use, but in Aristotle's case they are almost invariably translated as voluntary and involuntary. Why these words are so variedly translated (as voluntary, intentional, willed, etc.) in Plato and others while they are uniformly translated as voluntary in Aristotle is an enigma which I cannot solve here. In book 3 of the *Nicomachean Ethics*, which I shall argue is the first comprehensive study on the relationship between Intentionality and blame, *hekousios* and *akousios* actions are almost invariably translated as "voluntary" and "involuntary" actions. For the reasons expressed above, I do not wish to claim that it is necessarily a mistake to translate *hekousios* and *akousios* actions in this way, but not to point out that these Greek words can also mean "intended" and "unintended" action (or "intentional" and "unintentional" action) is surely a mistake which has misled many.

Aristotle discusses issues pertaining to a theory of culpability not in the context of framing a penal code, but in the context of laying the foundations of an ethical theory that still attracts the interest of moral theorists engaged in virtue ethics.[42] The general aim of embracing both the legal and moral realms that Aristotle has in mind is succinctly expressed at the outset of book 3 of the *Nicomachean Ethics*. There Aristotle tells us:

> Virtue however is concerned with emotions and actions, and it is only voluntary [*hekousios*] actions for which praise and blame are given; those that are involuntary [*akousios*] are condoned and sometimes even pitied. Hence it seems to be necessary for the student of ethics to define the difference between the Voluntary and the Involuntary; [between *hekousios* and *akousios*] and this also will be of service to the legislator in assigning rewards and punishments.[43]

---

41. David Charles, *Aristotle's Philosophy of Action* (Ithaca, NY: Cornell University Press, 1984), ix.

42. Alasdair MacIntyre is perhaps the best-known contemporary revivalist of virtue ethics; but even authors such as John Dewey can be viewed as presenting a version of virtue ethics. See my "Process Teleology: John Dewey's Reconstructed Virtue Ethics," *Revista Venezolana de Filosofía* (1996): 143–63 (in Spanish).

43. H. Rackham, trans., *Nicomachean Ethics*, by Aristotle (Cambridge, MA: Harvard University Press, 1926), 117.

Like Plato, Aristotle begins his analysis of different types of action by focusing on unintended ones. Aristotle presents two types of unintended action: "it is then generally held that actions are involuntary [*akousios*] when done (a) under compulsion or (b) through ignorance."[44] These two types of action are further subdivided. Actions done under compulsion can be either (a.1) those in which the agent contributes nothing, and (a.2) those in which the agent contributes something. The former type of action is always unintended and blameless; common examples are agents being carried away by strong winds onto someone else, and similar cases where agents are mere instruments. Here the agent is completely passive.[45]

Regarding the other type of action done under compulsion (where the agent contributes something), Aristotle recognizes that several difficulties arise. Consider Aristotle's example of someone being blackmailed into doing something under the threat of harm to her loved ones, or the famous example of throwing cargo overboard during a storm, in order to save one's life. Although Aristotle begins by characterizing these cases as "mixed," and though this strategy is reminiscent of Plato's treatment of deeds committed in anger, Aristotle quickly tells us that these cases are intended (*hekousios*), but only after one has taken into account the specific circumstances. This is a remarkable development. In our own times, when someone kills in self-defense we do not say that the person acted unintendedly, yet we do not blame this person for her action. Self-defense is a justification, and this means that the action itself is not unlawful, as we saw in chapter 1; to bring about the death of another human being in self-defense is not, strictly speaking, to do evil. The reason for calling these sorts of actions "mixed," of course, is that if they truly are unintended, they nevertheless seem to be more blameworthy than other unintended actions, and if they truly are intended they nevertheless seem to be less culpable than other intended actions. The problem haunting Aristotle and Plato, which continues to be difficult today, is how to map the purely descriptive realm of the intended and the unintended onto the normative realm of the more culpable and the less culpable. As we have seen, this mapping is further complicated by the fact that we typically move within the realm of the intentional and the unintentional, which fuzzily collapses the descriptive and normative realms.

In sum, however, we can clarify things as follows: among actions that can be said to be done under compulsion, only those in which the agent "contributes nothing" can be unequivocally called unintended and never culpable (hence they are frequently called unintentional). Yet, those actions

---

44. Rackham, *Nicomachean Ethics*, 117.
45. This is what John Austin, as we shall see in the next chapter, would consider an involuntary movement.

done under compulsion in which the agent "contributes something" are sometimes unintended but culpable (hence they are sometimes called intentional).

I turn now to Aristotle's class of actions caused by ignorance. Aristotle divides actions caused by ignorance (b) thoroughly, according to different criteria. For my purposes the most important criterion has to do with whether or not the agent feels regret after bringing about the evil outcome; thus actions are divided into two kinds. When the agent feels regret, then the action is unintended (or at least unintentional), but if the agent feels no regret then his action is neither intended nor unintended; it is nonintended. The evil act done through ignorance and not accompanied by regret afterwards constitutes, for Aristotle, a third ontological category of action: actions which are neither intended nor unintended. This is a very difficult point, and for my purposes very important too.

Regret seems to be an inadequate criterion, based on Aristotle's idiosyncratic focus on character-building and virtue-nurturing; what difference does any Intentional state accompanying the agent *after* the action is done make in our assessment of the blameworthiness of the way in which the action was done? Of course, in the big scheme of things regret does provide valuable information as to the nature of the wrongdoer's character, and these insights might affect, all things considered, the blameworthiness of her action. But for the reasons explained in the previous chapter, a theory of culpability should restrict itself to the Intentional states that the agent has when she acts. Whether or not the agent regrets what she did cannot help us determine whether she intended it or not, whether she was aware of what she was doing or not, and these above all are the issues with which a theory of culpability is concerned.

I have stated that intended and unintended actions are truly contradictories, and I have shown that this thesis holds for Plato, but I cannot possibly do the same in Aristotle's case. I have suggested that Plato's "third category" (acts committed in anger) is merely a category of epistemic uncertainty or vagueness; but in Aristotle's case the third category is ontologically distinct. Now, what is crucially important is that whatever categories we might allow at the descriptive level, we should allow a corresponding category at the normative level. If this or that set of Intentional states constitutes a relevantly different way of doing things, a theory of culpability must of course indicate how severely this way of doing this should be blamed.

Aristotle also distinguishes between acting *through* ignorance and acting *in* ignorance; thus, a drunken agent acts in ignorance but not through ignorance. The ignorance that can make the action less blameworthy is of several sorts: (1) ignorance regarding who is doing the act, (2) ignorance regarding what the act is, (3) ignorance about what or to what the act is aimed, (4) ignorance about the instrument with which the act is being carried out, (5) ignorance regarding with what purpose the act is carried out, and (6) ignorance regarding in what way the act is done. Of course, Aristotle points out that no one can be ignorant of all these simultaneously (and one can hardly be ignorant in the first case). But, in any case, whenever an agent acts in ignorance of any of these factors, her action is properly deemed blameless, if it is also regretted afterwards.

It is clear, then, that Aristotle discriminates between two conceptually distinct types of unintended action; a move which by itself constitutes a development from Plato's theory of culpability, where only different types of homicides or injuries were discussed. Richard Sorabji refers to the two reasons that justify Aristotle's two types of unintended action, compulsion and ignorance, as "excusing factors."[46] I think Sorabji's choice of words is unfortunate for two reasons; first, it obscures the fact that what Aristotle had in mind here were *modes of culpability*, not excuses. And of course, the term "excuses" is a term of art in contemporary criminal law, which is prone to be misleading in the analysis of Aristotle's incipient forays into a theory of culpability.

But, even more interestingly, Sorabji further attempts to show that Aristotle was not, of all things, parsimonious, having presented *just* a twofold classification of unintended action. If my thesis is correct, to defend Aristotle from the charge of excessive parsimony in his treatment of unintentional action seems like an instance of the fallacy of the straw man. Aristotle is, after all, actually the first thinker to distinguish different types of unintended action. Whether his classification is insufficient or defective (I think it is both) should not cause us to lose sight of the historical context in which it is found.

Sorabji provides a somewhat lengthy list of additional "excuses" that render action unintended: mental abnormality, upbringing, physiological defects, passion, lust, and fear. It would take considerable time to analyze each of these excuses in order to elucidate whether they are truly excuses or simply different types of unintended action, and such an enterprise is not relevant for my purposes here. If Sorabji's "excuses" indeed constituted different types of unintended action, this would further support my claim that rather than being parsimonious, one of Aristotle's most important contributions to culpability is to have expanded the types of unintended action.

The other crucial contribution of Aristotle's theory of culpability is that he provides, for the first time, clear-cut definitions of intentional and unin-

---

46. Richard Sorabji, *Necessity, Cause, and Blame: Perspectives in Aristotle's Theory* (Ithaca, NY: Cornell University Press, 1980), 257ff.

tentional action: "An involuntary [*akousios*] action being one done under compulsion or through ignorance, a voluntary [*hekousios*] act would seem to be an act of which the origins lies in the agent, who knows the particular circumstances in which he is acting."[47] Moreover, Aristotle also subdivides intentional action into two types, this division turns on the role that *choice* plays in bringing about an evil outcome.

> Having defined voluntary and involuntary [*hekousios* and *akousios*] action, we next have to examine the nature of Choice. For this appears to be intimately connected with virtue, and to afford a surer test of character than do our actions.
>
> Choice is manifestly a voluntary [*hekousios*] act. But the two terms are not synonymous, the latter being the wider. Children and the lower animals as well as men are capable of voluntary [*hekousios*] action, but not of choice. Also sudden acts may be termed voluntary [*hekousios*] but they cannot be said to be done by choice.[48]

> As then the object of choice is something within our power which after deliberation we desire, Choice will be a deliberative desire of things in our power; for we first deliberate, then select, and finally fix our desire according to the result of our deliberation.[49]

The result is an Aristotelian theory of culpability that strikingly resembles contemporary theories of culpability, at least regarding the ordinal gradation of blame. Intended action is divided into two kinds: actions chosen and actions not chosen. While these two subtypes of intended action do not exactly map onto the contemporary "purpose" and "knowledge" introduced in chapter 1, their normative implications are quite similar to those of the contemporary modes of culpability. Moreover, some of Aristotle's subtypes of unintended action also seem to precede contemporary modes of culpability whereby different types of unintended behavior can give rise to different degrees of blame. Chosen intended action is never less blameworthy than unchosen intended action, just as purposive intended action is never less blameworthy than knowing intended action; unintended action in which the agent contributes something is never less blameworthy than unintended action in which the agent contributes nothing (so much so that Aristotle refers to the former as "intentional");

---

47. Rackham, *Nicomachean Ethics*, 127. The definition of intentional action is further refined at 1135a25 (p. 299) where Aristotle tells us that by intentional action he means an action which is "within the agent's own control [and] which he performs knowingly, that is, without being in ignorance of the person affected, the instrument employed, and the result."
48. Rackham, *Nicomachean Ethics*, 129.
49. Rackham, *Nicomachean Ethics*, 141.

unintended action later regretted is never less blameworthy than unregret-
ted unintended action.

That Aristotle's theory of culpability aims to be a *general* theory
becomes even clearer in light of the discussion carried out in book 5 of the
Nicomachean Ethics. There, Aristotle links the analyses of modes of culpability carried out in book 3 with general issues of regarding justice. After
having discussed the nature of justice, Aristotle tells us, "such being an
account of just and unjust actions, it is their voluntary [*hekousios*] perfor-
mance that constitutes just and unjust conduct."[50] In book 5, Aristotle
also expands on the point that there are instances of unintended (*akousios*)
wrongdoing that are blamed (though not more severely than instances of
intended wrongdoing), and instances of unintended wrongdoing that are
not blamed.

> An injury done in ignorance is an error, the person affected or the act or the
> instrument or the result being other than the agent supposed. . . . When the
> injury happens contrary to reasonable expectation it is a misadventure [*aty-
> chema*]. . . . When though not contrary to reasonable expectation, it is done
> without evil intent, it is a culpable error [*hamartema*]; for an error is culpable
> when the cause of one's ignorance lies in oneself, but only a misadventure when
> the cause lies outside oneself.[51]

The distinction between *atychema* and *hamartema* only applies to
actions that are unintended in virtue of the agent's ignorance; thus it is not
entirely clear how Aristotle would have employed this distinction regarding actions that are unintentional in virtue of compulsion. It is probably
safe to assume that Aristotle would have considered unintended, com-
pelled conduct in which the agent contributes nothing *atychema*.
Atychema and *hamartema*, then, would exhaust the realm of (*akousios*)
unintended action. Aristotle calls the realm of possible condemnations for
(*hekousios*) intended action the realm of *adikia* or injustice. (There are,
necessarily, two types of *adikia* in Aristotle: (1) *hekousios* action, accompanied by deliberation or choice, and (2) *hekousios* action, not accompanied
by deliberation or choice.) Aristotle does not give different names to each
of these, he merely reminds us that it is only in (1) that the agent is properly held to be "unjust and wicked."

Before concluding my remarks on Aristotle's theory of culpability, I
would like to note one additional virtue of it. Aristotle's distinctions
between intended and unintended action, and the further subdivisions of
each of these, apply to all types of evil outcomes. This, I should continue

---

50. Rackham, *Nicomachean Ethics*, 299.
51. Rackham, *Nicomachean Ethics*, 301.

to claim, is necessary for establishing a sound and general theory of culpability. As Sorabji contrasts Aristotle's work with Plato's, he tells us that "Plato had mentioned particular examples of negligence . . . but Aristotle does not take the cases piecemeal, he creates a general category."[52] Aristotle does this not only with respect to negligence, but with other modes of culpability as well. I have shown, however, that Plato's theory of culpability is an obvious improvement because it abandons the piecemeal approaches of biblical times. But Sorabji is nevertheless right in pointing out the giant step that Aristotle takes in the direction of a general theory of culpability. A brief note on the similarity between the Aristotelian processes for praising and blaming should shed light upon the general nature of his theory of culpability.

Just as we praise the agent who intendedly brings about a good outcome more than the one who does not intend to do so, we blame the agent who intendedly brings about an evil outcome more (never less) than the one who does not intend to do so. Aristotle's theory of culpability is to an extent the reverse of his positive doctrine of virtue ethics. When Aristotle discusses virtues he is concerned with praiseworthy actions; when he discusses evil outcomes he is concerned with blameworthy actions. This partial symmetry between Aristotelian virtue ethics and Aristotle's theory of culpability has been traditionally ignored; the very fact that Aristotle has a full-blown theory of culpability has been neglected.

Of course, Aristotle's theory faces many difficulties. Some of them strike us as anachronisms, such as his concern for regret, which has been essentially extricated from modern theories of culpability, and perhaps also his overriding concern for knowledge and ignorance as the determining factors explaining action. Other difficulties stem from the peculiar agenda that engaged him, which perhaps explains why his definitions of intended and unintended action are a bit coarse, as a consequence of his emphasis on choice itself, which is crucial for virtuous action. Finally, Aristotle errs in a way in which all his predecessors erred, and many of his followers—even today—err. He failed to realize that the essential feature of a theory of culpability is to account for the variety in the degrees of blame for actions that produce the same evil outcomes and only differ with regard to the agent's Intentional states at the time she committed the action. Aristotle is mainly interested in showing that intentionality is a necessary condition for praise and blame. Moreover, in the case of praiseworthy actions, intentionality is not sufficient, because we need to add deliberation. Were we to push the analogy between praising and blaming, we should conclude that for Aristotle both intentionality and deliberation are

---

52. Sorabji, *Necessity, Cause, and Blame*, 293.

needed for blaming an agent for bringing about an evil outcome, and this is not true. In contrast, what Aristotle's theory and modern theories of culpability prescribe is that if an agent brings about an evil outcome intendedly and deliberately, she is *more* blameworthy than if she brings it about intendedly but without deliberation.

To conclude this chapter, I wish to turn our attention to the transition of Greek theory of action into the incipient Roman criminal law. The connection between Greek philosophy and Roman law, at least regarding the criminal law, is not commonly acknowledged. This connection, moreover, shows how firmly grounded in ancient philosophy is the continental theory of culpability.

Culpability in Roman Law

In historiographical contexts, to consider the fate of Roman law to be extremely obscure and complex is a veritable commonplace. Paul Vinogradoff, at the outset of his influential *Roman Law in Medieval Europe* tells us, "the story I am about to tell you [regarding the fate of the Roman law] is, in a sense, a ghost story."[53] The difficulties surrounding the history of Roman law extend, too, to its beginnings, or so I shall argue here. Moreover, the difficulties are truly exacerbated in relation to the origins of Roman *criminal* law, when contrasted to other branches of the law.

Law students in the continental tradition study Roman law not so much for historical reasons, but rather for practical purposes. Several branches of Roman legal science, such as the law of obligations, the law of contracts, family law, the classification of things, property law, estates, and commercial law, have full contemporary applicability. In some of these areas only minor changes upon classical Roman law have been made. But Roman criminal law was not well developed. It constitutes, as it were, the black sheep of Roman legislation, and this surely contributes to making its study and appraisal a rather thorny and unusual investigation.[54]

---

53. Paul Vinogradoff, *Roman Law in Medieval Europe* (Cambridge: Speculum Historiale, 1968), 13. Similar views are expressed by other influential scholars, such as Fritz Pringsheim, in his "The Inner Relationship Between English and Roman Law," *Cambridge Law Journal* 5 (1935): 347–65, and R. C. Van Caenengem, in his *The Birth of the Common Law* (Cambridge: Cambridge University Press, 1973). I attempt to shed some light upon this undoubtedly complex issue in my "On Deference and the Spirit of the Laws," *Archiv für Rechts- und Sozialphilosophie* 82 (1996): 460–71.

54. There are, of course, some works on Roman criminal law, but they pale in comparison to the number of similar works on Roman civil law. Moreover, these rare works on Roman criminal law say precious little regarding culpability itself, as they focus on

I wish to focus on two issues in this section. First, I wish to emphasize that the classical Roman distinction between *dolus* and *culpa*, still in use today in most of the non-English-speaking West, can be traced back to the pre-Roman history of culpability that I have presented already. Second, I want to show how, just as the contemporary distinction between intentional and unintentional action exhibits a tension between normativity and description, the tension between normativity and description was also problematized by Roman jurists.

As Daube puts it, "Roman law is much admired for its three standards of liability: *dolus*, evil intent, *culpa*, negligence, and *casus*, accident."[55] Daube is wrong, though, in translating "culpa" into "negligence." "Culpa" should be translated into "unintended (and culpable) action." (I shall come back to the discussion of this mistake in the last section of next chapter.) The traditional view is that these three Roman modes of culpability map onto the Aristotelian tripartite classification along the following lines:

Dolus is equivalent to *adikia*,
culpa is equivalent to *hamartema*, and
casus is equivalent to *atychema*.

Daube seems to be a lonely critic of this otherwise widely accepted view.[56] In spite of my agreement with the spirit of Sorabji's and Schofield's counterobjections to Daube's theses, I wish to analyze Daube's views.[57]

Daube has few qualms with equating *dolus* with *adikia*, and not too many qualms either with equating *casus* and *atychema*.[58] Most of his criticisms are aimed at undermining the equation of *hamartema* with "negligence." Daube is partially right, for negligence is not the same as *hamartema*, but—and this he fails to see—negligence is not the same as *culpa* either. That negligence is not the same as *culpa* is a terribly pervasive

---

procedural law and specific crimes. For the classical sources regarding Roman criminal law, see Theodor Mommsem, *Romisches Strafrecht* (Graz: Akademische Druck, 1955), and Wilhelm Rein, *Das Kriminalrecht der Romer von Romulus bis auf Justinian* (Aalen: Scientia, 1962).

55. David Daube, *Roman Law: Linguistic, Social and Philosophical Aspects* (Edinburgh: Edinburgh University Press, 1969), 131.

56. For bibliographical information concerning some important adherents to the view which Daube criticizes, see Richard Sorabji's illuminating annotated bibliography in his *Necessity, Cause and Blame*, 299ff.

57. Sorabji, *Necessity, Cause and Blame*, 257–95; Malcolm Schofield, "Aristotelian Mistakes," *Proceedings of the Cambridge Philological Society* 19 (1973): 66–70.

58. Daube claims that "even *atychema*, which at first sight looks the same as *casus*, is not quite the same, precisely because it includes unintended harm even if caused negligently" (*Roman Law*, 133).

mistake that Daube (just as mostly everybody in the Anglo-American tradition) incurs.

Daube claims that Kübler (who is followed by many other continental scholars), "sharing a common misunderstanding which finds its main expression in commentaries of Aristotle, translates *hamartema* by 'negligence.'"[59] But this is false. Kübler translates *hamartema* by *culpa*, and *culpa* and "negligence" are different. Let me repeat it once more: *hamartema*, the Aristotelian concept from which the Roman notion of *culpa* comes to exist, denotes those cases in which an evil outcome is, although unintendedly (*akousios*) brought about, not brought about accidentally.[60] This meaning of *hamartema* is preserved in the Roman notion of *culpa*, but not in the Anglo-American notion of "negligence." (Very briefly for now: negligence is merely one form of unintended action, whose essential feature is that the agent fails to show the standard of care the society would expect from a reasonable agent in his situation.)

At any event, *dolus* and *culpa* are the Roman heirs of the Greek *adikia* and *hamartema*, which in turn are based on the concepts of *hekousios* and *akousios*. The thesis I wish to defend here must by now be obvious: the distinction between *dolus* and *culpa* maps onto the distinction between intentional and unintentional action. (*Culpa* is not, it should by now be clear, coextensional with "unintentional," since there are unintentional actions that are not blameworthy: accidents, *casus*, or *atychema*.

Dolus and *culpa* continue to be the cornerstones upon which contemporary continental theories of culpability are based. The crucial distinction in continental theories of culpability is that between intentional and unintentional action. The *role* that this distinction plays in contemporary continental theories of culpability is the same it has played throughout human history: to allow us—by focusing upon mental phenomena—to have different degrees of condemnation for agents who bring about identical outcomes.

The case has been different in the Anglo-American legal tradition, where the reception of Roman law was so peculiar and, above all, so different from the rest of the continent. Elsewhere I have pointed out some of the advantages of the British rejection of Roman canons; I want now to point out a hitherto unnoticed shortcoming of the way in which law evolved in the Anglo-American tradition.[61] Anglo-American theories of culpability have evolved in an insular fashion, disconnected from a rich philosophical past, and of course also disconnected from rich developments in the rest of Europe. By struggling against the attitude of deference with

---

59. Daube, *Roman Law*, 132 and passim.
60 . Cf. Rackham, *Nicomachean Ethics*, 299.
61. See, e.g., Zaibert, "On Deference and the Spirit of the Laws," passim.

which Roman statutes and principles were accepted in Europe, the Anglo-American legal tradition lost sight of important philosophical problems that were not exclusively Roman. Anglo-American theories of culpability as enacted in codes, as a consequence of this, remains to a certain extent lacking referents in the history of culpability. Anglo-American lawyers and jurists fail to see the points of contact between, say, section 2.02 of the Model Penal Code and book 3 of the *Nicomachean Ethics*, as well as between the aforementioned section of the Model Penal Code and many other ancient writings.

The Model Penal Code, the jewel of Anglo-American criminal legislation, and indeed a rather ambitious code, contains a sophisticated theory of culpability. Nonetheless, the distinction between intended and unintended action *seems* to play no *overt* role whatsoever in the Model Penal Code. (The very word "intention" is conspicuously avoided.) As noted in chapter 1, the view that the Model Penal Code has done a great thing by avoiding references to intentional and unintentional action is accepted by many American jurists. But, as my investigation shows, the Model Penal Code has merely avoided the word "intention," but not the concept of intention.[62]

Now, in spite of the fact that Roman lawyers were not adept at engaging in philosophical disquisitions, one of them, however, left an aphorism that captures well the complexity of the tension between normativity and description in theories of culpability. Paulus's aphorism reads as follows: *Magna negligentia culpa est: magna culpa dolus est.*[63] That Paulus was talking here about the normative element in these concepts should be obvious. Otherwise, he would hardly be making any sense at all, for given a definition of, say, unintended (and culpable) action (*culpa*), a given action *X* is either unintentional or it is not: from the descriptive perspective this is not a vague term. But, since these concepts are used for normative purposes (allowing us to have different condemnations for agents who bring about identical outcomes), Paulus's dictum is indeed interesting. Let us analyze this further.

First of all let me point out that the meaning of *negligentia* in Latin is different from the meaning that "negligence" has in Anglo-American theories of culpability. For the Romans, *negligentia* meant something akin to imprudence, carelessness, and even accidentally bringing *X* about. What Paulus means with the first part of the aphorism is that there are cases in which someone brings about an evil outcome unintendedly, but in so

---

62. See the references to Husak's review of Alan White's *Misleading Cases*, cited in chapter 1.
63. *Corpus Iuris Civilis*, trans. Theodor Mommsen and Paulus Krueger (Berlin: Apud Weimannos, 1928), 919. (Paulus, *Dig.*, 226.)

doing she has exhibited such a high degree of clumsiness, that she should nonetheless be blamed. Though she might perhaps be blamed, she should never be blamed more severely than if she would have intended to bring about such an evil outcome.

Think, for example, of Cyrano's death, caused by a falling beam. Let us suppose that we were in the presence of whoever let the beam fall, and let us suppose that this person was building a house and he was abiding to all the regulations concerning such an activity. This would be a good example of an accident (a case either of very slight *negligentia*, or of *casus*). But if it turns out that this person was improvising some sort of show in the public square and that while he stumbled on the tightrope, the beam fell and killed Cyrano, we would blame him more severely. The intuitive appeal of blaming the agent in the second scenario more severely than the agent in the first scenario is, I think, quite strong. Now paraphrasing Paulus, the agent's gross *negligentia* (clumsiness) amounts to *culpa* in the sense that the agent should be blamed for such an excessively imprudent behavior. (The real case of Cyrano's death was, if any credit is to be given to Rostandt's story, probably an unproblematic example of intended action.)

The second part of the aphorism should be interpreted similarly. Now consider Hamlet killing Polonius. Hamlet did not even know that the person behind the arras was Polonius (he wished it would have been Claudius behind the arras, of course). Hamlet did not intend to kill Polonius, yet this is the type of borderline case where it is difficult to *assess* whether the action (of killing Polonius) was intentional or unintentional. Therefore, it is hard to mete out a fitting amount of blame to Hamlet for his action. Let us tinker with the scene and suppose that Hamlet *knew* that Polonius was there hiding behind the arras, and that in his rage he did not mind killing him, in spite of the fact that the bulk of his hatred was aimed at Claudius. We would then perhaps be inclined to consider the killing of Polonius to be intentional, so we can justify a sterner condemnation of Hamlet for his action.[64]

Had Hamlet known about Polonius's location and had he not minded killing him, then Paulus would probably consider Hamlet's act of making a pass through the arras to be just too similar to killing Polonius intentionally. And so, in spite of the fact that from a purely descriptive perspective Hamlet acted unintendedly (with *culpa*, assuming he did not desire

---

64. Incidentally, Donald Davidson also discusses Hamlet's actions while in his mother's bedroom. He tells us: "Hamlet intentionally kills the man behind the arras, but he does not intentionally kill Polonius." Donald Davidson, *Essays on Actions and Events* (Oxford: Clarendon Press, 1980), 46. Although my very point in discussing this case is to illustrate the difficulties in determining the normativity of intentions, and in that much I agree with Davidson, I have reservations concerning Davidson's unequivocal assessment concerning the intentionality of the action of "killing the man behind the arras."

Polonius's death), he should be blamed as if he had acted intentionally (with *dolus*).

Although we continue to struggle with cases such as Hamlet's killing of Polonius, we have come a long way, and we are now better equipped with a conceptual apparatus that facilitates the apportioning of blame in difficult cases (see chapters 5 and 6 below). This conceptual apparatus informs our modern theories of culpability. The main difference between these modern theories and their ancient predecessors is that we now have subtle and clearly defined subdivisions between each general type of action. We have clearly distinguishable types of unintended action and different types of intended action. And of course, we have more and less stern condemnations corresponding to each of these types of action. Most of these new subdivisions have arisen as a consequence of considering other distinctions between mental states. In the next chapter, while preserving somewhat the historical tone exhibited so far, I shall steer our attention to the rationale for, and the plausibility of, these refinements in our methods for apportioning blame.

[3]

On the Proliferation of Modes
of Culpability

Throughout the history of culpability, the distinction between intended and unintended action has gained in depth and sophistication. In this chapter I wish to shed light upon further developments that allow us to more precisely specify the degree of blameworthiness to which more fine-grained modes of culpability give rise. I shall proceed as follows. First, I will analyze Aquinas's contribution to the study of culpability known as the doctrine (or principle) of double effect. The doctrine of double effect introduces an important distinction between intending and foreseeing—an Intentional state about which so far I have only made tacit and indirect references. While I acknowledge the importance of this distinction, I shall argue that the doctrine of double effect has many flaws, and that there are better ways of incorporating this undoubtedly important distinction into theories of culpability. Second, I shall discuss the often-neglected contributions to theories of culpability made by the two most important Anglo-American jurists in the eighteenth century: Jeremy Bentham and John Austin. In fact, I will argue that their approaches offer better ways of incorporating this distinction into theories of culpability than does the traditional doctrine of double effect.

As noted in the previous chapter, my analysis does not seek to be historically comprehensive; my treating Aquinas, Bentham, and Austin together in one single chapter is the result of thematic preoccupations. My major aim in this chapter is to examine how distinctions other than that between intended and unintended action begin to be part of theories of culpability, thus giving rise to more fine-grained set of modes of culpability. Already in Aristotle we witness incipient use of distinctions other than that between *hekousion* and *akousion*: those between choosing and not choosing, between contributing something or contributing nothing when acting under compulsion, and others. But Aristotle's theory of culpability did not clearly indicate a specific degree of blameworthiness corresponding to each of its incipient modes of culpability. Some of the subtle distinctions between modes of culpability are not always sufficiently developed in Aristotle's writings, and a great deal of work is left for us to carry out in the form of speculation and exegesis. In contrast, the theories of culpability endorsed by Bentham and by Austin are more sophisticated than Aristotle's insofar as that they do present rather punctiliously described sets of Intentional states in tandem with a similarly concrete degree of blame attached to each of these sets of Intentional states. Before I discuss Bentham and Austin, we will look at how theories of culpability can go astray: the famous doctrine of double effect.

We owe to Aquinas the first formulation of the doctrine of double effect. He presented it rather succinctly in the following passage:

> Nothing hinders one act from having two effects, only one of which is intended, while the other is beside the intention. Now moral acts take their species according to what is intended, and not according to what is beside the intention, since this is accidental. . . . Accordingly the act of self-defence may have two effects, one is the saving of one's life, the other is the slaying of the aggressor. Therefore this act, since one's intention is to save the one's own life, is not unlawful, seeing that is natural to everything to keep itself in *being*, as far as possible.[1]

There are several problems with Aquinas's doctrine of double effect, which I shall tackle individually. The first problem with Aquinas's doctrine of double effect is not really attributable to the doctrine itself, but to the way in which it is frequently translated. I shall discuss this problem briefly at the outset, simply in order to render *intelligible* some of Aquinas's remarks.

For example, and beginning with the truly obvious, the heading of Aquinas's *Summa Theologiae*'s question 64, in its original Latin reads, "De homicidio," yet this heading is sometimes translated into English as "Of Murder."[2] This is a mistake. The meaning of Latin term "homicidio," just as that of the corresponding English term "homicide," is neutral, in the sense that it does not include reference to any Intentional state whatsoever that the agent might have had when acting. "Homicide" in both Latin and English simply means bringing about the death of a human being; and to that extent it is merely a descriptive term. "Murder," in contrast, is not neutral, in the sense that its meaning includes reference to the Intentional states that accompany the agent's action.[3] The slogan in Anglo-American

---

1. Thomas Aquinas, *Summa Theologiae*, pt. 2, sec. 2, q. 64, a. 7 (Toronto: Burnes Oates & Washbourne, n.d.), 10:209ff. All subsequent quotations from the *Summa Theologiae* refer to this edition.
2. Aquinas, *Summa Theologiae*, 195. Or see, for example, the digital version of the *Summa* available at http://www.newadvent.org.
3. Translations of "homicidio" into Latin-based languages are not problematic because in these languages (just as in Latin), there is not a word meaning "murder." At the very

legal theory has it that murder is a homicide committed with malice afore-thought, but it seems clear that one crucial Intentional state of murder (included in malice aforethought) is an intention to kill. Murders are, par-adigmatically, intended killings. It remains puzzling, in any case, why translations into English of this section heading use "murder" when "homicide" is also available.

Therefore, it is rather hard to make sense of some passages in Aquinas's *Summa*, as they are sometimes translated, to wit:

> It would seem that one is guilty of murder through killing someone by chance.[4]

> Therefore one is guilty of murder through killing someone by chance.[5]

> If a man . . .without due care [and also without intention causes the death of a person] he does not escape being guilty of murder.[6]

Murder presupposes an intention to kill.[7] It therefore seems odd to claim, as the mistranslated passages seem to suggest, that someone could commit an unintended murder; while there is nothing odd in the claim that someone could commit an unintended homicide. It would be, too, at least pleonastic to claim that someone committed an intended murder, whereas it is indeed informative to claim that someone committed an intended homicide.[8] Of course, the source of the confusion here is one with which we are by now very familiar: the tension between normativ-ity and description. Some descriptions of Intentional states might corre-spond to more or less severe degrees of blameworthiness. It is possible, as we have already seen, that some unintended homicides are blamed

---

least, though some words more or less equivalent to "murder," say, "assassination," could be found in languages other than English, the word does not belong to the tech-nical vocabulary of criminal law theory. It remains enigmatic why the preferred transla-tion into English is murder, when "homicide" is also a word in English.

4. Aquinas, *Summa Theologiae*, 210.

5. Aquinas, *Summa Theologiae*, 211.

6. Aquinas, *Summa Theologiae*, 211–12.

7. The felony murder rule of Anglo-American criminal law constitutes an exception to this claim, insofar as it allows that if in cases in which the defendant did not have the specific intention to kill the victim but was nonetheless engaged in felonious behavior, she should then be treated as if the death was an instance of murder (and thus presum-ably intended). See: State v. Levelle, Supreme Court of South Carolina, 13 S.E. 319 (1891).

8. There exists a translation of Aquinas's work where this mistake is not committed, and thus that is in this respect better: St. Thomas Aquinas, *Summa Theologiae* (London: Blackfriars, Eyre and Spottiswoode, 1974), vol. 38. I am using here one of many flawed translations just to emphasize the existence of the problems that these translations cre-ate.

(and eventually punished) quite severely. I think it is likely that what one normally means by saying something along the lines of "someone is guilty of murder through killing someone by chance" is that although the killing is unintended it still deserves blame. Translational difficulties aside, Aquinas's doctrine of double effect faces serious, substantive difficulties as well.

Intention, Foresight, and Aquinas's Abandonment of Gradational Approaches

Insofar as Aquinas claims that we are accountable only for those consequences of our actions that we intend, he is committing the mistake of suggesting that to bring about an event intendedly is a necessary condition for being blamed. Aquinas thus misses the correct, gradational normative import of the distinction between intended and unintended action. We are by now familiar with this mistake: it is the one I attributed to Socrates and to Arendt in chapter 1. The doctrine of double effect, however, is a poignant case of such a mistake because the particular normative implications of the appeal to the distinction between foreseen and intended evil outcomes are rather dramatic.

Throughout the book I have been assuming that sometimes when authors say "intentionally" we can assume that they meant "intendedly"; similarly, since the distinction between the realm of the punishable and the realm of the blameworthy has not been historically clear, I have sometimes suggested that we could safely assume that when an author says "*X* is (not) punishable" we could safely extend the meaning and assume that the author means "*X* is (not) blameworthy." A similar methodological word of caution is in order. Aquinas's formulation of the doctrine of double effect does not mention blame, and yet I shall assume that when Aquinas talks about lawful (and unlawful) acts, he means blameless (and blameworthy) acts. Insofar as Aquinas was such a staunch defender of the doctrine of natural law, according to which immoral laws are simply not laws, my suggestion is, I think, rather unproblematic and indeed innocuous.

Aquinas must have been aware that there are unintended actions whose consequences are not even foreseen. But Aquinas's doctrine of double effect operates within the context of a false dichotomy: actions are either blameworthy, when intended, or blameless, when merely foreseen. Obviously, as a result of Aquinas's false dichotomy, any and all differences between types of unintended action are obliterated. In other words, since the lack of intention regarding the evil outcome that one brings about precludes the possibility of blame (in Aquinas's view), it becomes quite pointless to distinguish between cases in which we foresee or do not foresee those unintended consequences: in all such cases, agents are equally blameless.

That these distinctions between types of unintended actions are indeed obliterated is visible, notoriously, in Aquinas's discussion of killing by chance. In attempting to answer several biblical passages and later commentaries where people were blamed for unintended homicides Aquinas states: "I answer that according to the Philosopher (*Phys.* ii 6) *chance is a cause that acts besides one's intention.* Hence chance happenings, strictly speaking, are neither intended nor voluntary. And since every sin is voluntary, according to Augustine it follows that chance happenings, as such, are not sins."[9] But Aquinas is aware that things are more complicated, as Plato and Aristotle made clear when they grappled with the distinction between intended and unintended action. Aquinas tells us then that "nevertheless it happens that what is not actually and directly voluntary and intended, is voluntary and intended accidentally."[10]

What can Aquinas possibly mean by "intended accidentally"? How can someone bring about an outcome both intendedly and accidentally? The concepts of accidental action and intended action with which Aquinas was working would render the expression "intended accidentally" to be as problematic then as it is now. For the cornerstone of Aquinas's discussion of killing by chance is the concept of *casus*—this is the term that he uses in the original Latin, which is translated into English as "by chance." *Casus*, however, as we have already seen, has been opposed to intended action ever since Aristotle's times. In Greek the opposition is expressed by *adikia* (intended action) on the one hand, and the conjunction of *hamartema* and *atychema* (unintended action) on the other. So the claim that someone can bring about an outcome at the same time intendedly and accidentally seems to be a contradiction—and seems to have been recognized as such even as far back as in Aristotle's times. And though it is undoubtedly a contradiction, it is nevertheless important to explain why Aquinas proposed such a view. Aquinas distinguishes two types of homicides which are "intended accidentally": "first, when a man causes another death's through occupying himself with unlawful things which he ought to avoid: secondly, when he does not take sufficient care."[11] Aquinas clarifies this further, by echoing the "opinion of jurists,"[12] as follows: "Hence, according to jurists, if a man pursue a lawful occupation and take due care, the result being that a person loses his life, he is not guilty of that person's death: whereas if he be occupied with something unlawful, or even with something lawful, but

9. Aquinas, *Summa Theologiae*, 211.
10. Aquinas, *Summa Theologiae*, 211.
11. Aquinas, *Summa Theologiae*, 211.
12. Aquinas, *Summa Theologiae*, 211.

without due care, he does not escape being guilty of murder, if his action results in someone's death."[13]

Aquinas's suggestion that the action of someone who in the course of pursuing "a lawful occupation . . . but without due care" accidentally causes the death of a passer-by, and in so doing fails to abide by rational standards of care, should be considered *intended* is obviously problematic. For, "to bring about an evil outcome due to lack of care" presupposes that one did not intend to do it. Lack of due care is the gist of negligent behavior, and negligent behavior, by definition, is unintended. Yet, what allows Aquinas to admit that these cases are blameworthy is that he refers to these cases as cases of murder. But, more importantly, this passage creates yet another problem for the doctrine of double effect, for now Aquinas introduces a distinction between agents engaged in lawful activities and agents engaged in unlawful activities. As it turns out, then, it is not the distinction between intending and foreseeing *simpliciter* that will after all do the job of establishing the normative implications of the different Intentional states with which one could bring about an evil outcome.

Already Plato and Aristotle would have rejected Aquinas's thesis according to which actions can be simultaneously intended and accidental. After all, Plato grappled with killing in anger, and Aristotle with evil outcomes brought about through ignorance but later regretted, because these were cases in which it was difficult to establish whether an action was intended or unintended, and thus it was difficult to establish how severely a given action should be blamed.

Consider what by now should be a familiar example; while driving her car, Ann rushes to get to the theater, and in her hurry she carelessly brings about the death of an innocent pedestrian. Contrast her action to Betty's, who wishes to get to the theater before the start of a play she wants to see, and so goes out in her car and, although she is aware of an innocent pedestrian who crosses her path, she kills him because avoiding the collision would entail that she would miss the play. It follows from my thesis that Betty's action is more blameworthy than is Ann's action.

---

13. Aquinas, *Summa Theologiae*, 211–12. This inflicts a fatal blow upon the doctrine of double effect. For now a distinction is being introduced as to agents engaged in lawful activities and agents engaged in unlawful activities. It seems, then, that it is not after all the distinction between intending and foreseeing *simpliciter* that will do the job. As a matter of fact, more and more modifications have been made to the version of the doctrine of double effect upon which I am focusing here. None of these attempts succeeds in making of the doctrine of double effect a valuable system of apportioning blame. Some of these attempts achieve some measure of success, but by clumsily adding to the doctrine of double effect elements of theories of justification, excuses, and deontological constraints. The result is a doctrine of double effect which is a concoction of important theories belonging to the criminal law—and which the criminal law, for good reasons, treats separately.

Within the context of Aquinas's doctrine of double effect, however, there is no easy way to make a distinction between the blameworthiness of Ann's action and of Betty's action. Both would be unintended actions and since both Ann and Betty were engaged in lawful activities (assuming neither of them was speeding, etc.), they would, *eo ipso*, be blameless. Although these two actions are unintended, there are important normative differences between them, and these differences are much better taken into account by theories of culpability other than the one contained in the doctrine of double effect. The judgment of blame that we pass upon Betty should be sterner than the one we would pass upon Ann. Any theory of culpability should give us the tools to explain this gradational difference.

The tension between normativity and description which runs through the history of the theories of culpability, and that haunts mostly everyone dealing with this history, exerts a heavy toll on Aquinas's theory. For it seems that the reason that might explain his odd talk of "intending accidentally" is that he wishes to *blame* actions such as Ann's, and even more actions such as Betty's, and in order to blame these actions he is forced to describe them as intended. For, echoing Augustine and venerable Christian theology, Aquinas holds that what is brought about unintendedly can never be blamed. Succinctly put in Latin: "Et quia omne peccatum est voluntarium . . . consequens est quod causalia, inquantum huiusmodi, non sunt peccata."[14] Conversely, Aquinas wishes to provide a framework for not blaming certain actions, and in this respect the problems with the doctrine of double effect become downright dangerous. For, according to it, merely foreseeing an outcome is not equivalent to intending such outcome. But, since not intending an outcome is to render the agent who brings it about blameless, someone could kill another human being in order to, say, exalt God's glory, and yet argue that his intention was not to cause death (although this possible outcome was foreseen), but to save someone's soul, or to spread God's word, or something like that. The doctrine of double effect would hold that this person should not be blamed at all. Both the case in which one wishes to blame unintended actions and the case where one wishes not to blame intended actions reveal the same coarseness in the doctrine of double effect: all gradation of blame is eliminated. It is not simply that, by potentially arbitrarily denying that one intends an outcome while admitting that one foresees it, one will be

---

14. Aquinas, *Summa Theologiae*, 214. The imprint of the Socratic paradox (all evil is unintended but sometimes we do evil intendedly) that we discussed in chapter 2 should be obvious. Notice too that in this passage Aquinas uses "voluntary" and "intentional" as synonyms, a problem he probably inherited from the Greeks. I shall return to the discussion of the role that intentions play in voluntary actions next chapter.

blamed more leniently: one would, in accordance with the doctrine of double effect, not be blamed at all.

In the preceding chapter I debunked the widespread view according to which *lex talionis* was as crude and rigid as it is frequently, though uncritically, taken to be. There is also a widespread view according to which the doctrine of double effect inaugurates a more nuanced and benevolent way to gradate the blameworthiness (and the eventual punishment) of human actions. Yet, I have tried to show in this chapter that Aquinas's doctrine of double effect is, in a sense, a step backwards in the development of a sound theory of culpability. For while the doctrine of double effect does introduce a much-needed focus on the Intentional state of foresight, it introduces it in a way that opens the floodgates for normative abuses of the doctrine.

After all, some of the most important contributions that Greek philosophy and Roman law exerted upon the rudimentary biblical policies of retaliation included showing that different Intentional states give rise to different degrees of blameworthiness. Philosophers and jurists struggled to propose ever more refined modes of culpability that would give rise to more fine-grained degrees of blameworthiness. Aquinas's doctrine of double effect halts this process. Intending to bring about an evil outcome is not a sufficient condition of blameworthiness, as justifications and excuses (of the sorts sketched in chapter 1) reveal, nor is it a necessary condition either, as reckless and negligent actions reveal. Of course, not intending to bring about an evil outcome is neither necessary nor sufficient for the action that brings it about to be blameless.

Justifications and the Epistemology of Intentional States

To repeat, the basic tenet of my theory of culpability is that to bring about an evil outcome intendedly is never less blameworthy than to bring it about unintendedly; one of the central features of this theory, then, is that it is concerned with the ordinal gradation of blameworthiness. Something resembling this principle was present in the theories of culpability we have discussed so far, yet Aquinas's doctrine of double effect transforms the careful analysis of Intentional states into an out-of-control justificatory engine: to bring about an evil outcome intendedly is blameworthy, whereas to bring it about unintendedly is blameless. While a certain tendency to treat the distinction between the intended and the unintended along lines similar to Aquinas's lines has been a temptation throughout history, it was specifically the doctrine of double effect that gave rise to institutionalized arbitrariness. Before I discuss this arbitrariness, I would like to suggest that, theoretically speaking, Aquinas's principle betrays a confusion between two distinct types of theory: theories of culpability and theories of justification.

To be sure, Aquinas appeals to the doctrine of double effect as a response to the question of how it is possible to *justify* killing in self-defense. As we noted in chapter 1, there are no degrees of justification: actions whose consequences constitute evil outcomes are either justified or unjustified, depending on a series of factors, some of which have nothing to with Intentional states. Attending to the Intentional states that agents have when they act allows us, in contrast, to blame them *more or less* severely for what they bring about. Self-defense in particular is the paradigmatic justification; but when someone kills in self-defense the death of the attacker is brought about intendedly. As George Fletcher has put it: "the consensus of Western legal systems is that actors may avail themselves of justifications only if they act with justificatory intent."[15] The rationale for not punishing (and for not blaming) an agent who kills in self-defense is not primarily related to Intentional states, but to a weighing of evils and other external considerations. Although the act of killing in self-defense is intended, it is not blameworthy, and for reasons extraneous to a theory of culpability proper. In order to justify this act we need not appeal to the existence of Intentional states but to a series of circumstances external to the agent's mind. Moreover, as it turns out, one of the necessary conditions for an action to be justifiable is that it is done intendedly.

Aquinas's attempt to justify the bringing about of evil outcomes by attending to Intentional states is dramatically inconvenient. It is not simple deference to current distinctions that leads me to say this. I have after all pointed out some obvious problems with Aquinas's doctrine of double effect already. But now I would like to point out a certain problem regarding the obvious epistemological limitations that we have in knowing the Intentional states of others. (And I would like to complement this discussion with the remarks of a noted philosopher, Blaise Pascal, born some 400 years ago, as he wittily ridiculed the way in which the doctrine of double effect can be put to use to *justify* practically any conceivable action.)

Leaving aside (neo-) psychoanalytic theories of subconscious Intentional states, (neo-) Marxist theories of alienation, and the like, I take it to be a safe assumption that we have access to our own Intentional states. In other words, we *know* whether we ourselves wish, dislike, fear, believe, intend, and so forth, some object. Once the incorrigible self-referentiality of this kind of knowledge act is removed, that is, once we venture into making claims about someone else's Intentional states, things get complicated, since access to others' Intentional states is not always unproblematic.

---

15. Fletcher, *Rethinking Criminal Law*, 557.

The epistemological limitations that surely arise when we attempt to investigate someone else's Intentional states constitute a particularly poignant problem for proponents of the doctrine of double effect. For how is it that they know that Edward merely foresaw that Peter's death would ensue when he pushed the latter down the hill in order to, say, keep his honor unblemished? Certainly, similar sorts of objections can be leveled against most theories of culpability to the extent that they are vulnerable to epistemological limitation regarding our access to other minds. But there is an explanation as to why dealing with this objection is more pressing for a proponent of the doctrine of double effect than for anyone else. For, within the framework of Aquinas's doctrine, distinguishing between the two relevant Intentional states (intention and foresight) entails distinguishing between total blameworthiness and total blamelessness. In modern theories of culpability, however, distinguishing between diverse modes of culpability each composed of several Intentional states, entails distinguishing merely between ordinal *degrees* of blameworthiness.

There are cases, to be sure, in which our guesses regarding someone else's Intentional states allow less room for doubt. Consider, for example, James, whom we have seen taking lessons on how to use knives, whom we have just seen buying a knife, who has told us about the hatred he feels for Emma, and who has been studying Emma's movements and habits. Imagine that one day Emma's dead body is found, with many stab wounds, and that James is apprehended and confesses to having committed the crime but claims that it was an accident. I think it is safe to assume that in spite of whatever epistemological limitations might exist concerning our knowledge of James's mind, we would readily (and safely) assume that Emma's death was not accidental. Or consider, again, Holmes's felicitous *bon mot*: "Even a dog knows how to distinguish between being kicked and being stumbled upon."

Most epistemological problems in contemporary theories of culpability arise only in relation to attempts to gain access to subtly different modes of culpability. Given the nongradational nature of Aquinas's doctrine of double effect, however, the problem of knowing what an agent's precise Intentional state was is always the problem of total blame versus no blame whatsoever. And then the epistemological concerns become all the more pressing because, among other reasons, implementing the doctrine of double effect is prone to create abuses and injustice.

In his famous *Provincial Letters*, Blaise Pascal ridiculed the doctrine of double effect, which he mockingly dubbed the *method of directing the intention*, by attending precisely to the way in which the doctrine of double effect justifies too much.[16] Pascal's new name for the doctrine is elo-

16. Blaise Pascal, *The Provincial Letters: Moral Teachings of the Jesuit Fathers Opposed to the Church of Rome and Latin Vulgate* (Toronto: William Briggs, 1893).

quent in and of itself: people can "direct" their intention to whatever they wish, and then, in accordance with the doctrine of double effect, avoid all blame (and all punishment) for their actions. Most of Pascal's remarks in this regard are extremely cynical, witty, and quite devastating. The main aim of the *Provincial Letters* is to show the absurdities of Jesuit casuistry, and subsidiarily to defend the Jansenists—particularly Pascal's friend, Antoine Arnauld, and other members of the school of Port Royal. Pascal's attack on Jesuit casuistry concerns itself with many different topics, and many of these topics are discussed in dialogical form—the participants being an unnamed disgruntled Jesuit Father, and Pascal himself. Through the mysterious Father, Pascal presents abundant evidence of the atrocities that Jesuit casuistry, via the doctrine of double effect, justified. The two men begin to talk about the doctrine of double effect as follows:

> I wish to now show you this great method [the doctrine of double effect] in all its lustre, on the subject of homicide, which it justifies on a thousand occasions. . . . In this way our fathers have found a method for permitting the violence which is practised in defending honour. It is only to turn away the intention from the desire of revenge, which is criminal, to direct it to the desire of defending honour, which according to our fathers, is lawful. . . . This [method of directing the intention] the ancients did not know; this is due to our fathers.[17]

But, of course, the doctrine of double effect can make much more than the defense of honor permissible, the possibilities are indeed infinite. Pascal shows how Jesuit authorities made many seemingly un-Christian actions permissible. Pascal quotes Lessius de Just as saying: "He who has received an injury may not have the intention of avenging himself, but he may have that of avoiding infamy, and for this may, on the instant, repel the injury, and that with the sword: *etiam cum gladio*."[18] In another passage Pascal quotes Father Gaspar Hurtado's views: "A beneficed person may, without mortal sin, desire the death of him who has a pension from his benefice, and a son that of his father, and rejoice when it happens, provided it is only for the advantage which accrues from it, and not from personal hatred."[19] I shall refer the reader to Pascal's work for countless additional examples of the ridiculous directions morality can take when guided by the doctrine of double effect. The two passages cited above serve my purposes here insofar as they are eloquent in expressing the sorts of abuses which can be "justified" by the doctrine of double effect. Jesuit fathers "justified" many

---

17. Pascal, *Provincial Letters*, 134–35.
18. Pascal, *Provincial Letters*, 136.
19. Pascal, *Provincial Letters*, 137.

acts expressly prohibited in the scriptures by using the doctrine of double effect. Killing in a duel, in war, for benefit, to protect one's honor, to protect one's property, to protect one's friends, and so on, could all be made to appear permissible, simply by concocting some appropriate story about the perpetrator's Intentional states.

Intention, Foresight, and Culpability

The distinction between intention and foresight is indeed important, if used in ways other than the way in which Aquinas (and some of his followers) used it. In medieval times the distinction was used to *justify* actions, and not really to articulate new modes of culpability. Surprisingly, perhaps, the doctrine of double effect is alive and well in contemporary philosophical circles. In fact, amendments to it seeking to avoid some of the greatest flaws of the doctrine have thrived and now constitute a veritable cottage industry. Still, no matter how many amendments are made to the doctrine, and in how many ways its potential to justify too much is curbed, the crucial problem with the doctrine is as pressing today as it was when Aquinas first formulated it: the doctrine appeals to Intentional states in order to come up with justifications.

Consider a brief sketch of the role that Intentional states and the doctrine of double effect play in contemporary discussions of euthanasia and assisted suicide. For example, Tom L. Beauchamp's collection, *Intending Death: The Ethics of Assisted Suicide and Euthanasia*, demonstrates the continued influence of the doctrine of double effect.[20] With a few exceptions, most of the sixteen essays of this collection revolve around issues such as the distinction between intending and foreseeing, the distinction between killing and letting die, and the doctrine of double effect.

Almost no contributor to this collection seems interested in defining what an intention is or when an action is intended. Moreover, some authors explicitly deny the existence of secular philosophical work on Intentionality. For example Edmund Pellegrino considers that Intentionality "has not played much of a role in contemporary moral philosophy" (although he recognizes a handful of recent authors who are indeed interested in analyzing it).[21] In contrast to secular moral philosophers, Pellegrino claims that "on the other hand, intention has been a crucial element in Catholic moral theology."[22] As this book shows, however,

---

20. Thomas L. Beauchamp, ed., *Intending Death: The Ethics of Assisted Suicide and Euthanasia* (Englewood Cliffs, NJ: Prentice Hall), 1996.
21. Beauchamp, *Intending Death*, 164.
22. Beauchamp, *Intending Death*, 164.

there is no lack of interest in these matters by secular thinkers. Moreover, this book also shows that Catholic moral theology's treatment of Intentionality and culpability, at least in relation the doctrine of double effect, is highly problematic. Most of Pellegrino's opinions—as well as those of many other authors who are persuaded by Catholic moral theology—are spearheaded by a vehement defense of the doctrine of double effect. Of course, some authors disagree with the doctrine of double effect, but the mere fact that there still exists a somewhat evenly matched debate regarding this flawed and anachronistic theory is regrettable.

For example, consider how Mark Aulisio, writing in the *American Philosophical Quarterly,* began his "In Defense of the Intention/Foresight Distinction" with kudos for the doctrine of double effect, as if the doctrine were the only way of cashing out the important aspects of the distinction between intention and foresight: "The distinction between intention and foresight has long been held to be at the basis of the Doctrine of Double Effect. Far from being merely the arcane device of sectarian Roman Catholic casuistry, however, the intention/foresight distinction has been put forth by Thomas Nagel, Shelly Kagan and others as an important way of specifying the scope of deontic constraints."[23] Aulisio fails to realize that one can admit that the distinction between intention and foresight is normatively important while at the same time disagreeing with the use that proponents of the doctrine of double effect make of it.

The view that interest in the distinction between intending and foreseeing is tantamount to interest in the doctrine of double effect has become such a mainstay in the intellectual climate of our times that separating these two topics requires express, special clarifications. Gerald Dworkin begins an article entitled "Intention, Foreseeability, and Responsibility" with the following words: "This is *not* an essay on the doctrine of double effect"; the first few words of the second paragraph of his article are "This *is* an essay on the distinction between what we intend and what we merely foresee."[24] That Dworkin needs to emphasize the separateness of the discussion of the distinction between intention and foresight, on the one hand, from the discussion of the doctrine of double effect, on the other, attests, amply I think, to what I have called a mainstay, indeed a malady, of the current state of the debate of these issues.

In spite of the difficulties that it faces, the doctrine continues to be commonly used in attempting to shed light on all sorts of moral problems,

---

23. Mark Aulisio, "In Defense of the Intention/Foresight Distinction," *American Philosophical Quarterly* 32 (1995): 341.
24. Gerald Dworkin, "Intention, Foreseeability, and Responsibility," in *Responsibility, Character, and the Emotions,* ed. Ferdinand Schoeman (Cambridge: Cambridge University Press, 1992), 338 (emphasis in the original).

such as those surrounding euthanasia and assisted suicide. Some have tried to defend assisted suicide on the grounds that the physician's intention is to relieve suffering, whereas the possibility of death is merely foreseen. A recent landmark judicial decision regarding the legality of euthanasia discusses a commonly invoked version of the doctrine of double effect that has been used in trying to *justify* the termination of a terminally ill patient's life by a physician.[25]

> The term "double effect" originates in Roman Catholic moral theology, which holds that it is sometimes morally *justifiable* to cause evil in the pursuit of good. . . . The intent of palliative treatment is to relieve pain and suffering, not to end the patient's life, but the patient's death is a possible side effect of the treatment. It is ethically acceptable for a physician to gradually increase the appropriate medication for a patient, realizing that the medication may depress respiration and cause death.[26]

This sounds a lot like medieval casuistry writ large, like the maneuvers that Pascal lampooned. The judges of the decision, however, were not persuaded, and they echoed the opinion of the Council of Ethical and Judicial Affairs of the American Medical Association:

> The euphemistic use of "possible" and "may" may salve the conscience of the *AMA* [American Medical Association], but it does not change the realities of the practice of medicine or the legal consequences that would normally flow from the commission of an act that one has reason to believe will likely result in the death of another. In the case of "double effect" we *excuse* the act, or to put it more accurately, we find the act acceptable, not because the doctors sugarcoat the facts in order to permit society to say that they couldn't really know the consequences of their action, but because the act is medically and ethically appropriate even though the result—the patient's death—is both foreseeable and intended.[27]

The opinion contained in this passage brings welcome sobriety to our discussion. It emphasizes that to bring about merely foreseen evil outcomes is sometimes blameworthy. It emphasizes that foresight and intentionality are not even contraries, let alone contradictories. But more importantly, it echoes Pascal in denouncing the hypocrisy that surrounds the doctrine of double effect.

---

25. *Compassion in Dying v. Washington*, United States Court of Appeals for the Ninth Circuit (1996), 79 F3.d 790, passim.
26. *Compassion in Dying v. Washington*, 109. Concretely, the decision of the United States Court of Appeals for the Ninth Circuit is discussing the Council on Ethical and Judicial Affairs of the American Medical Association, "Decisions Near the End of Life," *Journal of the American Medical Association* 267 (1992): 2229–33 (emphasis added).
27. *Compassion in Dying v. Washington*, 109 (emphasis added).

In spite of the differences among the variegated contemporary discussions of the relevance which issues related to Intentionality might have on the normative assessment of assisted suicide and euthanasia, most of these approaches share some more-or-less visible shortcomings. I wish to just mention a couple of them briefly. First, there is a notorious absence of full-blown attempts to clarify the meaning of intention itself; the concept of intention is the most important concept for the philosophical treatment of the relationship between Intentionality and blameworthiness. That contemporary authors are indifferent to both the long history and the important recent developments regarding the relationship between Intentionality and the normative assessment of human action is illustrated by, for example, Albert Jonsen's thesis: "Suicide is perpetually fascinating to philosophers: from Seneca to Camus. Homicide, on the other hand, is repellant [sic] and crude."[28] Contra Jonsen, however, the preceding chapters show that homicide has been neither repellent nor crude to philosophers; in fact, it has been discussed with at least as much depth as suicide by thinkers from Plato onwards.

Second, there exists an account of the distinction between intending, foreseeing, and simply not caring, which is far more sophisticated than is the obviously anachronistic and inadequate doctrine of double effect. Such an account is found in theories of culpability, such as the one informing the Model Penal Code in the United States or other penal codes around the globe. But, what is worse, even the rudimentary Aristotelian theory of culpability was more sophisticated vis-à-vis the gradation of blameworthiness than the doctrine of double effect. It is surprising that contemporary scholars pay so little attention to the very laws that regulate (let alone to the history which sheds light upon) issues related to Intentionality and to the gradation of blame. These oversights account for the repetition of some fundamental errors, and these errors extend rather widely, as the doctrine of double effect is invoked in order to defend a host of practices, such as affirmative action, homosexuality, and many more.[29]

The flawed assumption which Aquinas introduced—that to merely foresee (without intending) an act renders it permissible—remains irritatingly pervasive today. Of course, no contemporary legal system recognizes this assumption, though this seems unimportant in some circles. The distinction between intending and foreseeing does not mark the distinction between morally wrong and morally permissible, as is too often suggested. Rather, the distinction between intention and foresight is meant to shed light upon the *degree* of blameworthiness of different acts that produce

---

28. Beauchamp, *Intending Death*, 48.
29. See, for example: William Cooney, "Affirmative Action and the Doctrine of Double Effect," *Journal of Applied Philosophy* (1989): 201–4.

identical outcomes. This misconception arguably arises from the preeminent role that the doctrine of double effect continues to play. But, as long as people continue to look to the doctrine of double effect for guidance in the apportioning of blame rather than to theories of culpability, it is unlikely that much progress will be made in understanding how and why we blame each others in the way that we do.

Jeremy Bentham's Analysis of Intentionality

Bentham's and Austin's contributions toward clarifying the meaning of intended and unintended action are of great importance. Bentham carried out a highly sophisticated analysis of action. As a matter of fact, Bentham's *The Principles of Morals and Legislation*, aside from the famous sections on the principle of utility, contains rather far-reaching discussions as to the nature of human action and of some Intentional states. Sadly, these discussions have not received the same attention as Bentham's general views on normative ethics.[30] Some aspects of Bentham's and Austin's views are strikingly similar to aspects of contemporary theories of action and even to specific modes of culpability in the Anglo-American legal tradition. Bentham's distinction between direct and oblique intention, for example, is the basis of the distinction between "purpose" and "knowledge" in the Model Penal Code. Austin's discussion of rashness is the basis for the Model Penal Code's treatment of recklessness.

Benthamite utilitarianism and Austinian positivism are landmark contributions to Anglo-American legal and moral theory. Of course, this is not to say that utilitarianism or legal positivism does not exist beyond the Anglo-American world, just as to refer to British empiricism is not to deny that there are empiricists outside Great Britain. But clearly Benthamite utilitarianism and Austinian positivism exerted greater influence in the Anglo-American world than anywhere else. From the perspective of the history of ideas, it is noteworthy that these authors were self-admitted admirers of the continental legal tradition (Austin) or at least of codification (Bentham).

My concern with Bentham and Austin, however, does not exclusively belong to my overall interest in the history of ideas in general. These authors are particularly useful for my purposes of laying bare the foundations of a theory of culpability. The notions of *dolus* and *culpa* which we examined in the preceding chapter continued to figure prominently in penal codes during the Middle Ages throughout Europe, but not so in theories of culpability in Great Britain. Given the idiosyncratic interest that

---

30. Jeremy Bentham, *The Principles of Morals and Legislation* (New York: Haffner Press, 1948).

these authors had on European developments, they each had interesting things to say about *dolus* and *culpa*.

Bentham presented a detailed and sophisticated description of the Intentional states that accompany our actions—one which captures many important insights regarding sound theories of culpability. The most famous, indeed the emblematic, Benthamite contribution to the theory of action is the distinction between direct and oblique intention. Although this is a very important distinction, it is just one among many important distinctions Bentham drew. Aside from this famous distinction between different types of intended action, Bentham analyzed unintended action thoroughly as well, a fact which might also be obscured because he did not discuss unintended action in the chapter of *The Principles of Morals and Legislation* entitled "Of Intentionality," but in a chapter entitled "Of Consciousness." The chapter entitled "On Intentionality" does not discuss Intentionality in general, as a property of mental states, but rather the intentionality of actions, that is, the different types of actions that arise from the different types of intentions associated with them. In this context, then, the by-now familiar terminological warnings presented in chapter 1 are particularly pressing. Unless otherwise noted, what Bentham means by intentional and unintentional action is what I mean by intended and unintended action; that is, unless otherwise noted, Bentham uses "intended" and "intentional" as synonyms and "unintended" and "unintentional" as synonyms. The chapter entitled "Of Consciousness" does not discuss the problems that one would expect, that is, the famous problem of consciousness discussed, emblematically, by philosophers of mind. By "consciousness" Bentham merely means *being aware* of this or that circumstance surrounding this or that *individual* act, that is, I might be unconscious (unaware) that my car spews noxious fumes, but I am not thereby unconscious *tout court*.

Immediately following our discussion of the doctrine of double effect, Bentham's work is refreshing insofar as it redirects our discussion back to modes of culpability and to degrees of blame and away from those strange issues of justification that preoccupied Aquinas. But, independently of whatever relation they may have with the doctrine of double effect, Bentham's views have value in and of themselves, as I will show immediately. If Bentham's analyses of Intentional states and their impact on human action were not already enough, they come with a bonus. Bentham is interesting for my purposes insofar as he is one of the few Anglo-American scholars to show an interest in the traditional institutions of culpability which I have discussed so far (*dolus* and *culpa*). And although Bentham expresses disdain regarding these institutions of "Roman Law" (which I think is unjustified), his opinions on matters related to these concepts are enlightening.

Bentham began the chapter "Of Intentionality" in *The Principles of Morals and Legislation*, by listing the ontological presuppositions underlying his analyses. As he analyzes the possible Intentional components of intentions, that is, those things that can be intended, he concludes that we could intend either acts themselves or some of their consequences. If we intend an act itself, then the sense in which an act is intentional is the same in which an act is voluntary, or the consequences of an act. In a long footnote Bentham recommends ignoring the words "voluntary" and "involuntary" "on account of the extreme ambiguity of their signification."[31]

As we have seen, ever since Plato and Aristotle there has been an unresolved tension between intentionality and voluntariness, which one would have hoped Bentham did not disregard in such cavalier fashion (and which I will discuss briefly in the section on Austin at the end of this chapter, and at length next chapter). But from this view it necessarily follows that for Bentham acts are different from their consequences. Moreover, Bentham also distinguishes an act's consequences (or "incidents," as he also calls them) from its circumstances. The chapter of *The Principles of Morals and Legislation* dealing with intentionality focuses on consequences, and the chapter dealing with consciousness focuses on circumstances. For, according to Bentham, one intends or fails to intend this or that consequence of our action, but one does not intend this or that circumstance of one's action—rather: one is aware or unaware of this or that circumstance surrounding our action.

As far as possible, I shall avoid Bentham's complicated ontology of action, because it is either irrelevant for my purposes, and, as shall become clear, because it gives rise to misunderstandings. I prefer to put to use the Searlean framework of Intentionality and thus gather together Bentham's "consequences" and "circumstances" all under the heading "states of affairs" and then discuss the Intentional ways in which we can relate to states of affairs. Part of the reason for this preference follows from a sort of ontological parsimony: it is unnecessary to distinguish between consequences and circumstances. But the main factor that explains the difference between Bentham's approach and mine is that I am interested in Intentionality understood generally, and being aware, or being conscious, in Bentham's sense, are, quite like intentions themselves, Intentional states. Both Bentham's chapter on intentionality and his chapter on consciousness deal with Intentionality, with the ways in which our Intentional states relate to states of affairs.

I think that there are clear advantages to focusing on Intentionality rather than following Bentham in distinguishing between "intentionality"

---

31. Bentham, *Principles*, 84.

and "consciousness." For example, Bentham admits that "acts, with their consequences, are objects of the will as well of the understanding: circumstances, as such, are objects of the understanding only."[32] "Willing," according to this passage, is a synonym of intending; what Bentham means is that we can both intend (or will) and be aware of consequences (and acts) but we cannot intend (or will) circumstances. And the fact that Bentham admits that consequences belong both to the understanding and to the will reveals that the distinction between what he calls "intentionality" and what he calls "consciousness" is not terribly sharp. Yet, this Benthamite distinction between the will and the understanding—between intending and being aware—has been influential; it can be viewed as a forerunner of many contemporary attempts to explain modern theories of culpability, and of criticisms to the modes of culpability found, say, in the Model Penal Code, by suggesting that they conflate two different sets of distinctions: one set is conative while the other is cognitive.[33] While I recognize that there are differences between conative and cognitive Intentional states, I do not wish to make too much out of them. Modes of culpability are, precisely, collections of Intentional states, some of which are conative and some of which are cognitive. Moreover (and as I will discuss at length in chapters 6 and 7), intentions, the most important of the Intentional states with which my theory of culpability is concerned, themselves contain both cognitive and conative elements. I shall thus focus only on the ways in which Intentional states (those Bentham calls "intentional states" and those he calls "states of consciousness") relate to the outcomes of our actions (those things Bentham calls "consequences" and those he calls "circumstances").

Bentham distinguishes consequences which we directly intend from those that we intend obliquely as follows:

> A consequence, when it is intentional, may either be *directly* so, or only *obliquely*. It may be said to be directly or lineally intentional, when the prospect of producing it constituted one of the links in the chain of causes by which the person was determined to do the act. It may be said to be obliquely or collaterally intentional, when, although the consequence was in contemplation, and appeared likely to ensue in case of the act's being performed, yet the prospect of producing such consequence did not constitute a link in the aforesaid chain.[34]

Here Bentham nicely points out to the conceptual difference between the set of Intentional states one has when one directly intends some-

---

32. Bentham, *Principles*, 88.
33. See, for example, Kenneth W. Simons's valuable "Rethinking Mental States," *Boston University Law Review* (1992): 463–554.
34. Bentham, *Principles*, 84.

thing and those Intentional states one has when one obliquely intends something. Bentham's use of the expression "in contemplation" in relation to obliquely intended consequences amounts to, roughly, "with foresight." Right off the bat, then, we can see an important difference between Bentham and Aquinas, insofar as Bentham actually admits that some consequences which are merely foreseen should be considered as fully (yet obliquely) intended. Some of the cases which Aquinas would have term unintended (insofar as they are merely foreseen), and therefore blameless and permissible, Bentham would hold to be intended, and thus presumably blameworthy to a certain degree (certainly not blameless by default).

Let me use Bentham's own examples to further illustrate the important way in which he differs from Aquinas. Bentham's examples are diversifications and modifications of the following incident that Hume reported in his *History of England*: "William II. king of England, being out a stag-hunting, received from Sir Walter Tyrrel a wound, of which he died."[35] Bentham then goes on to offer specific examples, which serve to emphasize his distinctions between intended actions, to wit: "He [Tyrrel] killed the king on account of the hatred he bore him, and for no other reason than the pleasure of destroying him. In this case the incident of the king's death was . . . directly intended."[36] This case is straightforward and it is unproblematic in that Aquinas and other proponents of the doctrine of double effect would agree with Bentham's description and, assuming that killing the king is an evil outcome, would presumably blame Tyrrel for bringing about this evil outcome.

Now, let us analyze Bentham's example of an obliquely intended outcome: "He [Tyrrel] saw a stag running that way, and he saw the king running that way at the same time: what he aimed at was to kill the stag: he did not wish to kill the king: at the same time he saw, that if he shot, it was as likely he should kill the king as the stag: yet for all that he shot, and killed the king accordingly. In this case the incident of his killing the king was intentional, but obliquely so."[37] Aquinas would probably disagree with Bentham here, insofar as for them the king's death was merely foreseen and therefore not intended. Moreover, according to the doctrine of double effect, Tyrrel's act should not be blamed (or punished). Of course, sophisticated proponents of the doctrine of double effect may counter my claims here by noting that in most sophisticated renderings of the doctrine of double effect it is necessary that the good outcome sought must outweigh the evil outcome brought about, and this is hardly

35. Bentham, *Principles*, 85–86.
36. Bentham, *Principles*, 86.
37. Bentham, *Principles*, 86.

the case in the example at hand. To the extent that Pascal's remarks on this subject relate to real events in history, it is clear that some past adherents of the doctrine treated cases such as this one as if they were blameless—at least they would be guilty as charged, even if some contemporary, savvier defenders of the doctrine of double effect would allow for blaming (or punishing) Tyrrel. But even these savvier authors would have to respond to the more general objection that these are issues of justification and not of culpability.

Bentham, however, does not directly tackle the issue of how this distinction might affect how much blameworthiness each of these two ways of doing things merits—a normative issue. There is no reason to suppose that he would disagree with the general principle I defend in this book, that to bring about an evil outcome intendedly is never less blameworthy than to bring it about unintendedly. And further, there is no reason to suppose that if Bentham were to accept a normative distinction between direct and oblique intention this would be an all-or-nothing distinction, such as proponents of the doctrine of double effect would have it. In all likelihood, given all the punctilious distinctions Bentham drew, had he been explicit about the normative import of this particular distinction, it would had been a matter of degrees of blame. In any case, the most important difference between Bentham and Aquinas is that Bentham would not call an action unintended simply because it was not intended directly. Moreover, given what Bentham says about the connection between these distinctions he makes and the Roman law, we could be practically confident that he would have indeed accepted pretty much the same normative distinctions as I do.

Yet, in a roundabout way, Bentham also succumbs to the temptation of conflating the descriptive and the normative analyses of Intentional states and their relationship to action; normative considerations creep into what he takes to be a merely descriptive affair. This will become clear in the next section, where I discuss Bentham's analysis of what he calls "consciousness," and where I show a case in which Bentham argues that given certain conditions, a certain action "must have been intended," in spite of the fact that there was no relevant intention.

Advisedness, Heedlessness, and Rashness

According to Bentham, the distinction between advised and unadvised acts is the following: "He [a man who acted] may either have been aware of the circumstance, or not aware: it may have either been present to his mind, or not present. In the first case, the act may be said to have been an *advised* act, with respect to the circumstance: in the other case, an *unadvised* one."[38] Quite simply, if one is aware of this or that circumstance, then the act is advised with respect to this or that circumstance. Bentham further tells us, however, that whenever an agent acts with consciousness of all the circumstances, then not only the consequences, but also the act itself must have been intended:

> Advisedness, with respect to the circumstances, if clear from the mis-supposal of any preventive circumstance, extends the intentionality from the act to the consequences. These consequences may be either directly intentional, or only obliquely so: but at any rate *they cannot but be* intentional.[39]

> If Tyrrel intended to shoot in the direction in which the king was riding up, and knew that the king was coming to meet the arrow, and knew the probability there was of his being shot in that same part in which he was shot, or in another as dangerous, and with that same degree of force, and so forth, and was not misled by the erroneous supposition of a circumstance by which the shot would have been prevented from taking place, or any other such preventive circumstance, it is plain that he could not but have intended the king's death. Perhaps he did not positively wish it; but for all that, *in a certain sense* he intended it.[40]

I have emphasized the ways in which these two passages end "*they cannot but be* intentional," and "*in a certain sense* he intended it," because I think that these passages contain veiled normative claims. For it is after all possible that Tyrrel was aware of all the circumstances in the example just presented, and yet, strictly speaking and from a purely descriptive point of view, he did not really intend, did not really form an intention, to kill the king (say, because he did not desire the king's death). In these passages Bentham *ascribes* intentions, he does not merely describe them.

For all that Bentham did in the way of clarifying, organizing, and distinguishing among Intentional states, he did not offer enough in the way of definition of intended (or unintended) action. From the preceding example (which, incidentally, is found in the chapter on consciousness and not in the chapter on intentionality), we can merely surmise certain things about his definition of an intention. For example, though he never says it explicitly, we can conclude that Bentham did not consider desiring an outcome to be a necessary condition for intending such an outcome. And as for the rationale of Bentham's insistence on the intended character of advised actions, I can see none other than his belief that there is no rele-

---

38. Bentham, *Principles*, 89.
39. Bentham, *Principles*, 92 (emphasis added).
40. Bentham, *Principles*, 92 (emphasis added).

vant difference, in terms of blameworthiness, between intended acts and fully advised acts.

The bulk of the chapter on consciousness, in any event, revolves around different types of what I would claim are unintended actions. Consider the following claims:

> Whether a man did or did not suppose the existence or the materiality of a given circumstance, it may be that he *did* suppose the existence and materiality of some circumstance which either did not exist, or which, though existing, was not material. In such case the act may be said to be *mis-advised*, with respect to such imagined circumstance: and it may be said, that there has been an erroneous supposition, or a mis-supposal in the case.[41]

An act is unadvised when the agent is unaware of the existence or the materiality of a certain circumstance, and it is misadvised when the agent believes that there exists a certain circumstance or that it is material when in fact the circumstance does not exist or it is not material.

> An act which is unadvised, is either *heedless*, or not heedless. It is termed heedless, when the case is thought to be such, that a person of ordinary prudence, if prompted by an ordinary share of benevolence, would have been likely to have bestowed such and so much attention and reflection upon the material circumstances, as would have effectually disposed him to prevent the mischievous incident from taking place: not heedless, when the case is not thought to be such as above mentioned.[42]

In other words, the unadvised agent is also heedless when he carries out his act, in spite of the fact that we would have expected a reasonable agent to have realized the risk-creating nature of this act. Quite possibly, an unadvised and heedless act would be nowadays considered a case of negligence. An unadvised and not heedless act would be considered nowadays a case of a mere accident (blameless). Let us now analyze Bentham's distinction between rash acts and acts which are not rash:

> What heedlessness is in the case of an unadvised act, rashness is in the case of a misadvised one. A misadvised act then may be either rash or not rash. It may be termed rash, when the case is thought to be such, that a person of ordinary prudence, if prompted by an ordinary share of benevolence, would have employed such and so much attention and reflection to the imagined circumstance, as, by discovering to him the non existence, improbability, or immateriality of it, would have effectually disposed him to prevent the mischievous incident from taking place.[43]

---

41. Bentham, *Principles*, 90.
42. Bentham, *Principles*, 89–90.
43. Bentham, *Principles*, 92.

Given the first sentence of this passage, which establishes a parallel between the role that rashness plays within misadvised acts and the role that heedlessness plays regarding unadvised acts, we can conclude the following: a misadvised and rash act would coincide with what we now call negligence. A misadvised and nonrash act would correspond to a mere accident.

Both Aquinas and Bentham were interested in examining the importance of certain cognitive states in the description and evaluation of action. Yet, there is a vast difference between the Benthamite theory of culpability and the theory of culpability arising from the application of the doctrine of double effect. Aquinas's conclusion as to the normative role of the distinction between intention and foresight is highly problematic. Undoubtedly Bentham's taxonomy has its problems, most of which, in my opinion, stem from the overemphasized distinction between intentionality and consciousness. For example, Bentham fails to sufficiently address the relationship between an unadvised and an unintended act. In principle, and following Aristotle, we can suppose that someone who is unadvised about all of the circumstances surrounding a given act is acting unintendedly. However, Bentham leaves us in the dark as to whether or not to be unadvised about *some* of the circumstances surrounding the act affects the intendedness of the act. Similarly obscure is the relationship between misadvised acts and intended acts. It seems clear that Bentham would accept that there are intended acts which are advised (with respect to certain circumstances) and intended acts which are unadvised (with respect to certain circumstances) but it is not clear if there are for him misadvised intended acts.

In spite of its limitations, Bentham's taxonomy of the ways in which we can act is a robust and useful starting point for the development of a theory of culpability. Again, in spite of its limitations, it is hard to see how one could turn Bentham's analysis of Intentional states into a justificatory engine of the Thomistic sort, so wittily lampooned by Pascal. If anything, the main complaint against Bentham might be that he puts too much emphasis on the pure description of these Intentional states, without really engaging with the (all of the) normative implications of these different ways of acting. Yet, as I shall show next there are at least two reasons justifying the claim that Bentham was indeed interested in the normative dimension of his analysis.

Bentham, Normativity, and *Dolus* and *Culpa*

One thing that might be puzzling about my discussion of Bentham is the fact that Bentham cared so much about these distinctions regarding the mental states with which we act. As a hard-core utilitarian, why should he have paid attention to all of these details? What on earth could Bentham, one of the fathers of utilitarianism, have found important about these details? The answer to these questions is, I think, very interesting. Famously, Bentham believed that "all punishment is mischief: all punishment is in itself evil."[44] (I think he was wrong about this, but this is not the place to carry out such discussion.[45]) Since he thinks that punishment is evil, Bentham goes to great lengths in permitting punishment only in those cases in which it would without a doubt produce a larger increase in general welfare than any alternative course of action. According to Bentham, then, punishment should not be inflicted in cases in which it is groundless, inefficacious, unprofitable, or needless, and he discusses cases "unmet" for punishment because they fall within any of these four general categories.[46] Among the cases in which punishment is inefficacious Bentham lists some cases of unintended and unconscious acts. The main point is that, in the end, these fastidious distinctions are relevant in practical ways; whether or not an act is intended, whether or not the agent is aware of this or that circumstance, could be the determining factor of whether or not that agent gets punished.

I do not agree with the purely consequentialist justification of punishment that Bentham defends. The obvious question suggests itself: Why in some cases of unintended or unconscious behavior is punishment necessarily inefficacious? Bentham's stock utilitarian reply is that in those cases "it cannot act so as to prevent the mischief,"[47] just pushes the question one level up, for then we should ask: Why in some cases of unintended or unconscious behavior is punishment incapable of preventing mischief? Bentham did not really address this question. I suggest that the reason, whether or not Bentham realized it, has to do with the fact that some unintended acts, for example, are blameless, and to punish in the absence of blameworthiness is, in principle, not efficacious.

I do not wish to suggest that my account based on blameworthiness is somehow coextensional with Bentham's utilitarian account. I believe that my account is simply more fundamental, and that there are probably similarities between my account and Bentham's, simply because, again, whether Bentham was aware of this or not, his views agree with the most fundamental level of analysis with which I am concerned. Moreover, this aspect of the normative dimension of Bentham's analysis is, in the end, surprisingly coarse. After all, here he merely mentions a few cases in which

---

44. Bentham, *Principles*, 170.
45. See my *Punishment and Retribution* (Aldershot: Ashgate, forthcoming 2005).
46. Bentham, *Principles*, 171ff.
47. Bentham, *Principles*, 171.

punishment is allegedly inefficacious, and leaves it at that. Bentham does not at all analyze cases in which more or less severe punishment would be more or less efficacious; he does not show sufficient interest in the way in which his analyses of the subtly different ways of doing things can give rise to similarly subtle differences in the gradation of blame.

For my purposes, the most important passage which reveals Bentham's concern with the normative dimensions of human action is not the one about punishment, but the one in which he discusses the classical notions of *dolus* and *culpa* that we have already encountered in the previous chapter. Upon finishing his analysis of the different forms of action, Bentham discusses related institutions pertaining to the Roman law. Bentham's contempt for these institutions is explicit: "I pretend not here to give any determinate explanation of a set of words [*dolus* and *culpa*], of which the great misfortune is, that the import of them is confused and indeterminate. I speak only by approximation. To attempt to determine the precise import that has been given to them by a hundredth part of the authors that have used them, would be an endless task."[48] Although Bentham is correct to point out that treatment of these concepts has been rather confusing, he seems unaware of the history which traces the origin of these concepts to Plato and Aristotle; he treats *dolus* and *culpa* as if they would have been created by Roman jurists in a vacuum. To this extent Bentham's discussion of Roman law is lacking, and to this extent his somewhat excessively critical stance regarding Roman law might be unjustified. But no matter; Bentham's short discussion of these concepts is packed with valuable insights. First, it emphasizes the point that Bentham did care about the normative implications of his taxonomy of the ways in which we act. Second, it helps to situate Bentham in the context of the history of culpability that I am presenting here.

At any rate, Bentham is one of the very few classical Anglo-American scholars to discuss Roman law—the other one being his friend, John Austin, whose work I shall discuss in the next section. Bentham begins, strikingly, by suggesting that what he has said regarding intended action, consciousness, and unadvised and misadvised actions has relevance for the Roman law. "A few words for the purpose of applying what has been said to the Roman law," is the opening statement of the section in which he discusses *dolus* and *culpa*.[49]

Bentham half-heartedly attempts to build correlations between the institutions of Roman law and the concepts he has developed in *The Principles of Morals and Legislation*, as follows: "Unintentionality, and innocence of intention, seem both to be included in the case of *infortu-*

---

48. Bentham, *Principles*, 95.
49. Bentham, *Principles*, 94.

nium [*casus*], where there is neither *dolus* nor *culpa*."[50] Regrettably, Bentham's sources are not revealed; but this probably constitutes a misrepresentation of the institutions of the Roman law. For, as we have seen already, the realm of unintended action is divided in that tradition into *casus* and *culpa*, and in the Greek tradition into *atychema* and *hamartema*. The difference between these two subdivisions of unintended action in all traditions has been the same: one of these subtypes (*casus, atychema*) is unintended and blameless, whereas the other (*culpa, hamartema*) is unintended and blameworthy.[51] Therefore, it is not that unintended action is included in the case of *infortunium* or *casus*, but the other way around: cases of *infortunium* or *casus* are included in, they are a subtype of, cases of unintended action.[52]

But perhaps the reason why Bentham goes wrong is because he is understandably confused about the meaning of *culpa* in the continental tradition. He tells us: "*Culpa* upon any other occasion, would be understood to extend to blame of every kind. It would therefore include *dolus*."[53] And there certainly exists an ambiguous use of the term *culpa* in the continental tradition. In addition to the technical meaning that it has within theories of culpability, and that it has had for many centuries, the term *culpa* has another venerable sense, which is roughly the one Bentham alludes to. (This sense has been immortalized and popularized in the expression *mea culpa* which means something like "my fault" or "I am to blame.") But the technical sense of *culpa*, the meaning of *culpa* in the Roman law, is not the one to which Bentham alludes; rather, the technical sense of *culpa* is "unintended-but-blameworthy," which it has had since Aristotle's times.[54]

Bentham proposes other correlations, for example: "Unadvisedness coupled with heedlessness, and misadvisedness coupled with rashness, correspond to the *culpa sine dolo*."[55] We can witness in this proposed correlation a mistake similar to the one we saw regarding the previous correlation. After all, in the technical sense that we have been using the term *culpa* here, all cases of culpa are *sine dolo*. The expression *culpa sine dolo* is obviously redundant, insofar as by definition *culpa* means that there is no *dolus*. Whether or not the expression is redundant, Bentham is correct in that what he calls unadvisedness coupled with heedlessness and what he calls

---

50. Bentham, *Principles*, 94.
51. See the discussion in chapter 2.
52. I am using *infortunium* and *casus* as synonyms.
53. Bentham, *Principles*, 95.
54. In the next chapter I shall show how the manifold meanings of *culpa* have hindered fruitful communication between the continental and Anglo-American legal traditions.
55. Bentham, *Principles*, 94.

misadvisedness coupled with rashness constitute cases of *culpa*, that is, cases of unintended but blameworthy action. These cases deserve some blame; more than mere accidents, but less than intended action.

Finally, and merely as a corollary to the preceding discussion, Bentham thinks of his work on the description of human action to be normatively relevant, which is patently obvious in the last paragraph of the section:

> The above-mentioned definitions are far from being mere matters of specula-
> tion. They are capable of the most extensive and constant application, as well
> to moral discourse as to legislative practice. Upon the degree and bias of a
> man's intention, upon the absence or presence of consciousness or mis-sup-
> posal, depend a great part of the good and bad, more specially of the bad con-
> sequences of an act; and on this, as well as other grounds, a great part of the
> demand for punishment.[56]

Bentham is famous for his work on punishment and on utilitarianism in general. His work on Intentionality and the description of human action, though less well-known, is also of great importance. It is particularly note-worthy that Bentham, who devoted such punctilious attention to Intentional states, would remain silent on the complex Intentional state of blaming, apparently failing to notice that blaming is also an Intentional state. He thus failed to see that whatever connection exists between Intentionality and punishment is first and foremost mediated in crucial ways by the primitive relation between intentions and blameworthiness.

John Austin's Theory of Culpability

As noted, if Bentham was an adherent of codification, Austin was an ardent admirer not only of codification, but of continental law in general, and of German law in particular. Austin visited Germany in 1826, and very soon became fluent in the language and knowledgeable in German law. In the field of criminal law no other European country has exerted a greater influence than Germany has. It is a felicitous coincidence, then, that the contact which Austin—who was by no means a specialist in criminal law, but rather a generalist—had with the continental tradition took place in Germany, and from then on through German authors. (When Sarah Austin—Austin's widow—died, she donated the books of her late hus-

---

56. Bentham, *Principles*, 95–96. Bentham, however, assumed that lack of intention regarding a consequence and lack of awareness regarding circumstances were extenuations, and the presence of these Intentional states were criminative factors. As noted, these complex of Intentional states are best understood as modes of culpability, along the lines sketched in chapter 1.

band, which were filled with observations and analytical notes, to the Inner Temple Library. The vast majority of these books were German classics in their original editions.) Just as Bentham's work on utilitarianism and on punishment has eclipsed his discussion of issues pertaining to theories of culpability, Austin's huge influence in the development of positivism in the Anglo-American legal tradition has also obscured his many contributions to culpability.

Most of what Austin had to say about our subject is contained in his famous *Lectures on Jurisprudence or the Philosophy of Positive Law*.[57] The book is composed of the notes of Austin's courses at London University. Most of these notes are presented in a disorganized fashion, and there is a lot of repetition, yet the depth and subtlety of Austin's vast knowledge of our subject shines through.

Although Austin and Bentham saw eye to eye on many issues, Austin had some misgivings regarding Bentham's writings on culpability. Early in his lecture on "Intention," Austin admits that he had been mistaken in using the term "act" for internal workings of the mind and for external bodily movements. He then explains the source of his mistake: "I hastily borrowed the distinction [between external and internal acts] from the works of Mr. Bentham: A writer, whom I much revere, and whom I am prone to follow, though I will not receive his dogmas with blind and servile submission."[58] Austin's abandonment of Bentham's insufficiently differentiated treatment of acts and consequences also leads him to part company with Bentham's view that, in some cases, "will" and "intention" are synonyms. Indeed, Austin is emphatic in distinguishing the Intentional state that is relevant for acts from the one that is relevant for consequences: "To desire the *act* is to *will* it. To *expect* any of its *consequences*, is to *intend* those consequences."[59] Austin's remark has momentous importance. The first sentence contains, in embryo, the basic elements of the volitional theory of action. As we have seen time and time again, historically it has been difficult to distinguish between the normative aspects of voluntariness and the normative aspects of intentions, between the Intentional states having to do with actions themselves (whatever these are) and the consequences of actions. I shall deal with

---

57. John Austin, *Lectures on Jurisprudence: Or the Philosophy of Positive Law* (London: John Murray, 1861).
58. John Austin, *Lectures*, vol. 1, 420. The continuation of the passage is not important for my purposes here, but it is uplifting and eloquent: "Impostors exact from their disciples 'prostration of the understanding' because their views will not endure examination. A man of Mr. Bentham's genius may provoke inquiry; and may rest satisfied with the ample and genuine admiration which his writings will infallibly extort from scrutinising and impartial judges" (420–21).
59. John Austin, *Lectures*, 421.

these issues in detail in next chapter, after I am finished with the historical analyses that have occupied my attention thus far.

The second sentence contains a rather stunning claim: expecting X is sufficient for intending X. The claim, as it stands, is indefensible, for I expect that the sun will rise tomorrow, and obviously I do not intend to make it rise. As noted, Austin's *Lectures* were notes and they were not always organized or even properly prepared for publication. But even if we add all the obvious qualifications to this claim, such as that X must be our own action, that "expecting" in this context presupposes a very high likelihood, and so on, Austin's thesis is problematic in that intentions are rather complex Intentional states containing both conative and cognitive aspects.

Austin's emphasis on the connection between intentions and awareness causes problems for his account of intended action. Where Bentham allowed two fundamental types of intended action (direct and oblique), Austin allows for three:

> 1st. The agent may *intend* a consequence; and that consequence may be the *end* of his act.
> 2ndly. He may *intend* a consequence; but he may desire that consequence as a *means* to an end.
> 3rdly. He may *intend* the consequence, without desiring it.[60]

An example of the first type of intention would be the following: "You hate me mortally: And in order that you may appease that painful and importunate feeling, you shoot me dead."[61] This type of intention, of course, is the least problematic. But problems multiply as we begin to consider Austin's additional types of intended action. An example of an action in which a consequence is intended as a means is the following: "You shoot me, that you may take my purse. I refuse to deliver my purse, when you demand it. I defend my purse to the best of my ability. And, in order that you may remove the obstacle which my resistance opposes to your purposes, you pull out a pistol and shoot me dead."[62] As he comments on this example, Austin laconically says: "Now here you *intend* my death, and you also desire my death."[63] This is, of course, not an argument; it is merely an assertion. We could surmise that the argument can be gleaned from the context, and that the reason why Austin would claim that here you intend

---

60. John Austin, *Lectures*, 423. Bentham also allowed for the distinction between mediately and ultimately intended actions, and also between exclusively and inexclusively intended actions, but these were but sub-types of intended action, not on the same level with it.
61. John Austin, *Lectures*, 423.
62. John Austin, *Lectures*, 423.

my death is based on the fact that I expect your death to ensue from my bodily movements. Things get worse, though, as we examine the third type of intendedness:

> You shoot at Sempronius or Styles, at Titius or Nokes, desiring and intending to kill him. The death of Styles is the end of your volition and act. Your desire of his death, is the *ultimate motive* to the volition. You contemplate his death, as the probable consequence of the act.
>
> But when you shoot at Styles, *I* am talking with him, and am standing close by him. And, from the position in which I stand with regard to the person you aim at, you think it not unlikely that you may kill *me* in your attempt to kill *him*. You fire and kill me accordingly. Now here you *intend* my death without *desiring* it. . . . since you contemplate my death as a probable consequence of your act, you *intend* my death although you *desire* it not.[64]

While Austin's move linking intentions to awareness is somewhat appealing, and while it has been extraordinarily influential, I would like to suggest that it faces difficulties.[65] Aside from the quite obvious objection I raised above regarding intending that the sun rise tomorrow, the view faces the difficulty when it comes to dealing with unintended acts, as we shall see.

Austin's discussion of unintended actions is complicated here more than elsewhere because here the discussion of Intentional states is tangled up with the discussion of the nature of actions. Austin distinguishes between omissions and forbearances. An omission is "a *not* doing . . . without thought of the act which is not done."[66] A forbearance is, in contrast "a *not* doing . . . with an *intention* of not doing."[67] For Austin, then, all forbearances are intended. This is a strange view insofar as it constitutes an unexplained, uncomfortable asymmetry. Recall that for him acts are only willed, never intended. But then, if I am considering whether to perform act *X*, I am at that moment *willing* it, yet at the moment I am considering not to perform act *X*, then I am *intending* not to do it. During the process of deliberation of acts, then, our Intentional state transforms from willing to intending, back to willing, and back again to intention, depending on whether we think we are doing or not doing the act in question. This sort of problem is typical of the volitional theory of action, which I will criti-

---

63. John Austin, *Lectures*, 423.
64. John Austin, *Lectures*, 424.
65. For an enlightening discussion (with references to landmark cases in the United Kingdom) of the exact relation between intention and awareness, see Duff's *Intention, Agency and Criminal Liability*, 1–11, 76ff., and passim.
66. John Austin, *Lectures*, 426.
67. John Austin, *Lectures*, 426.

cize in chapter 5. For now, I wish to focus on the types of unintended actions Austin discusses.

According to Austin, among the many things we constantly omit, some of them are culpable, that is, some of them we should not omit. If we omit to do something which was a positive duty, then our action is considered negligent; if we omit to refrain from doing something, thus breaking a negative duty, then our action is considered heedless. Again, the distinction between positive and negative duties to which Austin appeals here is somewhat unnecessary, for Austin also tells us: "the states of mind which are styled 'Negligence' and 'Heedlessness' are precisely alike. In either case the party is inadvertent."[68]

In addition to negligence and heedlessness, Austin claims that there exists another way of doing harm unintendedly: what he calls "temerity" or "rashness" (the two expressions are synonyms for Austin). Unlike the heedless/negligent agent, who is inadvertent, "the party who is guilty of rashness *thinks* of the probable mischief," and then Austin continues, "but, in consequence of a missupposition begotten by insufficient advertence, he assumes that the mischief will not ensue in the given instance or case."[69]

Now, given Austin's insistence that awareness is enough for intention, it seems hard to see why cases of rashness are not simply intended. It seems to follow from Austin's views that at the very least in the early stages of rash acts there is an intention, given that before the rash agent mistakenly concludes that there is no risk, he was aware of the risk, and thus, from Austin's perspective, he intended it. About the fact that Austin considers negligence, heedlessness, and rashness unintended, there can be no doubt, as I shall show in the next section.

Austin, Normativity, and *Dolus* and *Culpa*

Like Bentham, Austin was interested in connecting his analyses of issues regarding culpability to the tradition of Roman law. Like Bentham, moreover, Austin treats the institutions of Roman law as if they would have been *ex nihilo* created by Roman lawyers. Several shortcomings of the Bethamite and the Austinian theories of culpability, and indeed of many contemporary theories of culpability, can be traced back to the neglect of the story that I told in chapter 2. This story is important not so much for general enlightenment purposes, but quite pointedly because it reveals that the problem of culpability is a philosophical problem; that the notions of *dolus* and *culpa*, for example, have their origins in philosophers' attempts to

---

68. John Austin, *Lectures*, 427.
69. John Austin, *Lectures*, 427.

answer the general question that inspires this book: "How do the Intentional states of agents when they act affect the blameworthiness of what they do?"

Austin concludes his discussion of unintended wrongdoing with the following observation: "By the Roman Lawyers, Rashness, Heedlessness, or Negligence is, in certain cases, considered equivalent to 'Dolus:' that is to say, to intention."[70] Austin believes that Roman lawyers are wrong, and his explanation of why they are wrong is very interesting. "Now this (it appears to me) to be a mistake," Austin notes. "Intention (it seems to me) is a *precise* state of mind, and cannot coalesce or commingle with a different state of mind."[71] And one of the things that Austin stresses repeatedly is that the distinction between the intended and the unintended is dichotomous, which is for present purposes an important point.

> Some injuries are intentional. Others are consequences of *negligence* (in the large signification of the term). . . . It is absolutely necessary that the import of the last-mentioned expressions should be settled with an approach to precision. For *both* of them run, in a continued vein, through the doctrine of injuries or wrongs; and of the rights and obligations which are begotten by injuries or wrongs. And *one* of them (namely 'Intention') meets us at *every* step, in *every* department of jurisprudence. . . . And since 'Negligence' implies the absence of a *due* volition and intention, it is manifest that the explanation of that expression supposes the explanation of these.[72]

It is noteworthy that Austin takes care to remind us that the "negligence" he is referring to in this passage is the "broadly-understood negligence," which encompasses all other forms of blameworthy unintended action. But nowadays "negligence" in the Anglo-American legal tradition refers to a specific mode of culpability. It is a frequent occurrence to encounter Anglo-American scholars interested in continental culpability, who translate the distinction between *dolus* and *culpa* as the distinction between intention and negligence. Although they sound a lot like Austin, they are in fact saying something very different and very pernicious, as I shall show in the last section of this chapter.

There at least two problems with how to interpret the assertion that "intention is a precise state of mind." First, it is hard to understand what Austin means by saying that intentions cannot coalesce or commingle with other Intentional states. For obviously intentions frequently coalesce with other Intentional states. Moreover, and as we shall see in the later chapters of this book, intentions are themselves composed of

---

70. John Austin, *Lectures*, 428.
71. John Austin, *Lectures*, 428.
72. John Austin, *Lectures*, 423.

diverse Intentional states, which in fact coalesce in order to give rise to an intention.

Austin comes close to seeing the problem that occupies significant amounts of my attention here, and that led me to distinguish so sharply between the intended, the intentional, and the culpable in chapter 1: the tension between normativity and description. By reminding Roman lawyers that an intention is a "precise" mental state, Austin might be reminding them that whether or not a given Intentional state is an intention is a purely empirical affair, and that how to apportion blame to this or that Intentional state is a different enterprise altogether. Not so—Austin had something else in mind.

> The mistake (I have no doubt) [of the Roman Lawyers] arose from a confusion of ideas which is not infrequent:—from the confusion of *probandum* and *probans*:—of the *subject* of an inquiry into a matter of fact, with the *evidence*.
> When it was said by the Roman Lawyers, 'that Negligence, Heedlessness, or Rashness, is equivalent, in certain cases, to *Dolus* or Intention,' their meaning (I believe) was this:—Judging from the conduct of the party, it is impossible to determine whether he intended, or whether he was negligent, heedless, or rash. And, such being the case, it shall be presumed that he intended.[73]

I have no doubt that these sorts of epistemological confusions are common; and I have myself referred to (different sorts of) epistemological concerns in attacking the doctrine of double effect. But this diagnosis fails to address the central problem of the relationship between Intentionality and culpability. Many, including Roman lawyers, when considering a case such as the juggler's case discussed in chapter 1, say something along the lines of "whether or not the juggler intended to explode a grenade, he exploded it intentionally." To repeat, to say that someone has an intention is an empirical affair (in spite of whatever epistemological limitations we might face) but to say that someone did X intentionally is not a purely normative affair. Austin is right in that whether or not the juggler has an intention to explode a grenade is an empirical "precise" affair. True, Roman lawyers were not clear about the distinction between the analysis of Intentional states themselves and the analysis of the normative implications of those Intentional states; but neither are contemporary philosophers, and neither is Austin himself. For, as he discusses Roman lawyers' error, Austin further explains that part of their mistake was to suppose that there was some sort of middle category between

---

73. John Austin, *Lectures*, 430; Austin correctly notes that this presumption would only hold in civil cases, and that in criminal cases, the presumption is the opposite, i.e., that there was no intention (430).

intended and unintended, or between conscious and unconscious. Regarding this possibility, Austin says:

> Now a state of mind between consciousness and unconsciousness—between intention on the one side and negligence on the other—seems to be impossible. The party thinks, or the party does not think, of the act or the consequence. If he think of it, he intends. If he do not think of it, he is negligent or heedless. To say that negligence or heedlessness may run into intention, is to say that a thought may be absent from the mind, and yet (after a fashion) present to the mind.[74]

From the purely descriptive perspective Austin is right, again, in that no matter how intensely I have, say, the Intentional state of believing that X, it simply is not going to become another Intentional state, say a desire that X or an intention to X. (By the way, this is probably not true of all Intentional states: a very intense dislike of X, for example, could become abhorrence of X, and I think disliking and abhorring are two different Intentional states). From the normative perspective, however, there could, of course, be intermediate modes of culpability, that is, modes of culpability which give rise to more blame than negligent behavior but less than intended behavior. Austin's rashness, which is a forerunner of the Model Penal Code's recklessness, is just one of those intermediate modes of culpability. Even assuming that Roman lawyers had no difficulty whatsoever knowing what the mental states of a given agent were, upon knowing that she was rash they would have difficulties dealing with her behavior, from the normative perspective. They would not know exactly how blameworthy the behavior was.

Theories of Culpability Today

The interest that Bentham and Austin showed in analyzing *dolus* and *culpa* has all but disappeared in the English-speaking world. Division of labor has set in; philosophers of mind might work on problems regarding Intentionality, philosophers of law typically work on the debate between positivism and natural law, ethicists might work on blameworthiness, and so on. Most English-speaking scholars, whether in philosophy or the law or ethics, are virtually wholly ignorant of the very existence of *dolus* and *culpa*, and I have no doubt that these terms sound, to such ears, like arcane, probably useless and uninteresting notions. As I have shown, *dolus* and *culpa* are important in that historically they have been the key modes

---

74. John Austin, *Lectures*, 428–29.

of culpability in most theories of culpability in the West. Most of Bentham's and Austin's criticisms of *dolus* and *culpa* stemmed from the fact that these notions had been used in different ways by different people through the ages. Still, they thought it important to attempt to map their own modes of culpability onto those "belonging to the Roman law." (As I pointed out before, the sense in which *dolus* and *culpa* belong to the Roman law is debatable, at least to the extent that this way of referring to them obscures the fact that these modes of culpability can be traced all the way back to Plato's notions of *hekousios* and *akousios* actions. Part of what I wish to do in this chapter is to discuss the ways in which contemporary theories of culpability relate to each other, and to some of the traditional theories of culpability presented so far.

Modern criminal law cannot help but have a theory of culpability (this does not at all mean that jurists and much less legal practitioners need to engage in philosophical analysis of the underlying foundations of theories of culpability). Thus I would like briefly to take a look at the theories of culpability of the two most important legal traditions of the West: the common law, and the tradition based on Roman law. Aside from providing some sort of closure to the story that I have been telling, this comparative stance shall serve two important purposes. First, the comparison shall allow me to highlight a rather widespread problem that strains the communication between the two legal traditions. Second, and much more important for my purposes, the comparison shall allow me to highlight once more the eminently philosophical nature of the main problems associated with theories of culpability. This shall be revealed, concretely, by the fact that the main difference between each legal tradition's theory of culpability is the way in which the distinction between what counts as intentional and what counts as unintentional is drawn. Remember, the distinction between intentional and unintentional action is a convoluted distinction which encompasses descriptive elements (whether or not the agent's action is intended) and normative elements (how blameworthy/culpable the agent's action is). How to draw this distinction is a monumental problem both at the purely descriptive and at the normative level. We first need a clear definition of intention (and other Intentional states). Yet, even if we are absolutely clear on the definition of an intention (and other Intentional states), it might still be difficult to determine exactly the difference in terms of blameworthiness between similar modes of culpability.

Most emphatically, my goal is not to solve technical issues pertaining to legal theory (though I of course would not mind it if my work helped with this task), but rather to shed light on the nature of the philosophical problem of how and why we blame people for the bad things that they bring about. What I shall here use as the representative model of the theory of culpability of each of these legal traditions might be from the internal perspective of legal practitioners, idiosyncratic, or it might even be considered inadequate, though from the philosophical perspective my choices are unproblematic.

As a representative from the theory of culpability of the common law tradition I will use the Model Penal Code.[75] As a representative of theory of culpability associated with the Roman law I have chosen the Standard Penal Code for Latin America.[76] I would just like to say a few words about these choices. While in some respects these codes are revisionist, at times admittedly so, they are also particularly valuable in that they critically summarize and systematize the received views on culpability of each of these legal traditions. The Model Penal Code is almost unanimously considered one of the most sophisticated and comprehensive penal codes in the tradition of the common law. Its influence upon specific enacted codes, moreover, has been great, as numerous jurisdictions in the United States have looked up deferentially toward the Model Penal Code, for enlightenment and guidance, as they enact their own codes. The Standard Penal Code for Latin America is also a collaborative effort that gathers the product of several years of work by Latin America's leading legal scholars.[77] We could refer to the Standard Penal Code, in a way, as the Latin American Model Penal Code (or to the Model Penal Code as the Anglo-American Standard Penal Code).

---

75. American Law Institute, *Model Penal Code*. The Model Penal Code is the most sophisticated and comprehensive code in the Anglo-American tradition of criminal law. This justifies my decision of focusing upon one single text, when I could have studied instead many interesting court decisions which shed light on the Anglo-American theory of culpability.

76. *Código Penal Tipo Para Latinoamérica* (Santiago de Chile: Editorial Jurídica de Chile, 1973). This is a collaborative effort which gathers the product of several years of work by Latin America's leading legal scholars. For information on its influence, cf. Henry Dahl, "The Influence and Application of the Standard Penal Code for Latin America," *American Journal of Criminal Law* 17 (1990): 235–62. There is another good reason for choosing a Latin American work as representative of the continental tradition. Latin American philosophy is European in origin; it constitutes a chapter in the history of Western philosophy. Latin American legal philosophy, in particular, is even more drastically dominated by European ideas. Whereas in the case of general philosophy, Anglo-American ideas may have attracted some attention and gained some acceptance, the contribution which Anglo-American law may have exerted upon Latin American systems has been, until recently, relatively insignificant. For more information on Latin American philosophy of law (and on how closely it follows European developments), cf. Leo Zaibert and Jorge J. E. Gracia, "Philosophy of Law in Latin America," in *The Philosophy of Law: An Encyclopedia*, ed. Christopher B. Gray (New York: Garland Publishing, 1999).

77. For information on its influence, cf. Dahl, "Influence and Application," 235–62. Admittedly, Latin American criminal law, and Latin American law in general, are European in origin. While it might have been then perhaps more orthodox to choose as a representative of the Roman law tradition a German code, for example, the Standard Penal Code has the advantage of being a representative compendium of many European codes and ideas.

The theories of culpability popular in legal systems identified with Roman law tradition are based in the concepts of *dolus* and *culpa*. To that extent, they are the heirs of a long and rich history, jurisprudence, and philosophy, and they fit better within the context of the story I have been telling. It is, I think, rather unproblematic to see how they evolved from the sorts of modes of culpability that we have been studying.

The Standard Penal Code defines intended and blameworthy action (*dolus*) as follows: "A person acts with *dolus* when he wishes the occurrence of the legally described act, or when he accepts it, foreseeing it at least as possible."[78] Unintended (blameworthy) action (*culpa*) is defined as follows: "A person acts with *culpa* when he commits the legally described act due to the lack of respect for the duty of care that is required according to the circumstances as well as his personal conditions, and, in the case of representing [to himself] the consequences as possible, trusts that he will be able to avoid them."[79] There are then two different modes of culpability embedded in the definitions of intended blameworthy action (*dolus*) and of unintended blameworthy action (*culpa*) in the Standard Penal Code. There are two kinds of intended action: first, when the agent desires exactly what she produces; and second, when the agent does not desire the side effect, but foresees it as at least possible and *accepts* the possibility of its eventuation. The first case is known as *dolus* (blameworthy intended action *simpliciter*), the second case is known as *dolus eventualis*.

In the case of unintended action the two modes of culpability are the following: first, when the agent, due to lack of care or prevision, brings about an unwanted outcome. Second, when the agent foresees the outcome but *trusts* that she will be able to avoid it. The first case is known as *culpa* (blameworthy unintended action *simpliciter*). The second case is known as conscious *culpa* (blameworthy unintended conscious action).[80]

The modes of culpability of the Standard Penal Code are then:

(1) *Dolus*
(2) *Dolus Eventualis*

---

78. *Código Penal Tipo*, 29 (article 25).
79. *Código Penal Tipo*, 29 (article 26). These are my own translations; for reasons that shall become evident later, I am not using José Canals and Henry Dahl's translation of the Standard Penal Code. See José Canals and Henry Dahl, "The Standard Penal Code for Latin America," *American Journal of Criminal Law* 17 (1990): 236–301.
80. Also known as "*culpa* with representation." The two expressions are synonymous. Throughout I use "conscious *culpa*" instead of "*culpa* with representation," given that the traditional distinction in Anglo-American law between recklessness and negligence is established in terms of "awareness of the risk" or consciousness of the risk. Hence, to use "conscious *culpa*" instead of "*culpa* with representation" while posing no problems to continental scholars, should facilitate understanding among Anglo-American scholars.

(3) Conscious *Culpa*

(4) *Culpa*

The Model Penal Code also operates in the context of four modes of culpability. An agent acts "purposively" if the outcome of her action is her "conscious object." An agent acts "knowingly" when she brings about a side effect of her conduct, knowing that it is practically certain that such side effect will occur. An agent acts "recklessly" when she consciously disregards a substantial and unjustifiable risk arising from her action. Finally, an agent acts "negligently" when, due to lack of care, she ignores the risk-creating nature of her conduct.[81] Each of these modes could be divided further, but for my purposes the breakdown of action stated above is sufficient.

The modes of culpability in the Model Penal Code are then:

(1) Purpose

(2) Knowledge

(3) Recklessness

(4) Negligence

Unlike the modes of culpability in the Standard Penal Code, the modes of culpability of the Model Penal Code cannot easily be situated in the context of the history of the theories of culpability I have described so far. Of course, they can indeed be traceable to the Austinian and Benthamite discussions of culpability, and the very names of the modes of culpability of the common law reveal the penchant for ordinary language terms already present in Austin and Bentham and emblematic of much of Anglo-American philosophy. In spite of this difference, however, there are striking similarities between the two theories of culpability. In the order in which they are presented, each mode of culpability in one tradition roughly corresponds to the same one in the other tradition, at least from the normative perspective. The ordinal gradation of blame in each of these theories is virtually identical, purpose is never less blameworthy than knowledge, and in turn never less blameworthy that recklessness, and so on, in pretty much the same way in which *dolus* is never less blameworthy than *dolus eventualis*, and in turn *dolus eventualis* in never less blameworthy than conscious *culpa*, and so on.

In both traditions, and reliving the historical problems we have analyzed, the most vexing and relevant problems arise in relation to the so called *borderline concepts*. Borderline concepts define modes of culpability

---

81. American Law Institute, *Model Penal Code*, sec. 2.02.

that correspond either to the maximum degree of blame for unintentional action or to the minimum degree of blame for intentional action. In other words, borderline concepts are those contiguous to the boundary (or "border") between intentional and unintentional action. In the continental tradition, the difficulties are found in the attempts to distinguish between *dolus eventualis* and conscious *culpa*. In the common law tradition, problems arise with the subtle distinction between acting knowingly and acting recklessly. There is nothing in the words themselves that would indicate that I am right in assuming that reckless behavior is unintentional and that knowing behavior is intentional. And although this is indeed the accepted view among contemporary legal scholars in the common law tradition, the history I have presented here should leave no room for doubt. The connection between recklessness and rashness/heedlessness on the one hand, and the connection between knowledge and oblique intention, on the other, is sufficient to justify my claim.

It is of course a shame that people no longer do what Bentham and Austin did, that is, try to relate their own theories of culpability to the classical theories of culpability dating back to Roman law and beyond to Plato and Aristotle. The advancement of theories of culpability within legal theory is, of course, hindered by failing to realize the fundamentally philosophical nature of issues relating to culpability. But it is also hindered by the parochial way in which each legal tradition develops. These two factors combine together in such a way that communication between the two legal traditions is made difficult by rather superficial mistakes, mistakes which would probably not exist if attention were paid to the history of culpability presented here.

For example, a crucial notion in the history of culpability, *culpa*, is almost invariably mistranslated into English (not surprisingly, I think the best rendering of *culpa* into English is Austin's).[82] Consider George P. Fletcher's, one of the world's leading experts in comparative criminal law, referring to the "classic distinction between *dolus* (intention) and *culpa* (negligence)." But, as we have seen, this is not the classic distinction that has occupied philosophers and legal theorists; rather, it is the distinction between intentional and unintentional action—negligence is but a form of unintentional action. But the plot thickens; as Fletcher goes on to claim that "recklessness is a form of *culpa*—equivalent to what German scholars

---

82. There are difficulties with giving a name to all the systems I am referring to here as "continental law." It is not accurate to gather them under the widely known heading of "Latin law" since Roman law contributed little to criminal law. It is inaccurate, too, to gather them under the heading of "German law" exclusively, since I am encompassing other systems as well. I am gathering under this label the legal systems of most of the non-English-speaking countries of the West.

call 'conscious negligence.'"[83] But then Anglo-American scholars would be justified in concluding that in Europe "recklessness'" is a form of "negligence," whereas recklessness and negligence constitute two different modes of culpability.

These sorts of translational difficulties are truly endemic. In evaluating the German Draft Criminal Code of 1960, Gerhard O. W. Mueller tells us: "The German draft code is in accord with our Common Law in requiring intentional production of the harm (section 15) except when the penal law explicitly makes *negligent* production of the harm adequate for liability."[84] Johannes Andenaes, in his illuminating comparison between the Study Draft of Proposed New Federal Criminal Code and continental penal codes, expresses the following view: "Negligence includes in European systems, the conscious risk taking ('conscious negligence,' roughly corresponding to the American 'recklessness') as well as the inadvertent creating of a risk ('unconscious negligence')."[85] In a similar vein, Mirjan Damaska refers to the primordial distinction in continental theories of culpability as follows. "'General parts' of civil law Codes usually define only two basic kinds of culpability: intent and negligence. The latter is subdivided into advertent negligence (most of the situations the Study Draft classifies as recklessness) and inadvertent negligence (negligence as defined by the draft)."[86]

These are respected scholars in the field of comparative criminal law. Their views have at least one important similarity: they present continental penal codes as containing two main modes of culpability: "intention" and "negligence." Granted, they all tell us that negligence in continental codes can be divided into what in America are called recklessness and negligence, but that does not entail that their terminology is less misleading. The classic distinction that informs virtually all continental legal systems is that between *dolus* and *culpa*, which should be properly translated as the distinction between intended and unintended action. What continental codes subdivide into advertent or inadvertent (conscious or unconscious, etc.) is not negligence, but unintended action.

---

83. Fletcher, *Rethinking Criminal Law*, 443. Notice that the first principle is identical to that presented by Austin and which I analyzed in the previous chapter. Yet, Austin's notion of "negligence" encompasses both the contemporary notion of "recklessness" and the contemporary notion of "negligence."

84. Gerhard O. W. Mueller, "The German Draft Criminal Code 1960—An Evaluation in Terms of American Criminal Law," *University of Illinois Law Forum* 25 (1961): 46 (emphasis added).

85. Johannes Andenaes, "Comparing Study Draft of Proposed New Federal Criminal Code to European Penal Codes," *Working Papers of the National Commission on Reform of Federal Criminal Laws* 3: 1455.

86. Mirjan Damaska, "Comparing Study Draft of Proposed New Federal Criminal Code to European Penal Codes," *Working Papers of the National Commission on Reform of Federal Criminal Laws* 3, 1487.

To be sure, there is an ambiguous use of the word *culpa* (or *colpa*, or *Fahrlässigkeit*, etc.) in the continental tradition, which, as we have seen, had already exasperated Bentham. The same word is used to describe unintentional action generally (*culpa latu sensu*), and to describe what in Anglo-American law is known as negligence (*culpa strictu sensu*). This ambiguity is present in most continental penal codes, regardless of the language in which they are written. In that respect, the Anglo-American law offers a clear advantage over its continental counterparts inasmuch as there are different words for each mode of unintentional action: "recklessness," "negligence," and so forth.[87] In continental systems the same word is used for "unintentional action" and for a particular form of "unintentional action," ("negligence" or *culpa strictu sensu*). This is, as stated, an obvious shortcoming of continental systems. Moreover, only in English, the language of the Anglo-American legal tradition, "negligence" has the technical meaning of unconscious-unintended-blameworthy action: only in the Anglo-American tradition does negligence constitute a standard mode of culpability.

These terminological details, however, do not justify the erroneous translations. Arguably, these would not be as common if the discussion of theories of culpability were placed correctly within their historical and philosophical contexts.

---

87. The problem of whether or not these terms mean the same in the technical legal realm or in the realm of ordinary language has played a central role in recent discussions of legal theory in the Anglo-American law. In any case, to have two different names for two different concepts is advantageous. Concerning the tension between the colloquial and technical use of the terms, see: John Austin, "A Plea for Excuses," 39–54; Alan R. White, *The Grounds of Liability* (Oxford: Clarendon Press, 1985); and Duff, *Intention, Agency and Criminal Liability*.

[4]

Intentions, Volitions, and Actions

Before discussing intentions specifically, it seems appropriate for me to address the great confusion regarding whether there is any difference between acting voluntarily and acting intendedly. In the course of the preceding discussion, it has become clear that Plato and Aristotle did not make distinctions between acting intendedly and acting voluntarily. As we saw in chapter 2, the term *hekousion* of ancient Greek is frequently translated into English interchangeably as "voluntary" and as "intentional," and the term *akousion* is similarly interchangeably translated as "involuntary" and as "unintentional." The Greeks did not have two different concepts. Surprisingly, perhaps, though now we have two different expressions, still today these two expressions are frequently used as synonyms.

The proliferation of modes of culpability that we have analyzed has been accompanied not merely by a more nuanced approach to the sorts of Intentional states that relate to the gradation of blame, but also by a more complicated ontology of action. While I believe that a more nuanced map of modes of culpability is a welcome improvement upon earlier theories of culpability, in this chapter I wish to argue for a simplified ontology of action. Aquinas paved the way for this complicated ontology by distinguishing between acts and their effects; Bentham and Austin also made much of the distinction between acts, their consequences, and their circumstances. Here I will insist in the abandonment of these superfluous distinctions.

In the common law tradition, in order for an agent to be punished for the commission of a crime, two things must be proved: the *actus reus* and the *mens rea*. The most general import of this distinction is this: in order to punish someone we need to prove two different things. First, that the person acted "voluntarily" (and that the act he voluntarily performed was previously described as crime) and, second, that he had the appropriate set of Intentional states which allow us to actually blame him for what he did: we need to prove that the person had a "guilty mind." The *actus reus* requirement is not a single requirement; it contains a rather varied set of requirements.[1] Among these requirements is that the agent must have acted voluntarily. The *mens rea* requirement is met when, at the time the agent committed the crime (when she acted voluntarily), she had one of the sets of Intentional states which the law requires for there to be any liability whatsoever. (Some crimes admit of only some Intentional states, i.e., some crimes cannot be committed negligently or recklessly.) Similarly, in the continental tradition, in order for an agent to be punished for the commission of a crime, it must be proved that the agent acted voluntarily, and that the agent is culpable; that is, she committed the crime with one of the required sets of Intentional states.

The maxim *actus non facit reus, nisi mens sit rea* is intuitively appealing: it seems wrong to say that someone should be punished, or indeed blamed, for having done this or that if, for example, the person did not know (an Intentional state) and could have not known that he was doing it. This intuition has as much currency outside the law as it does within the law. For example, a terrorist puts a bomb on a plane, and programs it to explode at 25,000 feet of altitude. The pilot of the plane, who is wholly ignorant of the fact that there is a bomb on the plane, actually pilots the plane until it reaches an altitude of 25,000 feet, and then the plane explodes. Imagine the pilot somehow survives the explosion. It seems absolutely clear that though the pilot acted, he is not to be blamed at all—he does not have a guilty mind. And the blamelessness of his action transcends the criminal law.

The categories that mark the boundaries between intendedness and voluntariness in the criminal law are useful for my purposes, for these categories underscore an important difference between acting voluntarily and acting intendedly. Issues of voluntariness belong to the discussion of the *actus*, or in other words, to the discussion of acts, facts, or states of affairs. Issues of intendedness belong to the discussion of the *mens*, or in other words, to the discussion of Intentional states. This, as I shall argue, is the central difference between intendedness and voluntariness. (It is mainly this difference which, too, lends support to my thesis that the most plausible translation of Aristotle's and Plato's key concept *hekousion*

---

1. Though I will later in this chapter criticize Michael Moore's defense of volitional theories of action, his account of the relationship between the *actus reus* requirement and related requirements such as the voluntary act requirement or the double jeopardy requirement is the best I have seen. See, e.g., Michael Moore, *Act and Crime* (Oxford: Oxford University Press, 1993), especially 17–60 and passim. For criticisms as to the unity of the voluntary act requirement see Paul H. Robinson, *Structure and Function in the Criminal Law* (Oxford: Clarendon Press, 1997), passim. See also my "Philosophical Analysis and the Criminal Law," *Buffalo Criminal Law Review* 4, no. 1 (2001): 100–39.

is "intentional" and not "voluntary," since these authors used the Greek term primarily in contexts where the existence of an action was not in doubt.)

One would have hoped that in criminal law theory, where these terms mark foundational distinctions, the meaning of these terms would be clearly spelled out. Yet, in spite of the obvious attractiveness of the categories just mentioned, *actus reus* and *mens rea*, legal theory does not fare much better than general philosophical approaches. Regrettably, there exists at least as much confusion surrounding the meaning of these terms in the field of the legal theory as exists elsewhere. A tradition of sorts exists in Anglo-American criminal law, for example, of not defining certain concepts, so as not to limit judges or juries in their interpretation of these terms. As it turns out, the Model Penal Code, for example, provides no definition of intended action and no definition of voluntary action, and this is obviously unhelpful.

In search of light, then, we must turn to philosophical works. There exists a venerable theory of voluntariness which, until relatively recently, was held in almost unchallenged high esteem, as it galvanized the opinion of many philosophers regarding this issue. This theory is known as the volitional theory of action, and also as the general doctrine of the voluntary act. Alvin Goldman eloquently tells us that the volitional doctrine "was once regarded as virtually self-evident by practically everyone."[2] The obscurities and inadequacies of this theory have been made clear in the twentieth century by Ludwig Wittgenstein and along similar lines by H. L. A. Hart, and by Alan R. White, among many others. These authors' solutions to the problems surrounding the definition of voluntariness, however, are not acceptable. In this chapter I shall show the shortcomings of the traditional doctrine of the voluntary act and of the amended theories which these authors put forth. My strategy will be to analyze these theories from the normative perspective, a rather unusual move. I shall conclude by sketching an account of the voluntariness of action that avoids the problems facing other definitions and also serves as the criterion to distinguish actions from other events.

Ever since Descartes' sharp distinction between mind and body, the idea that there exist some entities called "acts of will" has been popular. These "acts of will" have been, in turn, used to explain the distinction between the voluntary and the involuntary and the distinction between action and nonaction. In the seventeenth century, Locke succinctly presented the doctrine of the voluntary act:

---

2. Alvin Goldman, "The Volitional Theory Revisited," in *Action Theory*, ed. Myles Brand and Douglas Walton (Dordrecht: Reidel, 1975), 68.

This power which the mind has thus to order the consideration of any idea, or the forbearing to consider it; or to prefer the motion of any part of the body to its rest, and vice versa, in any particular instance, is that which we call the *Will.* The actual exercise of that power, by directing any particular action, or its forbearance, is that which we call *volition* or *willing.* The forbearance of that action, consequent to such order or command of the mind, is called *voluntary.* And whatsoever action is performed without such a thought of the mind, is called *involuntary.*[3]

Thomas Hobbes, David Hume, William James, and Oliver Wendell Holmes, among many other famous figures, held versions of this influential volitional theory of action. Contemporarily, there are many revivalists of the doctrine, such as Lawrence Davis, Alvin Goldman, Wilfrid Sellars, and above all, Michael Moore. John Austin was, however, perhaps the first to discuss voluntariness in relation to intendedness and other Intentional states *from a normative perspective.* John Austin is, moreover, frequently credited with having first introduced a distinction between voluntariness and intendedness. And so, among the many volitional theories of action, I shall begin the discussion of voluntariness by considering Austin's views.

Let us recall that for Austin the ontology of action involves three distinct elements: "The bodily movements which immediately follow our desires of them, are acts (properly so called). But every act is followed by *consequences*, and is also attended by *concomitants*, which are styled its *circumstances.*"[4] Bentham's treatment of intentionality and of consciousness as two different subjects is of a piece with the Austinian tripartite distinction. The ways in which we can Intentionally relate to these three building blocks of Austin's ontology of action are different. In spite of the apparent simplicity of Austin's talk of "desires" for bodily movements, a simplicity which, as we shall see in the next section, Hart overemphasizes, Austin in fact believed that these bodily movements—in his view the only real acts— are indeed *willed*: they are necessarily caused by a volition. For Austin insists that "to desire the act is to will it."[5] Moreover, though Austin criticizes Bentham for not distinguishing enough between willing and intending, Austin still believed the two notions were closely related: "In order that we may settle the import of the term 'Intention,' we must settle the import of the term 'Will'. For although an intention is not a volition, the facts are inseparably connected."[6]

3. John Locke, *An Essay Concerning Human Understanding* (Oxford: Oxford University Press), bk. 2, chap. 21, 5.
4. John Austin, *Lectures,* 421.
5. John Austin, *Lectures,* 421.
6. John Austin, *Lectures,* 411.

For Austin, then, regardless of whether or not we intend a *consequence* of an act (or are aware of an attendant *circumstance* of an act), a more fundamental question arises: are the bodily movements tending to bring about such an evil outcome preceded by a volition or "act of will"?[7] Austin considers this question to be central in our efforts to understand the nature of voluntariness. If we answer this question negatively, then we are not in the presence of a human act at all (because, for Austin, there are no involuntary *acts*—but mere involuntary *movements*). For a bodily movement to be considered an act, in Austin's sense, it must be the result of a volition or of an "act of will."[8] If we answer the question affirmatively, then we can proceed to analyze other factors relevant for the normative appraisal of the action. So, in order to even begin a discussion of Intentionality and other factors that might alter how we blame an agent, we must decide first whether or not a volition preceded the bodily movements which caused the evil outcome. If volition was absent, then there is no point in investigating further, for the movement (which is not an action) gives rise to no judgment of blame.

I agree with Austin and the defenders of volitional theories of voluntary action in one respect. An important lesson, at least for the purposes of clarity, that Austin gives us is that the distinction between action and nonaction, on the one hand, maps onto the distinction between so-called voluntary action and so-called involuntary action, on the other. The distinction between intended and unintended action belongs, wholly and unproblematically, to the discussion of Intentional states (intentions), and given that there clearly exist unintended actions, but not involuntary actions, it is clear that the two distinctions are different. Insofar as I care so much about Intentionality, it might be somewhat surprising that I will criticize volitional theorists of action for appealing to Intentional states in order to define actions. But I think that as crucially important as Intentional states are for the determination of the degrees of blame that people deserve for their wrongdoing, the ways in which they may help determine whether or not an event is an action are much more complicated.

---

7. I shall use here "acts of will," "willings," and "volitions" as synonyms.
8. Contrast my reading of Austin's theory (see chapter 3) with James W. Child's reading. He claims: "John Austin believed that all action was intentional and, therefore, all culpable action was intentional." James W. Child, "Donald Davidson and Section 2.01 of the Model Penal Code," *Criminal Justice Ethics* (1992): 31. This error is not a minor one. In light of the sophisticated analyses of modes of culpability which Austin carried out (again, see the previous three), it is beyond doubt that Austin did not believe that all consequences of actions were intended. Child's confusion is in part the result of the overcomplicated ontology of action peculiar to the volitional theory of action, and it reveals the deep misunderstandings that surround contemporary debate of these issues.

Volitional theories of action such as Austin's rather uncritically base the voluntariness of action, that is, the very condition of an event being an action, on the fact that the event was caused/preceded by an Intentional state. The Intentional state of choice has historically been termed a "volition" (hence the name of the theory), though synonyms like "acts of will" or "willings" have also been used. I shall echo many scholars who believe that in some important ways volitions are obscure and mysterious entities. Some of the recent revivals of the volitional theory of action, most notably Michael Moore's, try to overcome the difficulties associated to the mysteriousness of volitions by turning volitions into less mysterious Intentional states. While I believe that the mysteriousness of volitions constitutes a serious problem for traditional volitional theories, I also believe that even if the efforts to turn volitions into less obscure, garden-variety Intentional states were to succeed, volitional theories would still face other difficulties.

Objections to Traditional Volitional Theories

Wittgenstein, notoriously, reacted against volitional theories of action, and his criticisms of the doctrine have been seminal, as they greatly influence contemporary theories such as those of G. E. M. Anscombe and Gilbert Ryle. Alan R. White and H. L. A. Hart in particular, along Wittgensteinian lines, have aimed their attacks directly toward Austin's theory which, in the Anglo-American legal tradition, is known as the "general doctrine of the voluntary act."[9] The attacks on volitional theories of action have much in common; perhaps the most conspicuous commonality is that all these attacks censure the overcrowded ontology that arises from the volitional theory. It is possible, however, to suggest a peculiar tendency in each of the three attacks that I shall discuss in this section (although there is considerable overlapping among them). Wittgenstein is primarily concerned with bringing much-needed perspicuity to philosophy of mind, Hart is primarily concerned with showing that volitional theories contradict common sense, and White with showing that these theories contradict the way in which we ordinarily speak about these issues. I first present our authors' criticisms of volitional theories of action, then suggest a method for deciding whether or not a theory of action is correct, and then go back to our authors and analyze their views under the light of this method.

---

9. Perhaps even more notoriously, Gilbert Ryle has reacted against this view. His *The Concept of Mind* (Chicago: University of Chicago Press, 1949; passim) is the *locus classicus* for modern attacks on theories relying too heavily on Intentional mental states. Notoriously, though the book has chapters on "the will," "dispositions," "emotions," and other mental phenomena, there is no chapter or discussion of "intention."

Wittgenstein presents a devastating attack on volitional theories of action. His argument goes roughly as follows. Since theories such as the general doctrine of the voluntary act posit the existence of "acts of willing," then it would be possible to have an "act of will" for another "act of will," but this is inconsistent. Wittgenstein tells us:

> In the sense in which I can bring anything about (such as stomach-ache through over-eating), I can also bring about an act of willing. In this sense I bring about the act of willing to swim by jumping into the water. Doubtless I was trying to say: I can't will willing; that is, it makes no sense to speak of willing willing. "Willing" is not the name of an action; and so not the name of any voluntary action either. And my use of a wrong expression came from our wanting to think of willing as an immediate non-causal bringing-about.[10]

Wittgenstein's expression "noncausal bringing about" is itself somewhat obscure and difficult to understand. We normally think that whenever an event X brings about a different event Y, then X causes Y, or in other words, the expressions "bringing about" and "causing" are roughly synonymous. Wittgenstein suggests that this idea of noncausal bringing about arises in the minds of those who talk about acts of will and then face difficulties in explaining what exactly this act of will is. Some modern defenders of the volitional theory confirm Wittgenstein's hypothesis. Lawrence Davis states: "Precisely what it means to say that a particular doing was an action, according to the volitional theory, is that it was generated by a volition. But if generated by a volition, then neither preceded nor caused by a volition."[11] How can an event X generate another event Y, with neither X preceding Y nor X causing Y, is indeed difficult to grasp.

Wittgenstein suggests that it is a mistake to suppose that the relation between the "act of will" and the muscular contractions is one of the former "bringing about" the latter. The "act of will" is not the instrument we use in order to realize the muscular contractions. To be sure, "when I raise my arm 'voluntarily,'" Wittgenstein tells us, "I do not use any instrument to bring the movement about."[12] As shall become clear in the following chapters, this peculiar "*causal* bringing about" to which Wittgenstein alludes to in this passage is always present in the case of intended actions. It is this "bringing about," moreover, which allows a distinction between intended action and voluntary action, and between "intendings" and other related but importantly different Intentional states. For now, however, a sketch of the difference should suffice. Roughly, when an agent intends X,

---

10. Ludwig Wittgenstein, *Philosophical Investigations*, trans. G. E. M. Anscombe (New York: MacMillan, 1953), 159 (§613).
11. Lawrence Davis, *Theory of Action* (Englewood Cliffs, NJ: Prentice Hall, 1979), 40.
12. Wittgenstein, *Philosophical Investigations*, 160.

she wants to bring X about, and she wants also that X be brought about *because* she so intended. For example, if Ludwig intends to paint his house, and goes to town to buy the paint, but upon returning finds that Arnold already painted the house, his intention "to paint the house" has not been satisfied. The mere fact that the mental representation realizes itself (unlike in the cases of beliefs, hopes, wishes, desires, etc.) does not satisfy an intention. In some way (again, to be explained fully in the following chapters), the house being painted must be "brought about" by the intention of painting it, which is its cause. And in some way, then, "intentions" (but generally not "wishes." and much less "acts of will," as Wittgenstein correctly points out), cause our intended action.

Since for Wittgenstein, "willing" is not itself an act, and not a separate entity of any sort either, he tells us that "[w]illing . . . must be the action itself. It cannot be allowed to stop short of the action."[13] And so Wittgenstein convincingly debunks the volitional theory; willing to swim is swimming, willing to speak is speaking and so on. Wittgenstein expresses a similar concern elsewhere:

> How is 'will' actually used? In philosophy one is unaware of having invented a quite new use of the word, by assimilating its use to that of e.g., the word 'wish'. . . . 'Want' is sometimes used with the meaning 'try': 'I wanted to get up, but was too weak.' On the other hand one wants to say that wherever a voluntary movement is made, there is a volition. Thus if I walk, speak, eat, etc., etc., then I am supposed to will to do so. And here I can't mean trying. For when I walk, that doesn't mean that I try to walk and it succeeds.[14]

Thus, Wittgenstein hints at reasons for skepticism regarding volitions, and indirectly, also at reasons for being skeptical about distinguishing actions from their consequences. These hints are also taken up by Hart.

Hart's attack on the doctrine of the voluntary act is composed of two arguments: I am only interested in one of them. (The argument I am ignoring here shows that the volitional theory cannot adequately deal with omissions.) Hart, following in Wittgenstein's footsteps, considers the general doctrine of the voluntary act to be "nothing more than an outdated fiction—a piece of eighteenth century psychology which has no real application to human conduct."[15] Hart's most important substantial argument against the way in which the Austinian doctrine has been interpreted is that the exact meaning of the expression "act of will" is hopelessly obscure and

---

13. Wittgenstein, *Philosophical Investigations*, 160 (§615).
14. Ludwig Wittgenstein, *Remarks on the Philosophy of Psychology*, trans. G. E. M. Anscombe (Chicago: University of Chicago Press, 1980), vol. 1, 12–13.
15. H. L. A. Hart, *Punishment and Responsibility: Essays in the Philosophy of Law* (Oxford: Clarendon Press, 1968), 101.

vague. Hart believes that the obscurities inherent in this talk of volitions have become accentuated as the theory has propagated. In a condemning tone, Hart points out:

> It would be interesting to trace in detail the descent of this [Austinian] doctrine [of the voluntary act] to the modern writers on the criminal law whom I have quoted. I cannot do that here; I will however observe that the terminology in which the doctrine is expressed has, in the course of the descent, become very much less precise. For later authors do not ever plainly say that the psychological element which makes conduct 'voluntary' is just a desire for muscular contractions. Instead we are told that it is 'an element of will' or 'operation of the will' (from which muscular contractions 'result') or a 'mental attitude to conduct' as distinct from a 'mental attitude to the consequences of conduct.'[16]

But Hart, after quoting profusely from Austin's *Lectures on Jurisprudence*, tells us that what Austin had in mind, although flawed, was much simpler than his followers have taken it to be. Hart's paraphrasing of Austin is perhaps clearer than Austin's own original:[17] "Conduct is 'voluntary' or 'the expression of an act of will' if the muscular contraction which, on the physical side, is the initiating element in what are loosely thought of as simple actions, is caused by a desire for those same contractions. This is all [that] the mysterious element of the will amounts to."[18]

Hart's defense of Austin's volitional theory of action insofar as its "acts of will" are not as mysterious as the "acts of will" of other volitional theories, is extremely charitable. It is true that Austin wants to avoid appealing to strange Intentional states. After all, Austin bemoans that fact that he has to talk about the will at all: "the structure of established speech forces me to talk of 'willing;' and to impute the bodily movements, which immediately follow from our desires for them, to 'the Will.'" By way of explanation he adds, "a familiar expression, however obscure, is commonly less obscure, as well as more welcome to the taste, than a new and strange one."[19] Yet Austin also clearly distinguishes volitions from intentions, as I noted above, and he incessantly repeats that "a consequence of the act is never *willed*." But it is clearly possible to desire a consequence of an act, thus rendering suspicious both Austin's supposedly unhappy use of "willings" and Hart's simplistic equation of Austinian "willings" with

---

16. Hart, *Punishment and Responsibility*, 99. Hart provides in a useful footnote what he takes to be the main stages in the descent of the theory; see p. 99, n. 24.
17. This is understandable given the fact that the *Lectures on Jurisprudence* are sometimes disorganized and repetitive. They are after all, Austin's class notes, which were collected after his death by his widow, Sarah Austin, who, in her deceased husband's honor, did not attempt to alter the state in which he left these notes.
18. Hart, *Punishment and Responsibility*, 99.
19. John Austin, *Lectures*, 419.

desires.[20] For if willings were merely desirings, of course, the obvious question would arise as to why Austin claims that it is not possible to will the consequences of our acts.

Hart is not alone in this extremely charitable reading of Austin. R. F. Stalley, for example, has argued that Austin (influenced greatly by the philosophy of Thomas Brown) wanted to get rid of "volitions." But for the same reasons that I find Hart's reading of Austin too charitable, I also find Stalley's conclusion too charitable:

> It is paradoxical that the Brown-Austin theory should have been treated as a standard case of a volitional theory of action. Both Brown and Austin thought that the great merit of their theory was precisely that it did away with the mysterious entities called volitions. Their attempt to dispose of these entities leads to the conclusion that Hart finds so unsatisfactory. So those modern critics who have used the Brown-Austin theory as a target, without playing adequate attention to its historical context, have been attacking a would-be St. George rather than an authentic dragon.[21]

In spite of his charitable reading of Austin's formulation of the doctrine of the voluntary act, however, Hart still criticizes the doctrine because even if it does not appeal to strange Intentional states, it does nevertheless require that we adopt a rather complicated ontology of action, one in which for every act there are (at least) three elements: first, "desires" for muscular contractions; second, the contractions themselves; and third, the consequences (which can be "desired," foreseen, intended, etc.).[22] It indeed seems counterintuitive to suggest that when we, say, go for a bike ride, we both "desire" (will) the muscular contractions needed for our ride, and also desire (intend or foresee, etc.) the consequences of the muscular movements needed for the ride. Many of Hart's arguments in this regard rest on the fact that ordinary people rarely, if ever, perceive (much less talk about) their acts in this threefold manner. It is unlikely that our actions are really like this, and we rarely ever experience them like this.

Later in the chapter, I will develop a point that I think is at the core of Hart's suspicion regarding even the Austinian rendering of the volitional theory of action. Even if we were to admit that on this or that volitional theory of action, volitions are identical to desires, or identical to intentions

---

20. John Austin, *Lectures*, 421.
21. R. F. Stalley, "Austin's Account of Action," *Journal of the History of Philosophy* (1980): 453.
22. Incidentally, the Model Penal Code has bought into the Austinian ontology of action wholesale: Model Penal Code, 1.13(9). See also Moore's remark to the effect that the Model Penal Code slightly, but problematically, alters the Austinian ontology in *Act and Crime*, 190, n. 5.

(much more likely), or to any other garden-variety Intentional state, the volitional theory must give rise to this sort of threefold analysis of action. For as long as we admit a distinction between actions and their consequences, we cannot escape the overcrowded, threefold ontology of action. (Incidentally, it is for this reason that, in the previous chapter, I did not follow Bentham or Austin in separating these two phenomena.)

White's misgivings regarding the volitional theory of action stem from his concern for ordinary language. I do not believe that ordinary language is the last word on any philosophical matter, but taking a look at the ways in which we ordinarily talk about this or that issue frequently is at least enlightening. In this vein, White tells us: "One can surrender, withdraw, or resign unwillingly, though quite voluntarily, and be persuaded or dragged off willingly, though neither voluntarily nor nonvoluntarily. There is nothing self-contradictory in the *Digest*'s phrase '*Coactus volui*'. 'Unwilling', but not 'nonvoluntary' or 'involuntary', is related to grudgingly and reluctantly. There are degrees of willingness but not of being voluntary."[23] White is suggesting that, based on the way we ordinarily speak, to act willingly and to act voluntarily are different things, although the general doctrine of the voluntary act has it that an act is voluntary if and only if it is "willed." Of course, the force of this remark depends on the importance we attach to ordinary language. In his famous Lionel Cohen Lecture at the Hebrew University of Jerusalem, Glanville Williams, commenting on Ryle's views on the relationship between willingness and voluntariness (comments that apply as well to White), stated: "'Voluntary' is the adjective corresponding to the noun 'will', so it is somewhat difficult to see why Ryle [or White] should reject the noun but accept the adjective."[24]

Appeals to ordinary language are somewhat problematic for my purposes; after all, sometimes the way we ordinarily speak about certain things is inadequate. For example, the very distinction that I am emphasizing in this book, that between intended and unintended action, purports to be a more accurate way of describing what in ordinary language people sloppily describe by appealing to the much more complicated distinction between intentional and unintentional action. What we have said so far regarding the distinction between the intended and the unintended, on the one hand, and the distinction between the intentional and the unintentional, on the other, is relevant for the discussion of the distinction between the voluntary and the involuntary. Like the distinction between intentional and unintentional action, the distinction between voluntary and involuntary movements serves, in ordinary language, both descriptive and norma-

---

23. White, *Grounds of Liability*, 51.
24. Glanville Williams, *The Mental Element in Crime* (Jerusalem: Magnes Press, 1965), 18.

tive purposes. Like the distinction between the intended and the unintended, if a given movement is voluntary, then it is not involuntary, and if it is involuntary then it is not voluntary. This seemingly obvious remark is necessary in order to stave off suggestions that there are other ways of acting which are neither voluntary nor involuntary, that is, claims of the following tenor: victims of blackmail do not give in to the blackmailer's demands voluntarily, though they do not give in involuntarily. For my purposes, as long as the agent was aware of what was happening, as long as he *chose* to give in to the blackmailer's demands, he acted voluntarily. Whether my view contradicts ordinary language or not is not important to me.

White, in any case, presents two more substantial objections to the general doctrine of the voluntary act. Echoing Wittgenstein's insightful indictment of the volitional theorists' unusual talk of "non-causal relations of bringing about," White tells us that regarding this doctrine

> [t]here is the difficulty of characterizing the relation between the volition and the bodily movement which follows from it, for this seems to be at the same time logical and causal. It is logical in that the volition which is alleged to cause, for example, a movement of the index finger is necessarily the volition to do exactly that and it is causal in that it is the cause of the movement. But a cause of something ought to be logically independent of it.[25]

The hope shared by Wittgenstein, Hart, and White is not to have to appeal to extra, unnecessary entities; I am sympathetic to those hopes. Wittgenstein bases his criticisms mainly upon the fact that there can exist no relation of "bringing about" between the "willing" and "the thing willed." Hart builds his ontology mainly by relying on the way in which we ordinarily experience our actions; he relies on our common sense, if you will. And White bases his criticisms on the combining of the two types of objections previously mentioned, while he adds to this eclectic view considerations concerning ordinary language. Inspired by the arguments already presented, I wish to mention a famous objection to volitional theories and then supplement it with my own "normative" criticism.

As Ryle has so clearly demonstrated, some formulations of the volitional theory of action lead to an infinite regress.[26] Indeed, Wittgenstein only explains part of the problem of the volitional theory of action, merely hinting at another aspect of it. For he does not explicitly refer (nor do Hart or White) to the obvious problem that the ontology of human action underpinning the doctrine of the voluntary act faces. For if we were able to have an "act of will" for another "act of will," that is,

---

25. White, *Grounds of Liability*, 30.
26. Ryle, *Concept of Mind*, 62ff.

if "willings" were acts in themselves, then we could also have a third (and a fourth, and so on) "act of willing" for the "act of willing" for the first "act of willing."

Fine, but why is this a problem? (It might be retorted.) Can we not desire "to have a car," and also desire "to have a desire to have a car," and also desire "to have a desire to have a desire to have a car," *etceteras ad infinitum*? We can, of course, however silly such a practice might be. This analogy with desires, however, does not hold. For "willing" is a necessary condition for the event willed to be realized as an act, and therefore to talk of "acts of will" it is necessary to *explain* human action, whereas "desiring" is not necessary in the same way. The sorts of infinite regresses that one *could* end up with regarding, say, desires, are not explanatory. Those infinite regresses that one would *necessarily* end up with regarding "acts of will" are explanatory. Just as there are nonvicious circular arguments, there are nonvicious infinite regresses. "Contingent" infinite regresses, such as "she knows that I know that she knows that I know that she knows. . . ," although sometimes silly, are not necessarily vicious, because these regresses are not meant to *explain* a given action. But with "acts of will" the regress is vicious, in that each act (including the "act of will") must be preceded by another "act of will," and we are, after all, searching for an end to these "acts of will" so that we can explain a given action.

From the normative perspective there is a sense in which issues of voluntariness are more fundamental than issues of Intentionality (and even nonvolitional theorists should agree with this). Lack of voluntariness entails lack of action, and thus it entails no responsibility (unless one wishes to talk about responsibility for mere thoughts or for character traits, a discussion I avoid in this book). Voluntariness and the lack thereof are contradictory: either what one does is voluntary or it is not. If our movements are voluntary, then discussions such as those relating to the sets of Intentional states that constitute this or that mode of culpability might be pertinent. If our movements are involuntary, then these discussions of modes of culpability are pointless—for these movements did not constitute an action. But if, as the doctrine of the voluntary act would have it, there are mental phenomena called "willings," which are representations of states of affairs which they in turn cause, the doctrine would face all sorts of additional difficulties. For then either all actions are by default willed, even if they are unintentional, or else the relation between the "willing" and the action could be as varied as in the case of the authentic Intentional states which authors like Bentham and Austin reserved for consequences of action. In other words, the general doctrine would allow the following sorts of descriptions: "John intentionally did X voluntarily," "John recklessly did X voluntarily," and so on, since it would be possible that "John intentionally willed X," "John recklessly willed X," and so on. I shall come back to this point when I discuss Moore's defense of the volitional theory of action below.

In spite of the thoughtful criticisms that our authors have raised against the volitional theory of action, they have not been able to put forth normatively useful theories of voluntariness (nor, either, to convince contemporary defenders of the volitional theory). In order to show that Wittgenstein's, Hart's, and White's theories of voluntariness are indeed flawed, I first need to explain my strategy for appraising these theories of voluntary action, and then I shall return to our authors' accounts of voluntariness.

Alternative Accounts of Voluntariness and the Problem of Normativity

In order to appraise the usefulness of the different accounts of voluntariness which have been put forth as substitutes for the general doctrine of the voluntary act, let us now turn our attention to the following principle, which I suggest captures the normative role of voluntariness:

> To bring about an evil outcome voluntarily is a necessary (but not sufficient) condition of blameworthiness; bringing about an evil outcome involuntarily is a sufficient (but not necessary) condition of blamelessness.

Keeping in mind what I have already argued, that is, that the distinction between the voluntary and the involuntary is dichotomous, it seems to me that this principle is in obvious agreement with our moral intuitions. Another way of expressing it would be the following:

> Acting is a necessary (but not sufficient) condition of blameworthiness, and not acting is a sufficient (but not necessary) condition of blamelessness.

This principle is one of the most basic principles of modern criminal law. The Model Penal Code, for example, establishes: "A person is not guilty of an offense unless his liability is based on conduct which includes a voluntary act."[27] The drafters of the Model Penal Code, moreover, have referred to this principle (as stated in the preceding quotation) as "the fundamental predicate for all criminal liability."[28] (Not surprisingly, similar provisions are expressed or assumed in penal codes all around the globe: this principle clearly agrees with deep-seated moral intuitions.)

---

27. American Law Institute, *Model Penal Code*, vol. 1(3), 212 (Sec. 2.01 [1]).
28. American Law Institute, *Model Penal Code*, 213.

I think that the fact that criminal liability presupposes an acting agent is as intuitively appealing as we could hope for. In spite of the fact that debates as to the exact meaning of voluntary and involuntary acts rage in the field of criminal law, the principle itself is virtually never challenged. Categorically, A. T. H. Smith, has stated: "It has never been seriously questioned that without an *actus reus* [which presupposes voluntariness], there can be no liability at all."[29] (A few years later, however, White put forth a challenge to this principle which I shall analyze below.) I think, moreover, that the fact that this principle is universally accepted in the legal realm is also good evidence of its bedrock status in our moral psychology. Now, if a certain theory of voluntariness rendered "involuntary" some cases that from the normative perspective are clearly voluntary (insofar as the allegedly involuntary agents do not seem necessarily blameless), this would be a major problem facing such a theory. If when we examine a given definition of voluntariness through the lens of this principle, cases which are in tension with our deepest-seated moral intuitions, also captured by our legal institutions, multiply, something is probably wrong with such definition.

In what follows I shall show that the accounts of voluntariness that Wittgenstein, Hart, and White have put forth are, in light of the normative import of issues of voluntariness, inadequate. I shall give a general explanation of why they fail which, in spite of the differences between each of the three theories, is applicable to all of them.

Let us, then, now turn to Wittgenstein's response to the inadequate talk of "willings." He tells us:

> Examine the following description of a voluntary action: "I form the decision to pull the bell at 5 o'clock, and when it strikes 5, my arms makes this movement."—Is that the correct description, and not *this* one: ". . . and when it strikes 5, I raise my arm"?—One would like to supplement the first description: "and see! my arm goes up when it strikes 5." And this "and see!" is precisely what doesn't belong here. I do *not* say "See, my arm goes up!" when I raise it.
>
> So one might say: voluntary movement is marked [instead of "by an act of will"] by the absence of surprise.[30]

If we apply the test afforded by the normative principle just stated to Wittgenstein's thesis, we shall attain unsatisfactory results. Consider Carol, who works at a candle store and is in charge of closing every day at five o'clock. Friday, she closes the store, unaware of the fact that a girl is locked inside the store. Monday comes and the girl has died trying to escape. It is to be expected that Carol would be surprised (among other things, and

---

29. A. T. H. Smith, "On *Actus Reus* and *Mens Rea*," in *Reshaping the Criminal Law: Essays in Honour of Glanville Williams*, ed. P. R. Glazebrook (London: Stevens and Sons, 1978), 97.
30. Wittgenstein, *Philosophical Investigations*, 162 (§627, §628).

to say the least) to find out that she locked the girl in the store and thus contributed to bringing about her death.

One ought to be careful here. Wittgenstein merely claims that voluntary action is *marked* by the absence of surprise. This does not entail that absence of surprise is a sufficient condition of voluntary action. And it does not entail either that the presence of surprise is the mark of involuntary action. Wittgenstein's use of "mark" is not too helpful. Yet in order to make some sense out of this passage I shall suggest that although it is clear that there is no logical necessity involved, it is possible to interpret Wittgenstein as holding something along the following lines. Voluntary actions tend not to be accompanied by the agent's surprise at the eventuation of the outcome; involuntary actions tend to be accompanied by the agent's surprise at the eventuation of the outcome.

According to this interpretation of Wittgenstein, then, Carol's action would arguably be involuntary (because it caused her surprise), and therefore, in accordance with the normative import of voluntariness, it would give rise to no judgment of blame. Again, if my interpretation is correct, Wittgenstein's account would open the floodgates for many acts which we would intuitively treat as voluntary to be counted as involuntary. We would not normally (in the law or in moral introspection) deny Carol's responsibility for her action.

Moreover, it seems that there are cases of certain movements that Wittgenstein, given my interpretation, would be inclined to consider voluntary, insofar as they do not surprise us, but these cases are prototypical examples of what we normally consider involuntary movements. For example, think of a visit to the doctor, and of the doctor testing our knee reflexes with the well-known rubber hammer. After he hits our knee, our leg moves, and this would hardly surprise us. Yet, we would not for that stop thinking that the knee movement in this scenario is a prototypical example of involuntary action. Now, I do not think that Wittgenstein is really forced to call the knee movement voluntary. But in order to see why not, we need to analyze further his notion of "being surprised," which is a rather subtle notion. Wittgenstein's element of surprise is closely related to the possibility of having a certain "observant" attitude toward events. He tells us:

> it has been said that when a man, say, gets out of bed in the morning, all that happens may be this: he deliberates, "Is it time to get up?", he tries to make up his mind, and then suddenly *he finds himself getting up. . . .* Now there is something in the above description which tempts us to contradict it; we say: "we don't just 'find', observe, ourselves getting up, as though we were observing someone else! It isn't like, say, watching certain reflex actions.[31]

---

31. Ludwig Wittgenstein, *The Blue and Brown Books* (New York: Harper & Row, 1960), 151.

Wittgenstein then presents an even more eloquent example in order to illustrate this point further:

> If e.g., I place myself sideways close to a wall, my wall-side arm hanging down outstretched, the back of the hand touching the wall, and if now keeping my arm rigid I press the back of the hand against the wall, doing it all by means of the deltoid muscle, if I then quickly step away from the wall, letting my arm hang down loosely, my arm without any action of mine, of its own accord begins to rise; this is the sort of case in which it would be proper to say, 'I *find* my arm rising'.
>
> Now here again it is clear that there are many striking differences between the case of observing my arm rising in this experiment or watching someone else getting out of bed and the case of finding myself getting up. There is e.g., in this case the absence of what one might call surprise, also I don't *look* at my own movements as I might look at someone turning about in bed, e.g., saying to myself "Is he going to get up?"[32]

Although it is true that in a colloquial sense we do not find it surprising that our leg moves after the doctor hits our knee with the rubber hammer, I think that in Wittgenstein's sense we are indeed surprised after this event. For being surprised in his sense means, or entails, being *able* to take an observant attitude, and we can take this attitude in the case of the rubber hammer hitting our knee just as much as we can in Wittgenstein's example of pushing our arm against a wall. Moreover, it can be argued further in Wittgenstein's defense that one is perhaps, even in the colloquial sense of "surprise," surprised if not with the fact *that* our leg moves then with *how* it moves. It is in respect to this "how" that we take an observant attitude.

But what about Carol's case? Is Wittgenstein really forced to call her action involuntary? I think he is. After all, it is hard to see a way in which Carol can take an "observant attitude" regarding any of her actions which led to locking the girl in the store. To be sure, Wittgenstein's main aim in talking about the will is to criticize the mentalistic element in volitional theories of action. And then it might be argued that my very suggestion that "being surprised" is a mental element is misguided.[33] There are, after

---

32. Wittgenstein, *Blue and Brown Books*, 151. Of course, the arm moving up of its own accord might not be in itself an action, but the whole behavior consisting of the leaning against the wall, the pushing hard against it for a few minutes, and so on, is an action. More on the ways of describing actions will come later in this chapter.

33. Perhaps this is the sort of warning which Stuart G. Shanker has in mind when he claims that it would be a mistake to claim that Wittgenstein is explaining the difference between voluntary and involuntary movements subjectively. See Stuart G. Shanker, "The Nature of Willing," in *Wittgenstein's Intentions* (New York: Garland, 1993), 201–2.

all, passages in which Wittgenstein bases the distinction between voluntary and involuntary movements on things other than surprise. Yet, these passages make reference to Intentional states even more clearly than the passages relating to surprise do.[34]

In *Punishment and Responsibility*, there is a section entitled "The General Doctrine Reconstructed," in which Hart puts forth a concept of voluntariness cleansed of the impurities of Austinian-based views. He provides a definition of involuntary movements from which a definition of voluntary movements can be easily constructed. According to Hart:

> we can then characterize involuntary movements . . . as those movements of the body which occurred although they were not appropriate, i.e., required for any action (in the ordinary sense of action) which the agent believed himself to be doing. . . . Such movements are 'wild' or not 'governed by the will' in the sense that they are not subordinated to the agent's conscious plans of action: they do not occur as part of anything the agent takes himself to be doing. This is the feature which the Austinian theory represents in a distorted form by identifying the involuntary movements as those which are not caused by a desire for them.[35]

Obviously, then, a definition of voluntary movement, for Hart, would run along the following lines: voluntary movement is a movement of the body that occurred and was appropriate, that is, required, for some action (in the ordinary sense of action) that the agent believed himself to be doing.

That Hart's conceptual scheme does get rid of the overcrowded ontology of the general doctrine of the voluntary act is clear (no appeal volitions, no relevant distinction between acts and consequences, etc.), but does his account of voluntariness work from the normative perspective? Consider Pat, who, driving his car to the theater, suddenly sees a child in front of him lying on the road. He makes no effort to avoid running over the child (although he could have easily changed lanes), and thus runs over the child and causes his death. Now, killing the child was not, in any conceivable sense of the relevant terms, either required or appropriate for the action that Pat thought he was doing, that is, going to the theater. Hart would presumably have to consider cases like this involuntary, and therefore (in accordance with the normative principle regarding voluntariness) blameless. This should be enough to render Hart's solution suspect, inso-

---

34. See, for example, in his *Remarks on the Philosophy of Psychology* (vol. 1) cited above, §841, where the criterion seems to be whether or not the movement is automatic; §902 where the criterion seems to be whether or not one is conscious, §761, where the criterion seems to be whether or not one is aware of what one is doing, or whether or not one is capable of doing otherwise.
35. Hart, *Punishment and Responsibility*, 105.

far as there is an immense variety of cases such as this one, in which Hart would presumably have it that the action is involuntary (and therefore that it gives rise to no judgment of blame), and which would be in opposition to our moral intuitions.

Let us then turn to the last of our authors. White presents the following definition of voluntary action: "To do something voluntary is to do it with the awareness that there is in the circumstances a genuine alternative open to one: that is, that one is a free agent and has choice."[36] For White, then, in order for an act to be voluntary it is not enough that there exists a genuine option open to the agent, the agent must be *aware* of that fact. And this gets his theory into trouble. Let us see how White's theory fares against cases such as the following. Consider Vivian, who, as she strolls by the market square one morning, spots a suspicious-looking person coming her way; terrified, she takes a handgun out of her purse and kills the person. In her defense, she claims that she was not aware of the fact that there were other alternative courses of action (i.e., running away, calling the attention of the policeman walking just behind her, or taking refuge in one of the many coffee shops around her). However unlikely, this is a *possibly* true account of her Intentional states; that is, it is possible that she was truly unaware of these options and that therefore she honestly believed she had no other choice. Quite clearly, she *should* have been aware, but that is not the issue here. Vivian's action, under White's scheme, would have to be considered not voluntary, since she did not act with the awareness that she had other options. And therefore, she should not be blamed for her action. This conclusion, again, contradicts the appealing normative force of the principle regarding the relationship between blameworthiness and voluntariness.

But White would, I suspect, disagree with my conclusion regarding the blamelessness of Vivian's act, because he disagrees with the normative implications of the distinction between voluntary and involuntary movements that I have suggested are so intuitively obvious. After all, White tells us that "we can be liable for our negligent acts, whether they are voluntary or not."[37] White would express himself along the following lines: "Fine, Vivian's action was involuntary (and obviously it was unintended too), but this is one of those actions that, though involuntary, is still blameworthy." Then, however, two obvious questions suggest themselves. First, how could there be involuntary acts (if voluntariness is the mark of action)? Second, what are the criteria that make some involuntary movements blameworthy and others not?

---

36. White, *Grounds of Liability*, 54.
37. White, *Grounds of Liability*, 48.

It is up to White to explain why he rejects the principle that voluntariness (understood as a mark of action) is a necessary condition of blameworthiness, and he never did this, at least not explicitly. I shall venture an interpretation of this unusual move that will also make visible the general problem with the three theories of voluntariness we have analyzed. White, a stereotypical representative of the ordinary language philosophy, focuses on everyday uses of "voluntary" and "involuntary." He discovers that in ordinary language people tend to characterize my inadvertently stumbling into your Ming dynasty vase and breaking it to be "not voluntary" or "involuntary"; of course, not only accidents, but even cases where an agent acts negligently of recklessly are sometimes described as "involuntary." Now, if White were to simultaneously accept that these cases are involuntary and that that involuntariness entails blamelessness, he would have to admit, *a fortiori*, that all these cases are blameless. This calling involuntary what is really (legally and morally) voluntary is exactly what happens as a result of Hart's and Wittgenstein's theories; White, unlike our other authors, opts for disagreeing with the normative implications of voluntariness in order to avoid this untenable result. Yet simply disagreeing with a sensible principle, without even explaining why he disagrees with it, renders White's thesis unacceptable.

I think, however, that the main problem with White's theory is that it requires the agent to be *aware* that she has another option. And awareness is an Intentional state, just as being surprised is (in Wittgenstein's case), and just as not considering something to be appropriate or required for the action one thinks one is doing is (in Hart's case). By demanding that the alternative course of action be known to the agent in order for his movements to be voluntary, White is forced to allow innumerable cases in which agents are unaware of alternative courses of action (even if they should have been aware) to count as involuntary movements, and then to be blameless by default.

The preceding examples are but prototypes that reveal how Hart's, Wittgenstein's, and White's theses are inadequate when analyzed from the normative perspective. The possibilities of expansion regarding these sorts of counterobjections are endless. If their theories were correct, many difficult questions in moral philosophy would be "answered." Think of reckless or negligent wrongdoing, for example. All these cases our authors would have unwittingly "solved": reckless agents do not necessarily consider the outcome which they recklessly bring about to be appropriate for the action they think they are doing and are at times surprised by their occurrence. Even more clearly, negligent agents (who are not even aware of what they do) are not aware of the outcome of their action. Even thorny problems associated with the weighing of evils, such as those exemplified by the well-known "trolley problem," do not require that the agent consider the undesired evil outcome which she brings about appropriate for the action she believes to be doing, and so it would be involuntary and therefore blameless by default.[38]

In general, regarding most outcomes (evil and beneficial alike) that we bring about negligently (and some cases of reckless wrongdoing too), the following three statements are true:

(1) We are surprised by their occurrence.
(2) We do not consider them required or appropriate for any act that we think we are doing, for we are not even aware that we are acting negligently at all (and we are unaware of the appropriateness of the act when we act recklessly).
(3) We are not aware that we could do otherwise, because we are not even aware that we are negligently behaving in such-and such-manner.

Yet, if we adopt any of the concepts of voluntary action that we have analyzed, many cases of unintendedly (certainly all cases of negligently) bringing about an evil outcome would give rise to no judgment of blame whatsoever. This is obviously problematic in that we do blame agents for their negligent and reckless conduct.

Michael Moore's Defense of the Volitional Theory of Action

The accounts of voluntariness that one could speculate are derivable from the writings of the authors who have famously attacked the volitional theory of action are not promising. Before I sketch the sorts of theoretical paths that a workable theory of voluntariness might take, I would like to pay attention to the most promising and ambitious contemporary defense of the volitional theory of action: Moore's theory as advanced in *Act and Crime*.[39] The discussion of Moore's defense of the volitional theory of action is important for my purposes for several reasons. First, because insofar as it is the most sophisticated defense of the volitional theory of action, showing it to be flawed should be seen as a final blow to the theory. But this discussion is also important insofar as Moore's sustained defense of the volitional theory of action is indeed attractive, and part of its attractiveness is the importance that it gives to intentions. For, as we shall see, Moore ends up claiming that volitions are after all intentions.

---

38. See, in relation to the Trolley problem, Judith Jarvis Thomson, "Killing, Letting Die, and the Trolley Problem," *The Monist* (1976): 204–17.
39. Michael Moore, *Act and Crime*, passim.

Moore takes seriously all the major objections to volitionalism. For example, unlike most contemporary volitionalists, Moore is quite generous to Ryle, and he admits that "there is much sting left to Ryle's objection," and then he continues: "to define acts like moving one's hands in terms of duplicate mental acts of willing the movement seems an ontologically expensive way of gaining very little ground, for acting is still left unexplained. . . . And if one is willing to give a non actional account of the act of willing, why put in the extra act (i.e. of willing)?"[40]

Thus, Moore is justifiably interested in determining exactly what sort of Intentional states volitions are. "The choice between . . . competing conceptions of volition is not a minor matter, for it determines the nature volitions can plausibly be thought to have."[41] Moore discusses and rejects the possibility that volitions are beliefs, or (à la Austin) that volitions are desires. Aside from admitting that volitions are *sui generis* Intentional states, an admission Moore sensibly wishes to avoid, Moore sees two options left: either volitions are intentions or they are what some authors call "choosings," "tryings," or "decidings." Moore favors the first option, that is, for him "'volition' names a species of intention."[42] Though Moore also believes that the opposition between these two options could be rather superficial: "In so far as these [choosings, tryings, decidings, etc.] are taken to be synonymous ways of referring to that subclass of bare intentions that execute our more general plans into discrete bodily movements, the disagreement is merely about the least misleading label with which to refer to a state whose nature is agreed upon."[43] In virtue of our previous discussion and in virtue as well of all that Moore himself recognizes is problematic in classical accounts of volitions, it is surprising that Moore would stick to volitions, when he could have used any of these other terms.

Though it might seem that by classifying volitions as types of intentions Moore avoids the embarrassment of postulating the existence of mysterious Intentional states, this is far from clear. Remember that according to Austin you can only have volitions for your acts, not for their consequences. In other words, volitions can only be about acts, understood as bodily movements, but if volitions are just intentions, then their scope must be as wide as the scope of intentions in general. Yet, Moore restricts the scope of that subclass of intentions that are volitions: they can only be about bodily movements. And then, functionally, Moore's move is similar to that of claiming that volitions are a unique Intentional state, for

40. Michael Moore, *Act and Crime*, 116.
41. Michael Moore, *Act and Crime*, 120.
42. Michael Moore, *Act and Crime*, 120.
43. Michael Moore, *Act and Crime*, 121.

although volitions are a subclass of a familiar Intentional state, they are a subclass with very peculiar characteristics.

I have no major objection to Moore's suggestion that (some) intentions (which he, infelicitously, calls volitions) display a crucially executory role. In fact, it is this executory role of *all* intentions which in part will allow me to show why it is true that to bring about an evil outcome intendedly is never less blameworthy than to bring it about unintendedly. Nonetheless, I think that Moore's ontology of action is still, in spite of the move that classes volitions as types of intentions, far too complicated. For example, Moore tells us that "volitions are specified by the role they play in proximately causing bodily motions and in being the effects of both our more general intentions and the belief-desire sets the latter execute."[44] Furthermore, Moore continues, "volitions are mediating states, and what they mediate between are our motivations and our intentions, on the one hand, and our actions, on the other."[45] Aside from the fact that Moore's way of speaking here seems to suggest that he forgets that volitions are themselves intentions, Moore's ontology of action faces the following difficulty. It turns out that whenever we act we need to have two different types of intentions at play: We need the garden-variety intention to do *X*, though Moore believes that this intention is "general" and somehow the result of a given set of beliefs and desires. For Moore this intention in and of itself is insufficient in getting us to actually do *X*; for that, we need a mediating sort of intention (a volition) to do *X* that makes our general intention to do *X* operative.

Classical objections to the volitional theory of action understandably exploited the obvious weakness of the classical proponents of the theory, according to which the only actions "properly so called" were bodily movements. So, objectors would claim, if Susan kills Bob, the killing is not an action, the action is just made up of some of Susan's bodily movements, which might have as a consequence that Bob is killed. Moore refers to this aspect of the volitional theory as "the exclusivity thesis," that is, actions are, exclusively, willed bodily movements.[46] Moore wishes to defend this thesis but he wishes to admit that killings, rapings, and the like are actions too. Roughly, the way Moore accomplishes this is by suggesting a strict identity between token bodily movements, which he calls "basic acts," and token killings, token rapings, and so on, which he calls token "complex actions," or token "complex action descriptions."

I don't think that Moore's identity thesis is itself without problems, insofar as Moore refers to the relationship between basic acts and complex

---

44. Michael Moore, *Act and Crime*, 131.
45. Michael Moore, *Act and Crime*, 131.
46. Michael Moore, *Act and Crime*, 109ff. and passim.

descriptions of actions not merely as a relationship of identity. At times he claims that basic actions are "the source" of complex actions,[47] at other times he admits that complex descriptions "ascribe properties to [basic] acts in addition to the properties of being a bodily movement caused by a volition,"[48] and at times he refers to the relationship between the basic action and the complex action as a causal relation, for example, when he asserts that "sounds and audience beliefs must be caused by some basic acts of the would-be conspirator."[49] These multifarious ways in which basic acts and complex acts relate is in spirit reminiscent of the multifarious ways in which volitions, in traditional renderings of the volitional theory of action, relate to actions.

But Moore is emphatic about his belief that there is an identity between basic acts (bodily movements) and complex actions (killings, rapings, etc.), so far and beyond the fact that it is not always clear whether for Moore the relation between basic and complex acts is only one of identity, I shall focus upon this alleged identity and show the problems that this thesis faces. This identity allows Moore to "say, with Austin and Holmes, that the only acts there are are bodily movements without also implying that killings etc. are not acts."[50] Moore presents a useful way of distinguishing among action theorists by attending to how they answer the question of whether or not basic acts and complex acts are identical. Those who answer this question affirmatively are "coarse-grained"; those who answer negatively are fine-grained theorists.[51] Of course, Moore himself is a coarse-grained theorist: he believes that basic acts and complex acts are identical.

But if moving my body in certain ways and, say, raping someone are (token-) identical, why should there be, as Moore is committed to asserting, two different sets of Intentional states at play? One Intentional state has as conditions of satisfaction one description and another Intentional state another description? After all, Moore would assert that regarding the token set of bodily movements themselves (which are identical to this token rape) I have volitions; whereas regarding the token rape (which is identical to this token set of bodily movements) I have intentions. The problem I suggest Moore faces here is in no way solved by remembering that Moore believes that volitions are best understood as a special subclass of intentions. For, even if all the Intentional states at play here are nonmysterious, surely it seems that there are too many of them floating around. According to Moore, when a rapist rapes, for example, he intends (in a special sense of

---

47. Michael Moore, *Act and Crime*, 300.
48. Michael Moore, *Act and Crime*, 169.
49. Michael Moore, *Act and Crime*, 221.
50. Michael Moore, *Act and Crime*, 110.
51. See Michael Moore, *Act and Crime*, 280ff., for a valuable classification of authors.

intending) certain bodily movements, and he also intends (in a somewhat different sense) the rape. But, to complicate things further, it turns out that the bodily movements and the rape are token identical, so it becomes even more confusing how it is that Moore believes that one could have two different sets of intentions regarding one and the same event.

In addition to the fact that Moore's ontology of action seems overcomplicated, there is a perhaps more pressing objection to it. There is a sense in which for Moore all actions are intended. For if Moore believes that all actions are willed bodily movements, and if by willed, he means caused/preceded by a volition, and if volitions are but one subclass of intentions, then it necessarily follows that all actions are, in this sense, intended. Of course, Moore can get away with this insofar as he does distinguish between (a) general intentions and (b) executory intentions (volitions). But this strategy is cumbersome, and it is not at all clear what these "ontologically expensive" moves (to use Moore's own phrase as he, echoing Ryle, described some appeals to "willings")[52] are supposed to attain. I think that Moore's moves face many difficulties, though I wish to briefly discuss only two of them.

First, in attempting to save volitions from being queer Intentional states, Moore pays a high price. Insofar as volitions are executory intentions that mediate between our general intentions and our actions, it is unclear why our general intentions are intentions at all. If something is characteristic of intentions, it is that they are more closely connected to action than other Intentional states are. Among the differences between desiring X and intending X is that intending X, in principle, has at least a tendency to make me act in such a way that I might bring X about. For example, I desire to lose weight, but at the moment I do not in any way intend to lose weight. If I intended to lose weight, in contrast, I would, in principle at least, attempt to start a diet or to exercise more, or something along those lines. Yet, for Moore this essential connection between (general) intentions and actions is somewhat inert, in the sense that garden-variety (general) intentions need a push from Moore's executory intentions (volitions) in order to really connect the former with our actions. There is a sense, then, in which it is difficult to distinguish Moore's general intentions from simple desires, and thus, in equating volitions to a type of intention, Moore strips the other type of intention of what is recognizably essential to intentions in general.

The second problem with Moore's identity thesis has two interrelated aspects. Since there is a sense in which for Moore all actions are by definition intended, this fact hinders both the correct description of actions and

---

52. Michael Moore, *Act and Crime*, 116.

the effort to determine of the normative implications of the intendedness of actions. Regarding the first of these issues, as he discusses the difference between doings and happenings, Moore claims that it is easy to "sense the difference between actions of other persons, like their arm being raised by them, and other events involving their bodies, such as their arm going up as a reflex."[53] Surprisingly, however, Moore illustrates the capacity we have to distinguish between doings and happenings with the famous phrase by Holmes which I have quoted already in chapter 1. Immediately following the sentence just quoted, Moore states: "In the familiar hyperbole of Oliver Wendell Holmes: 'Even a dog distinguishes between being stumbled over and being kicked.'"[54] But the distinction between being kicked and being stumbled over does not necessarily map onto the distinction between doings and happenings. Many a time I have stumbled over my dog, and what is true of most of those cases is that I have done it unintendedly, not that it was no action of mine. Moreover, I suspect that what dogs do pick up on is that on those occasions in which one stumbles over them, one did not intend to hurt them; I doubt that they can distinguish between doings and happenings.

This brings me to the second aspect of this problem, the difficulties to which Moore's identity thesis give rise in the normative realm. Since Moore requires two distinct types of intentions in the course of performing any act, even my unintended (in the general sense) stumbling over my dog, is intended (in the executory, volitional sense). It would turn out, then, that the distinction between the *actus reus* and the *mens rea* with which we began this chapter, that is, the distinction between actions and Intentional states, is hopelessly muddy. For in order to determine whether an event is an act, we need to know whether it was intended (in the volitional sense) or not.

Moore is not alone in this; the members of the American Law Institute, categorically express in the commentaries to the Model Penal Code a view similar to Moore's: "The term 'voluntary' involves inquiry into the mental state of the actor, and, indeed, the demand that an act or omission be voluntary can be viewed as a preliminary requirement of culpability."[55] Moore expressly agrees that an event is an action if and only if it is a willed bodily movement. Since nowhere does Moore disagree with the Austinian thesis that voluntariness is the mark of action, we can conclude that for Moore an event is an action if and only if it is voluntary; that some bodily movements are voluntary (and thus that they constitute an action) is true if and only if they are caused/preceded by the appropriate volition.

53. Michael Moore, *Act and Crime*, 134–35.
54. Michael Moore, *Act and Crime*, 135.
55. American Law Institute, *Model Penal Code*, 215–16.

But not being alone is not sufficient for being correct. I think that the admission of the drafters of the Model Penal Code, of a piece with Moore's view, is problematic in that it complicates the distinction between actions and Intentional states. It turns out that in the Model Penal Code, influenced as it is by the volitional theory of action, in order to establish that someone has *acted*, it is necessary to inquire into her Intentional states, to see if these included a volition to do what she did. This is also true of Moore's thesis. The main difference between the drafters of the Model Penal Code and Moore is that Moore is emphatic about the fact that volitions are but a form of intention. But then it is clear that when addressing the normative force of the distinction between the intended and the unintended Moore would have to distinguish between two different normative consequences arising from the two types of intentions with which he operates. First, a distinction within the realm of executory intentions: when there is no executory intention, then there is no act at all, and presumably no blameworthiness either; when there is an executory intention then there is an act, and a certain degree of blame might be attached to the person who acted. Second, at the level of general intentions, Moore would have to distinguish between those aspects of complex descriptions of basic acts which are intended from those which are not. One would presume that Moore would have no reasons to disagree with the account of the normative implications of the distinction between the intended and the unintended presented here. Yet, insofar as he renders the "general" intentions somewhat inert, it is not clear *what* exactly he would say is the normative import of the distinction between the intended and the unintended, or *why* he would say it.

In spite of the sophistication of Moore's defense of the volitional theory of action, I think it faces too many difficulties. In fact, in solving some of the classical difficulties of the volitional theory, Moore ends up creating new difficulties, both at the purely descriptive level, and more importantly, at the normative level.

Intentionality and the Logic of Action

In light of the problems facing the attempts to define actions in terms of this or that Intentional state, it is tempting to consider an account of action that would limit the appeal to Intentional states as far as this is possible. One could, perhaps, suggest something along the following lines:

> A movement is voluntary if and only if at the time it takes place there exists another option open to the agent (whether or not he is aware of this option being inconsequential).

Conversely,

> A movement is involuntary if and only if at the time it takes place there exists no other option open to the agent (whether or not he thinks there is one, of course, being inconsequential).

These definitions of voluntary and involuntary movements do not involve considerations of any Intentional state whatsoever. For this reason, they fare well when dealing with the sorts of cases that invalidated the nonvolitional theories analyzed above. Given these definitions, it is clear that since there exists a state of affairs whereby Pat could have changed lanes, another state of affairs whereby Carol could have checked carefully that no one was inside the store before she closed, and a state of affairs whereby Vivian could have taken refuge at a coffee shop or with the policeman, all these actions should be classed as voluntary. In other words, none of these actions would be of the sort that gives rise to no judgment of blame, at least not by default, as they would be if one applies any of the preceding nonvolitional but still Intentionalist accounts of the distinction between the voluntary and the involuntary.

White tells us that the agent must be aware of the existence of a "genuine" alternative course of action. But what does genuine mean? White would have it that if someone puts a gun to Tom's head, and orders him, say, to drink a glass of water, the drinking of the water is not voluntary. White has it that allowing oneself to be shot is not a "genuine" option, for we cannot (should not?) expect people to behave like this. And I think that this sort of consideration might play a role in explaining some reticence in accepting views which do not appeal to Intentional states, such as the one just sketched. Let there be no doubt, according to these definitions, Tom's drinking the water is a voluntary action. And many would suppose that a theory that fails to distinguish between these two scenarios (doing X when the alternative is being shot, and doing X when there are many alternatives, none of which jeopardize our very life) is a flawed, inhuman theory.

This sort of objection misses, however, that endorsing these definitions of voluntary and involuntary movements in no way commits us to not differentiating between these two types of scenarios. Endorsing these definitions simply commits us to the view that the differentiation should *not* be made in terms of voluntariness. People tend to miss the true normative import of the distinction between involuntary and voluntary movements; the distinction works like a binary switch, if you will. If the action is involuntary, then the switch is off, which means that our blaming apparatus will not be put to work, because involuntary movements, by default, give rise to no judgment of blame. Now, if an action is voluntary, then the switch is on, which *merely* means that our blaming apparatus is to be put to work.

Quite unproblematically, it might turn out that some voluntary movements bring about evil outcomes yet give rise to no judgment of blame, for considerations having to do with Intentional states and also with all sorts of other considerations, as we saw in chapter 1. Let us suppose that, at gunpoint, Tom would be asked to steal a bracelet from a store. Although his action is voluntary (refusing to steal the bracelet is an option, even though an unreasonable one), it will perhaps, in light of our moral intuitions, be blameless after all. In no way, then, do the definitions of voluntary and involuntary movement just sketched commit us to blaming agents too sternly, by condemning them for doing things when the only "genuine" alternatives they had were being killed, or tortured, and so on.

What if the agent did not know that an alternative option existed? In some cases we would probably assert that the agent should have known of the existence of such an option (Vivian, Carol, or Pat, for example, would fall under this class). In other cases, we would consider it unreasonable that agents know about the existence of alternative options. Yet, these epistemological considerations do not affect the fact that there exists at least another option, and then they do not affect the status of the action as such. In other words, cases in which an agent ignores the existence of an *unreasonable* option are still cases of voluntary movement. And since the fact that an event is an action (a voluntary movement) is not enough to conclude that the agent's action is in the final analysis blameworthy, not much is lost by the apparent expansion that the scope of the voluntary undergoes if one uses a criterion along the lines of the non-Intentional definitions sketched above.

Similarly, one might object that a distinction between the voluntary and the involuntary along the lines of the definitions above makes the realm of the involuntary action too restricted, for very rarely do agents really find themselves without options. And again, the reply to this objection could simply be: "granted, there are indeed very few cases of true involuntary movements; your objection is true but irrelevant." In general, and to use a well-known philosophical slogan, an agent has no option if and only if some force overcomes him. This force might be internal (epileptic seizures, St. Vitus Dance fits, etc.) or external (say, wind gusts, being pushed or pulled, etc.). In cases where agents are pushed, afflicted by epilepsy, or otherwise overcome by force, they are said not to be acting at all. And this can be explained without appealing to Intentional states, but only to the fact that they have no option available: whatever Intentional states agents in these cases might have are, in a sense, irrelevant for determining whether the agents acted or not.

Imagine Helen, whose hand is being used by Laura to beat Sylvia. Laura overpowers Helen, who cannot resist her superior strength. Suppose that as a consequence of the blows, Sylvia dies. According to my theory

Helen's movement is involuntary, since there was no alternative option available to her. Fine, the objector might say, but what about if as she was being overpowered, she was enjoying Sylvia's suffering and actually wishing that she would die. Would not her action give rise to a more stern judgment of blame than if she would have had a different mental state? The answer to this objection has two parts. First, I would simply answer that no one can be punished for thought alone, and this is all Helen engaged herself in (since her movements were not really *hers*). Now from a purely ethical perspective I shall answer that if we blame Helen in this case, we do not blame her for what she did (the blows), but for what she felt (pleasure). We find repulsive that someone would feel pleasure due to someone else's suffering, but in this case we are blaming a flaw of her character which is neither voluntary nor involuntary. We would blame Helen just the same if we would know that, imagining that she was under the effects of some machine which made her believe that she was actually inflicting pain (when in fact she was not acting at all) she would have felt pleasure, even if her arm was not used to actually hurt anyone.

While a theory of action based on the sketches of voluntary and involuntary movements presented above seems to solve some of the normative difficulties facing the other nonvolitional accounts of action, I think that this sort of approach, tempting as it is, is not as independent from Intentional states as it might superficially appear. The word "option" presupposes an agent, and so a mind, and a mind capable of Intentional states; the word "option" smuggles references to at least the capacity for Intentional states. And although the accounts of voluntary and involuntary movements presented above do presuppose the existence of a mind and with it of Intentional mental states, they do not presuppose any *specific* token Intentional state in that mind. And while I do think that there is really no way of completely avoiding references to Intentional states in an account of human action, the sort of approach which these sketches of voluntary actions exemplifies is better than any alternative, for two main reasons.

First, this approach is not committed to the existence of any particular Intentional state, let alone to the existence of obscure Intentional states like volitions. Granted, saying that someone has an option, even if we allow that the person is actually unaware of that option, is to appeal to Intentional states, at least in the sense that there is a different set of movements that a being capable of Intentional states could, perhaps should, have Intentionally apprehended. Yet this approach appeals to Intentional states differently from the way in which volitional theories appeal to volitions; this approach does the work of naturalizing volitions that Moore, with more success than other volitionalists, tried so hard to accomplish, without facing the sorts of difficulties that Moore's and other volitionalists' theses face. Second, this approach does not tie in any token action to any token Intentional state. And this is not an unimportant fact.

Donald Davidson has put forth an account of what makes an event an action, that is, an account of what distinguishes an action from other types of events. Davidson states: "a person is the agent of an event if and only if there is a description of what he did that makes true a sentence that says that he did it intentionally,"[56] and he further adds: "Action does require that what an agent does is intentional under some description."[57]

A clarification to Davidson's thesis is in order. In these passages, when Davidson speaks of "intentional" he means "intended." For Davidson, then, what distinguishes actions from other events is simply that if an event is an action then there exists at least one true proposition (although perhaps several) which describes that event as intended. If there is an event that cannot be described by any true proposition as intended, then such event is not an action. Furthermore, though Davidson does not talk here about voluntariness, his criterion for distinguishing actions from other types of events serves also as a criterion for determining which events are voluntary movements and which are not: an event which cannot be described in a true proposition as intended is involuntary, and it is voluntary if it can be so described by a true proposition. Consider any of the examples of involuntary movements I have presented, seizures, being pulled or pushed, and so forth; it is clear that these are examples of events in which there is no true description of what happens according to which it is an intended movement. They are not actions, they are merely involuntary movements.

One might, unsuccessfully, object to Davidson's thesis along the following lines. What he has done amounts to no more than a cosmetic change, a mere change of words, vis-à-vis the traditional volitional theory of action. Instead of making the existence of a volition preceding the movement the criterion for an event being an action, Davidson now claims that the criterion is the existence of an intention preceding the movement, in such a way that Davidson's move would be quite like Moore's. And even if intentions and volitions are not equally "mysterious" Intentional states, Davidson then would have to face the at least some of the same objections that volitional theorists face, although the objections shall be terminologically different in Davidson's case. Davidson, under this light, simply would have substituted "intentions" for "volitions."

Yet, an objector along these lines fails to see that for Davidson, in order for *X*'ing to be an action, it is not necessary that agent intend to *X*. What

---

56. Donald Davidson, "Agency," in *Essays on Actions and Events*, 46.
57. Davidson, *Essays*, 50.

is necessary is that the agent who *X*'s intends *something*, be it Y, Z, or W. In contrast, the volitional theory of action has it that in order for *X*'ing to be a voluntary act, the agent must will, must have the volition, to *X specifically*, and not just any volition whatsoever. Even in Moore's reformulation of the volitional theory of action, the bodily movements which constitute a basic action must be caused/preceded by a specific executory intention for those very movements. The difference is clear enough. Davidson's theory does not lead us into any sort of vicious infinite regress as some volitional theories do, nor does it commit us to the no less problematic thesis that every token action requires a corresponding token Intentional state having as its object that very action.

Volitions are about bodily movements only. It is this duplication of relationships between Intentional states and bodily movements on the one hand, and Intentional states and consequences of those movements on the other, which gave rise to the overcrowded ontology of action inherent to the volitional theory of action. Davidson is particularly interested in bodily movements, not as something distinct from the effects of those movements, but because in his view all our actions are simply bodily movements. That is why Davidson can safely, I think, hold the following two theses simultaneously. First: "We must conclude, perhaps with a shock of surprise, that our primitive actions, the ones we do not do by doing something else, mere movements of the body—these are all the actions there are. We never do more than move our bodies, the rest is up to nature."[58] And second: "This doctrine, while not quite as bad as the bad old doctrine that all we ever do is will things to happen, or set ourselves to act, may seem to share some of the same disadvantages."[59]

Moore and other volitionalist theorists might be right, after all, about the fact that every complex action's description is intimately related to some basic action composed of bodily movements, though not necessarily through a relation of identity; it could, rather plausibly, be that the bodily movements are *part* of the action, a whole that in turn constitutes the condition of satisfaction of an intention. Yet, the nature of the relationship between bodily movements is not the only problem facing volitional theories of action. To repeat, perhaps the stickiest problem is to suggest that each bodily movement that counts as an action must be preceded by an Intentional state linked to that specific movement. Insofar as Davidson does not claim this, the fact that he commits to the view that primitive actions are just bodily movements is, in this context, innocuous. What Davidson emphasizes is that primitive actions, constituted by bodily move-

---

58. Davidson, *Essays*, 59.
59. Davidson, *Essays*, 59.

ments, can be described in a great variety of ways, and that these are only actions if there is at least one true description of those movements or their consequences whereby they or their consequences were intended.

Davidson's insight regarding the fact that "it is a mistake to suppose there is a class of intentional actions,"[60] which could be extended to apply to "willed actions," finds no room within the context of volitional theories of action, insofar as volitionalist theorists presuppose that all actions are willed (and some of them, like Moore, equate willing to intending). Unlike volitionalists, Davidson can "without confusion speak of the class of events that are actions" and simultaneously insist that this "we cannot do with intentional actions."[61] After all, volitionalists do conflate actions with willed (or intentional) actions.

Paraphrasing Davidson's own examples, if I (1) move my fingers and thereby (2) turn the light switch on, (3) illuminate the room, (4) bother my partner, (5) spend money on electricity, and so on, I still made only one action—the moving of my fingers. The different descriptions of what I did are just that, descriptions. In this regard, Davidson is as coarsely grained an action theorist as is Moore. But to concede that ultimately every token action is identical to a token (set of) bodily movement(s) is not to become a volitionalist, in spite of the fact that Davidson himself fears that he might be perceived as one.[62] I think that Davidson's arguments, which seek to show how his theory does not really "face the same disadvantages" of the "bad old doctrine [of the volitional theory of action]" are convincing.[63] Yet I think that a promising way of explaining why Davidson is not a volitionalist in any recognizable sense of the term, is that his theory of action, in the spirit of the sketches of voluntary and involuntary movements presented above, seeks to reduce the ways in which the analysis of action is the result of looking directly and specifically at Intentional states. It is this spirit, I think, which explains Davidson's important observation: "If we can say, as I am urging, that a person does, as agent, whatever he does intentionally [intendedly] under one description, then, although the *criterion* of agency is, in the semantic sense, intentional, the *expression* of agency is itself purely extensional. The relation that holds between a person and an event, when

---

60. Davidson, *Essays*, 46.
61. Davidson, *Essays*, 47.
62. Yet, some still wonder whether or not Davidson is a volitionalist. Cf. Timothy Cleveland's "Trying Without Willing," *Australasian Journal of Philosophy* (1992): 324–42 and "Is Davidson a Volitionist in Spite of Himself?" *Southwestern Journal of Philosophy* (1991): 181–93; and Michael Gorr's, "Willing, Trying and Doing," *Australasian Journal of Philosophy* (1979): 237–49. Gorr actually considers Davidson to be a volitionalist of sorts: "I would attribute a belief in volitions . . . to someone like D. Davidson" (238).
63. Davidson, *Essays*, 59–61.

the event is an action performed by the person, holds regardless of how the terms are described."[64] I think that this spirit of attempting to disassociate the analysis of action from the analysis of specific token Intentional states necessarily tied in to token actions is also visible, perhaps even more clearly, in Searle's writings on the relationship between Intentional states and actions, writing to which I now turn my attention.

Davidson seems somewhat dissatisfied with his account of actions: "This formulation, with its quantification over linguistic entities, cannot be considered entirely satisfactory."[65] It is this sort of dissatisfaction with turning the analysis of the relationship between Intentional states and actions into an analysis of linguistic entities (used to represent that relationship) that motivates Searle's approach, an approach which seeks to analyze the facts and not the descriptions of the facts. Searle claims that his way of undertaking this discussion "differs somewhat from the standard methods of the philosophy of action because we don't stand back a long way from the action and see which *descriptions* we can make of it, we have to get right up close to it and see what these descriptions are actually describing."[66] Moreover, Searle is skeptical as to the usefulness of this other (Davidsonian) method: "The other method incidentally produces such true but superficial results as that an action "can be intentional under one description, but not intentional under another"—one might as well say that a fire-engine is red under one description but not red under another. What one wants to know is: What facts are these various descriptions describing?"[67]

Searle's method involves discussing four elements: actions, bodily movements, and two types of intentions, which he calls prior intentions and intentions-in-action. Searle admits that while all actions involve intentions-in-action, not all have prior intentions; for the sake of simplicity I shall just discuss intentions-in-action.[68] The distinction between prior intentions and intentions-in-action is quite unlike Moore's distinction between executory and general intentions; it is, for our purposes, irrelevant

---

64. Davidson, *Essays*, 46–47.
65. Davidson, *Essays*, 46. Immediately after this sentence Davidson states, "But to do better would require a semantic analysis of sentences about propositional attitudes," and on a footnote he refers to his "The Logical Form of Actions Sentences," ibid., 105–48, and to his "On Saying That," *Synthese* 19:130–46. Still, in these works Davidson is mostly concerned with linguistic entities, not with actions themselves.
66. Searle, *Intentionality*, 92.
67. Searle, *Intentionality*, 92.
68. Elsewhere I have argued against the usefulness of this distinction between intentions; see my "Intentions, Promises, and Obligations," in Smith, *Contemporary Philosophy in Focus*, 51–83. See also Brian O'Shaughnessy's view on this topic in his "Searle's Theory of Action," in *John Searle and his Critics*, ed. Ernest LePore and Robert Van Gulick (Oxford: Blackwell, 1991), especially pp. 271–79.

here. The fact that Searle frequently speaks of intentions *simpliciter*, rather than about prior intentions or intentions-in-action, supports my claim, although Searle has expressly admitted that in some contexts, the distinction is not terribly important.[69]

The crucial first step of Searle's method is to affirm that "an intentional action is simply the condition of satisfaction of an intention."[70] Although Searle admits that this account does not quite work, mostly in light of problems of deviant causal chains (which we shall discuss again in the following chapters), he still sticks to this general formulation, insofar as he later claims that "an action is, in some sense at least, the condition of satisfaction of an intention."[71] Having an intention to do X has as a condition of satisfaction that there be an *event X* in the world and that this *event* be caused by my intention to bring about this event.[72]

This event could be a bodily movement, but it could be something else as well. What Searle has in mind is that the account of simple bodily movements is fundamentally the same as the account of complex act descriptions. In other words, Searle rejects the mainstay of volitional theories of actions according to which there are basic acts and complex descriptions of those acts: "Complex intentions are those where the conditions of satisfaction include not just a bodily movement a, but some further components of the action, b, c, d, . . . which we intend to perform by way of (or by means of, or in, or by, etc.) performing a, b, c, . . . and the representations of both a, b, c, . . . and the relations amongst them are included in the content of the complex intention."[73] In other words, complex acts are simply the conditions of satisfaction of complex intentions, and simple acts are the condition of satisfactions of simple intentions, but the distinction between simple and complex intentions in no way hinges upon any distinction between Moorean executory and general intentions, and in no way depends upon any metaphysical distinction between acts themselves and their consequences. I think that Searle's maneuver allows us to avoid the complicated ontology of volitional theories of action. Not only does it allow us to deny the existence of different Intentional states which relate to different sorts of entities (volitions for acts and intentions for consequences of those acts), but also it allows us to get rid of the distinction between acts, consequences, and circumstances in the first place.

---

69. See John R. Searle, "Reply to O'Shaughnessy" in LePore and Van Gulick, *John Searle and his Critics*, 297ff.
70. Searle, *Intentionality*, 80. The by now familiar amendment is in order once again: here Searle means "intended" when he says "intentional."
71. Searle, *Intentionality*, 92.
72. The details of the special causation of intentions will be presented in chapter 6.
73. Searle, *Intentionality*, 99.

With this simplified ontology Searle undertakes to explain the nature of action. He presents the following example:

> Consider Gavrilo Princip and his murder of Archduke Franz Ferdinand in Sarajevo. Of Princip we say that he:
>
>> pulled the trigger
>> fired the gun
>> shot the Archduke
>> killed the Archduke
>> struck the blow against Austria
>> avenged Serbia.[74]

For Searle, all these events "together with the causal (or other sorts of) relations between them constitute the conditions of satisfaction of a single complex intention."[75] It seems clear that Princip intended all these things; that he neither willed some and intended others, nor that he was merely aware of some of them. Princip had precisely this complex intention; quite importantly, here "complex" does not entail a different type of Intentional state, but simply an intention that has all these events as conditions of satisfaction. As Searle puts it: "it is a remarkable and little-noted fact of human and animal evolution that we have the capacity to make intentional bodily movements where the conditions of satisfaction our intentions go beyond the bodily movements."[76] One should not be fooled by the apparent simplicity of Searle's remark; scores of great thinkers who have defended the volitional theory of action have had difficulty noticing this fact, and as noted above, these thinkers continue to exert influence upon, for example, the Model Penal Code, and its inherited Austinian tripartite ontology of action.

But a problem remains, of course: the list of events can be expanded, perhaps infinitely, and obviously, Princip's complex intention could not have been infinite. In this connection, Searle discusses Feinberg's famous idea of the accordion effect,[77] that is, the possibility of adding true descriptions of actions. Searle claims:

> Starting in the middle we can extend the accordion up or down . . . and off the side:
>
>> He produced neuron firings in his brain
>> contracted certain muscles in his arm and hand

---

74. Searle, *Intentionality*, 98.
75. Searle, *Intentionality*, 98.
76. Searle, *Intentionality*, 99.
77. Feinberg, *Doing and Deserving*, 33ff.

pulled the trigger
fired the gun
shot the Archduke   moved a lot of air molecules
killed the Archduke
struck a blow against Austria
avenged Serbia

    ruined Lord Grey's Summer season
    convinced the Emperor Franz Josef that God was punishing the family
    angered Wilhelm II
    started the First World War[78]

Searle then concludes: "none of these things above, below, or to the side are intentional actions of Princip, and I am inclined to say none of them are actions of his at all. They are just unintended occurrences that happened as a result of his action."[79] Searle's term "occurrences" is quite unlike the classical volitionalist "circumstances," "concomitants," and the like; in Searle's case this is not a term of art but simply means "events," and it is not meant to mark any ontological distinction between basic acts and other types of events. And then Searle adds: "As far as *intentional* actions are concerned, the boundaries of the accordion are the boundaries of the complex intention . . . but the complex intention does not quite set the boundaries of the *action*, because of the possibility of unintentional actions."[80]

Quite poignantly, Searle's analysis of cases such as Princip's lead me to stress, once more, the distinction between intended and unintended action on the one hand and intentional and unintentional action on the other. What Searle means is that none of these extra descriptions were part of Princip's complex intention, and thus, none of them are *intended* actions of his. But clearly they could in some cases be considered, from the normative perspective, intentional actions, in the sense that they might be considered very blameworthy. Searle is absolutely correct in that the boundaries of the complex intention constitute the boundaries of the accordion of *intended* action—this is purely a descriptive matter. Insofar as the term "intentional" is typically (and so has been historically) used in ways that conflate both descriptive and normative aspects, however, it is not correct to say that the boundaries of the complex intention are also the boundaries of intentional action.

Imagine, for example, that aside from Princip's complex intention, which, by stipulation, only contains the events appearing in the original

---

78. Searle, *Intentionality*, 99–100.
79. Searle, *Intentionality*, 100.
80. Searle, *Intentionality*, 100.

list, Princip was aware that by carrying out his complex intention it was practically certain that he was going to ruin Lord Grey's summer season (and assume that this is an evil outcome). Given what we have discussed so far, it is clear that this would be a case of acting with an oblique intention in Bentham's sense, or acting knowingly, or with *dolus eventualis*, in the terms of contemporary theories of culpability, and thus that it would be a case of intentional (not intended) action, almost as blameworthy as cases of direct intention. Moreover, imagine that angering Wilhelm II is another evil outcome, and suppose further that Princip not only did not intend to anger Wilhelm II, but was wholly unaware that his action might anger Wilhelm II. If it were true that angering Wilhelm II is something that Princip should have been aware of, then Princip could still be blamed for having brought this occurrence about. It would have been a case of acting negligently or with *culpa*.

The fact that Searle admits that the boundaries of the accordion of descriptions of action, unlike those of the accordion of descriptions of intended action, are not limited *ab initio* by the boundaries of Princip's complex intention suggests an obvious and important question. How shall we distinguish between events which are Princip's unintended actions from those which are simply "occurrences" and not Princip's actions at all?

Searle, by way of an answer to this question, presents the following example: "When Oedipus married his mother he moved a lot of molecules, caused some neurophysiological changes in his brain and altered his spatial relationship to the North Pole. These are all things he did unintentionally and none of them are actions of his. Yet, I feel inclined to say that marrying his mother, though it was something he did unintentionally, was still an action, an unintended action."[81] But Searle immediately asks: "What is the difference?" and then he humbly admits: "I do not know of a clear criterion for distinguishing between those aspects of intentional actions under which they are unintentional actions and those aspects of intentional actions under which the event is not an action at all."[82] It is indeed difficult to find a clear criterion for making this distinction, and to a great extent the difficulty flows from the fact that the distinction has a normative component. The criterion, if it exists at all, is not going to be the result of looking at Intentional states alone, though looking at them, of course, helps.

In the next chapters, I will have more to say about the interplay between description and normativity in assessing the blameworthiness of

---

81. Searle, *Intentionality*, 102. I think Searle would have been better served if he had avoided saying "things he did," given that he claims that these were not "actions of his"; he could have said instead "things he caused."
82. Searle, *Intentionality*, 102.

human action. But I would like to conclude this discussion by summariz-
ing the ways in which Searle's ontology of action is more convenient than
its alternatives. First, Searle's ontology of action gets rid of unnecessary
entities within the realm of events (no need for the tripartite distinction
between acts, consequences, and circumstances). Second, it also gets rid of
unnecessary entities within the realm of Intentional states (no need for
volitions and intentions, or for structurally different types of intentions),[83]
thus solidifying a sensible trend that is already visible even in modern ren-
ditions of the volitional theory of action, such as Moore's. Third, it stresses
the fact that the conditions of satisfaction of intentions can be quite varied, and could include bodily movements and other things. Fourth, it calls
attention to the fact that the relationship between bodily movements and
other possible conditions of satisfaction of complex intentions need not be
relations of identity; they could be part-whole relations, "by means of" or
"by" or "in" or "as," and so forth, relations. Finally, Searle's theory of
action, though it links actions to Intentional states, does not link them to
any specific token Intentional state that must necessarily precede every
token action. In this respect, it is similar to the spirit of Davidson's theory
of action as well as the aspiring non-Intentionalistic approach to the distinction between voluntary and involuntary movements sketched in this
chapter. I believe that the ontological parsimony visible in Searle's account
of action does not strip his theory of any explanatory power. To be sure,
there are important things which Searle's theory is admittedly incapable of
explaining, namely, the distinction between mere occurrences and unintentional actions, though the explanations afforded by alternative theories
offer are no better. In the remaining chapters of the book I shall attempt
to shed light on some of these issues.

---

83. As I admitted above, Searle does distinguish between prior intentions and intentions-in-action, but this is merely a temporal distinction, and he admits that there are
cases in which we act without having ever formed a prior intention.

[5]

The Distinction between Intentional and Unintentional Action

Let us take stock. Intentions, our preceding discussion showed, might have more than one normative dimension. Not only do intentions allow us to apportion blame differently to agents for their wrongdoing, but intentions, in an indirect and subtle way, allow us to determine whether or not an event is an action, and whether or not an event is an action has obvious normative implications, since we typically blame people for their actions. The distinction between actions and nonactions is equivalent to the distinctions between voluntary movements and involuntary movements; between so-called voluntary actions and so-called involuntary actions; and between doings and happenings. I am mostly interested in the former normative dimension of intentions; that is, the normative dimension of intentions that gives rise to more or less severe judgments of blame to agents for their wrongdoings.

I have insisted throughout the book, moreover, that there is an important difference between (un)intended action and (un)intentional action. When we talk about (un)intended action we merely describe, but when we talk about (un)intentional action we are typically engaged in both normative and descriptive enterprises. The theories of culpability that we have analyzed hitherto aptly attest to the muddled talk of (un)intentional action: *dolus*, and *dolus eventualis*, just as the Model Penal Code's *purpose* and *knowledge* are intentional even though they describe different modes of culpability, that is, different sets of Intentional states. As we saw, when an agent acts with *dolus eventualis* or when she acts with knowledge, she does not really intend to do what she is nevertheless aware she is going to do, but, in spite of the absence of the appropriate intention, we still call her action intentional.

As we saw in chapter 1, the muddle created by the overlap between the normative and the descriptive enterprises extends beyond the talk of intentional and unintentional actions: it covers all sorts of expressions such as "inconsiderate," "sloppy," "forgetful," "kind," and so forth. Perhaps most

149

germane to my purposes is Bentham's distinction between direct and oblique *intentions*. For, whatever an intention turns out to be (an issue which we will discuss at length in the next chapter), whether or not one has an intention is an entirely empirical affair. Bentham's rationale for talking about oblique intentions, I think, is that acting with such set of Intentional states is virtually indistinguishable, from the normative perspective, from acting with a direct intention.

The same sort of insight is also captured by the famous principle of criminal law: "The actor can be taken to intend not only the consequence that he positively desires, but also other consequences known to be inseparable from the consequence he desires, even though they are not themselves desired."[1] This principle is of a piece with Sidgwick's famous remark to the effect that we should be taken to intend "all the consequences of an act that are foreseen as certain or probable."[2] The adage would have it that if Robert intends to, say, turn the TV on, he also intends to spend some money on electricity, he intends to wake his partner Susan up, and intends to have his pupils dilated. This is problematic. What *might* be true is that Robert intentionally does some things that he did not intend to do, say, waking Susan up, or spending money on electricity (assuming, of course, that these other things are inseparable from watching TV). If someone intends *X*, and is aware that *X* is "inseparable" from *Y* and *Z* and if she acts in such a way that *X*, *Y*, and *Z* all happen (as expected), she could be "taken" to have intended *X*, *Y*, and *Z*. But, of course, she did not, *ex hypothesi*, intend *Y* and *Z*. What is correct about this principle is that an agent who brings about *Y* and *Z* in cases such as these, is as (or virtually as) blameworthy as the agent who brings about *Y* and *Z* intendedly. What is correct about this adage is better captured, I think in Paulus's aphorism, *Magna negligentia culpa est: magna culpa dolus est*, which I cited at the end of chapter 2, insofar as Paulus could be taken to be equating modes of culpability, not Intentional states.

So, the relationship between having an intention to do *X* and doing *X* intendedly is straightforward and simple: intending to *X* is a necessary condition for doing *X* intendedly. But the relationship between having an intention to *X* and doing *X* intentionally is not at all simple: having an intention to do *X* is not a necessary condition for doing *X* intentionally. In fact the view, held by many contemporary philosophers, according to which intending to do *X* is a necessary condition of doing *X* intentionally, has been termed (by Michael Bratman) "the simple view"—and here "simple" is a nice example of an expression that has both descriptive and normative elements.[3]

---

1. Williams, *The Mental Element in Crime*, 11.
2. Henry Sidgwick, *The Methods of Ethics* (London: MacMillan, 1907), 202.
3. Bratman, *Intention, Plans, and Practical Reason*, 111ff.

In what follows I shall discuss some useful contemporary accounts contemporary of the relationship between intentions and intentional action. I am sympathetic to these approaches and to the general conclusion regarding the falsity of the simple view, but I would like to emphasize that peculiar way in which the distinction between normativity and description in the case of the talk of (un)intentional action of shows the falsity of the simple view. Once we realize that the distinction between intentional and unintentional action serves both normative and descriptive purposes, it becomes rather surprising how frequently these two types of purposes are not distinguished, or even acknowledged, in the pertinent contemporary literature. I shall, then, discuss a few discussions of the distinction between intentional and unintentional action, and explain why I find them problematical.

The Simple View

I take it that it is unproblematic that "having the intention to x," "pure intending" as Davidson refers to this Intentional state,[4] is different from "doing x intentionally"—a person can (however strangely) have the intention to X without ever doing X. This is a common feature of Intentional states: I could desire to be a famous pianist without ever doing anything conducive to that end, I could believe things which are not true, and so on. (The converse relationship is similarly obvious, that I can do X without having the intention to X, i.e., whenever I do X unintendedly.) But, at least for the layperson who has not heard about the normative import of the talk of (un)intentional action, the converse claim, that an agent can do X *intentionally* without intending to X, would appear strange and counterintuitive. This claim negates what is known in the specialized literature as "the simple view," that is, the view that in order to intentionally X it is necessary that one intends to X.

But some reflection about the issues should convince even the most skeptical layperson, perhaps not that the simple view is false, but that its rejection is not at all strange: things are more complicated than they at first appear. Gilbert Harman usefully discussed the following example: "A sniper shoots at a soldier from a distance, trying to kill him. . . . In firing his gun, the sniper knowingly alerts the enemy to his presence."[5] Clearly the sniper intends to kill the soldier, and if he succeeds he would have killed the soldier intentionally. Two questions remain: (1) Does he also

---

4. Davidson, *Essays*, 83–103.
5. Gilbert Harman, "Practical Reasoning," in *The Philosophy of Action*, ed. Alfred R. Mele (Oxford: Oxford University Press, 1997), 151.

intend to alert the enemy? and (2) Does he alert the enemy intentionally? Harman, sensibly in my opinion, but also in ways that should be compelling the layperson, answers these questions in the following ways: (1) the sniper "certainly does not intend to alert the enemy to his presence," yet (2) the sniper alerts the enemy "intentionally, thinking that the gain is worth the possible cost."[6]

I entirely agree with Harman's answers, and in this book I have said quite a bit about the much more interesting reasons why these are the correct answers. Notice how Harman goes about explaining why this is so. He does not explain this directly, for he asks us to compare cases such as the one of the sniper who alerts the enemy with cases in which one succeeds in doing something without intentionally succeeding: "Henry tries to win a game of chess and succeeds. Does Henry win intentionally? Only if it was up to him whether he would win."[7] How does this relate to the sniper? Harman takes another detour: "at the firing range the sniper intentionally shoots a bull's eye only if that is something he can do at will. If it is only a lucky shot, he does not intentionally shoot a bull's eye. The reason why we say that the sniper intentionally kills the soldier but we do not say that he intentionally shoots a bull's eye is that we think that there is something wrong with killing and nothing wrong with shooting a bull's eye."[8] After presenting this comparison between the sniper's alerting the enemy and a person hitting a bull's eye, Harman states: We say that the sniper alerts the enemy to his presence intentionally "because the enemy acts in the face of a reason not to alert the enemy to his presence."[9] And then, he presents a final contrast: "On the other hand, we will not say in any normal case that the sniper intentionally heats the barrel of his gun, even though in firing the gun he knowingly does heat the barrel, because there is no reason for the sniper not to heat the barrel of the gun."[10]

Again, I find all of these remarks by Harman sensible. But I think that his explanation as to how it is possible to do things intentionally without intending to do those very things can be supplemented by the sorts of normative considerations that I put forth in this book. While I think that Harman is correct in claiming that the main difference between the alerting-the-enemy case and the heating-the-barrel case is the fact that only in the former is the agent acting against a reason, I also think that, from the normative perspective, this sort of explanation is wanting. The interesting questions as to which reasons are relevant in this context and why they are

---

6. Harman, "Practical Reasoning," 151.
7. Harman, "Practical Reasoning," 151.
8. Harman, "Practical Reasoning," 151–52.
9. Harman, "Practical Reasoning," 152.
10. Harman, "Practical Reasoning," 152.

so remain unanswered. Imagine the sniper particularly enjoys warm things. Is this a reason which would justify now saying that the sniper intentionally heated the barrel of the gun? Whatever the answer of this last question, it seems to me that it leaves too much to be decided by the contexts. And this sort of answer relies too heavily on ordinary language and on supposedly shared ideas as to when a reason is relevant. Most importantly from my purposes, to the extent that whether or not something is done intentionally depends on the perceived importance of the reasons that might exist for doing it or not, Harman's view might face a more serious difficulty. It might be that Harman's view would allow for the existence of actions done neither intentionally nor unintentionally. This is a problematic prospect, as I have noted, ever since Plato posited the existence of a borderland between intentional and unintentional action (a region where killings in anger reside). Bratman's stance vis-à-vis the simple view faces similar difficulties, as I shall show next.

Bratman also attacks the simple view, and he points out us that his argument against it "is rooted in [his] conception of intentions as elements in larger, coordinating plans, and the resulting demands for strong consistency."[11] I am quite sympathetic to Bratman's effort to analyze intentions as related to plans and also closely linked to practical reasoning. Indeed I shall come back to these aspects of intentions in the next chapter in order to explain why intentions have the normative force that I claim they have. Here, however, I wish to focus on some of the by-now famous examples that Bratman discusses and that he thinks show that the simple view is false.

The first example Bratman discusses develops in three stages. First, imagine that "I am playing a video game in which I am to guide a 'missile' into a certain target"; the game is difficult, but I am skilled at it; and though "I am doubtful of success . . . still, I aim at the target and try to hit it."[12] Suppose I succeed in hitting the target. Bratman then asks: "Do I hit the target intentionally?" and he responds affirmatively. If a proponent of the simple view were to agree that here I hit the target intentionally, she must thereby also accept that I intend to hit it. Second stage: "Suppose now that a second game is added, a game which also involves guiding a 'missile' to a certain target. Since I am ambidextrous and can play one game with each hand, I decide to play both games simultaneously. As before, the games are difficult and I am doubtful of success in either of them. As it happens I miss target 2 but I do succeed in hitting target 1 in the way I was trying."[13] Again, Bratman believes that I hit target one intentionally. A problem arises for a defender of the simple view who

---

11. Bratman, *Intention, Plans, and Practical Reason*, 113.
12. Bratman, *Intention, Plans, and Practical Reason*, 113.
13. Bratman, *Intention, Plans, and Practical Reason*, 114.

would agree with Bratman in claiming that I hit target one intentionally insofar as, since she is forced to admit that I intended to hit target one, she must also admit that, given the "symmetry of the cases" that I must have intended to hit target two as well. It is not yet clear why this is a problem for the defender of the simple view. But then comes Bratman's *coup de grâce*:

> Let us now suppose that the two games are known to me to be so linked that it is impossible to hit both targets. If I hit one of the targets, both games are over. If both targets are about to be hit simultaneously, the machines just shut down and I hit neither target. Both targets remain visible to me; so I can see which target I hit if I hit either one. And there is a reward for hitting either target. But I know that although I can hit each target, I cannot hit both targets. [I then endeavor to play, and then suppose that] I do hit target 1 in just the way that I was trying to hit it.[14]

And then Bratman concludes: "it seems, again, that I hit target 1 *intentionally*. So, on the Simple View, I must intend to hit target 1. Given the symmetry of the case, I must also intend to hit target 2." The reason why now, finally, the defender of the simple view faces a problem is that "given my knowledge that I cannot hit both targets, these two intentions fail to be strongly consistent. Having them would involve me in a form of criticizable irrationality."[15] It would be irrational for me to intend to do two things which, if I were to succeed in carrying out each of these intentions, this would be counterproductive, because, given the way in which the games are linked together, succeeding in carrying out each of these intentions would defeat the purpose of playing the game. One could of course argue that this game is strange indeed, and that whatever suspicion of irrationality in the intentions that we would form in playing it might be the inheritance of the irrational way in which the game is set up. But that, I think, would miss the point.

There is nothing irrational in the game, and, moreover, Bratman insists, there is nothing irrational either in my strategy: "the strategy of giving each game a try seems perfectly reasonable. If I am guilty of no such irrationality, I do not have both these intentions. Since my relevant intention in favor of hitting target 1 is the same as that in favor of hitting target 2, I have neither intention. So the Simple View is false."[16] I think that Bratman is correct in the ways in which he thinks intentions relate to rationality, but I do not quite understand exactly what Bratman thinks demonstrates so

---

14. Bratman, *Intention, Plans, and Practical Reason*, 114.
15. Bratman, *Intention, Plans, and Practical Reason*, 114.
16. Bratman, *Intention, Plans, and Practical Reason*, 115.

clearly that the simple view must be false. First, he has not *shown*, in any of the cases, that I hit any target intentionally. Bratman's conclusion relies too heavily on the fact that *it (merely) seems* that I am acting *intentionally*. But merely that this act *seems* to be done intentionally will not do, for a defender of the simple view can simply say that although hitting target one *seems* to be intentionally done, it is in fact not done intentionally.

But since I believe that Bratman is correct in asserting that I hit the targets intentionally in the cases where he says that it seems as if I do, I think that the most pressing objection to Bratman's handling of this example is the following. Bratman assumes that since there is nothing irrational in my playing the two games simultaneously and in trying to hit each target, then the only possible explanation of what is going on is that I have neither an intention to hit one nor an intention to hit two. But I think that Bratman overlooks another possible, more promising, and more direct way of dealing with his own example.

The way in which Bratman describes my intentions as I play the game is somewhat arbitrary. It is not clear why my intention might not have very well be a complex one, along the following lines: "I intend to hit either of the two targets but not both," instead of stipulating that perforce I had to have two separate intentions, as Bratman has it. As we saw in the last chapter when we discussed Princip's action and how it is affected by the accordion effect, it is very difficult to individuate actions. Similarly, there is a difficult problem in individuating intentions. This is a problem affecting many Intentional states; "How many different beliefs (or desires) do I have?" might be an impossible question to answer. But there are cases in which it is valuable to attempt to individuate intentions, and I think the example that Bratman discusses is one of those cases.

Save for insisting that intentions could be quite complex, I do not have a method, even a general one, for individuating intentions. And that intentions can be complex is something with which Bratman agrees. The overarching theme of Bratman's views on intentions (indeed the title of one of his books, which gathers many of his most influential articles—*Intention, Plans, and Practical Reason*) is that intentions operate in the context of more general plans and projects. In fact, plans and projects can be seen simply as very complex intentions: remarks of the following tenor abound in Bratman's writings: "intentions are the building blocks of larger plans,"[17] "plans . . . are intentions writ large."[18] I think that the connections that Bratman has made between intentions, plans, and practical reason are very illuminating, and I will discuss them at length in the next chapter. For now, however, I would like to articulate what I do when I play

---

17. Bratman, *Intention, Plans, and Practical Reason*, 32.
18. Bratman, *Intention, Plans, and Practical Reason*, 29.

the target game in terms of a plan; in Bratman's third stage of the game I have a plan along the following lines: *My plan is to try to hit each of the targets trying not to hit both simultaneously, because I know that if I hit both then I cannot continue playing.* And I would argue that this plan is a very complex intention, whose condition of satisfaction is that, as a result of my efforts, I hit one of the targets without hitting the other one.

Examples of this sort of complex intentions are, I think, perfectly familiar. If in order to please my partner, I decide to clean the house, my intention is not only complex but to some degree indeterminate, that is, I might vacuum the carpet, I might dust the coffee table, I might sweep the kitchen floor, and so on, and although I do not necessarily have an intention to do each and every single one of these chores, I nonetheless do each of them intentionally. Now, each of them (or at least each of several possible sets of chores) satisfies my intention to clean the house, and my cleaning the house is intentional and intended even if some aspects of the process are not specifically intended.

I take it that the reason why it would be irrational to simultaneously "intend to hit target one" and "intend to hit target two" would be that I also intend to keep playing, and I know that if I hit both targets simultaneously the game will end. What I am suggesting is that we describe my complex intention when I play the game incorporating the ways in which such intention is affected by the circumstances of the case. Of course Bratman could then argue that these "circumstances" include, for example, a belief (that the game will end if I hit the two targets simultaneously) and that such a belief somehow cannot be part of an intention. But then it is hard to understand Bratman's general thesis that intentions are plans writ large and that intentions are the building blocks of plans. After all, it is hard to imagine any sensible plan whatsoever which would not tightly interconnected with beliefs.

Furthermore, according to Bratman, in the third stage of the example I have no intention to hit target one and no intention to hit target two. (Incidentally, this is not an insignificant oddity, for in the previous stages I had intentions to hit one or the other target: How did it come to happen that in the third stage I have no intention that includes as a condition of satisfaction hitting one of the targets?) Just as we know what it is to have certain Intentional states, that is, what it is to have a desire, or an intention, or a belief, and so on, we also know what it is to fail to succeed in carrying out an intention. So, imagine that while trying (though not intending) to hit one of targets, somehow I end up hitting both, and the machine turns itself off. According to Bratman, none of my intentions has been unfulfilled, since I neither intended to hit one nor intended to hit two. But it seems to me that if this were to happen to me, hitting both targets simultaneously would feel as I failed to carry out my complex intention of hitting-one-of-the-targets-but-not-both-so-as-to-keep-playing. I would be disappointed, and this can best be explained by the fact that my intention is a complex one, along the lines sketched. Bratman might, of course, suggest that my disappointment could be explained by my failed *desire* to hit-only-one-of-the-target-but-not-both-so-as-to-keep-playing, but then he would owe us an explanation as to why this Intentional state must be a desire and not an intention.

Bratman presents two other famous examples, and I wish to discuss them briefly. The first of these additional examples concerns the difference between two bombers, strategic bomber and terror bomber. They both share several intentions associated with the general intention of weakening the enemy. Terror bomber intends to bomb a school in enemy territory, attempting thereby to terrorize the enemy. Strategic bomber's plan is somewhat different; he intends to bomb a munitions plant, though he knows that it is next to the school and that children will surely die with the explosion.[19] While it might be true that, like terror bomber, strategic bomber intentionally kills the children, unlike terror bomber, he does not intend to kill the children. Bratman recognizes that the difference between the Intentional states of the two bombers is "thought by some to make an important moral difference," though he admits that his "primary interest" does not lie in the discussion of this moral difference "but in the commonsense psychology that underlies it."[20]

The other example is the following: "suppose I intend to run the marathon and I believe that I will thereby wear down my sneakers."[21] Though in his discussion of this example Bratman is not interested in the simple view either, once again, I agree with Bratman in claiming that though I do not intend to wear down my sneakers, if I run the marathon and thereby wear them down, I do wear them down intentionally. In order to strengthen the view that I wear down the sneakers intentionally, Bratman adds two features to the example: "first, I not only believe that I will wear them down; I consciously note this while I am running," and "second, wearing them down has some independent significance to me; perhaps they are a family heirloom."[22]

Bratman's merely secondary interest in the moral implications of the distinctions between Intentional states has a price. He fails to notice the ways in which intuitively (very) appealing moral principles help to show the problems facing the simple view. These moral principles are not less appealing than some of the principles of commonsense psychology to which

19. Bratman, *Intention, Plans, and Practical Reason*, 139ff.
20. Bratman, *Intention, Plans, and Practical Reason*, 140.
21. Bratman, *Intention, Plans, and Practical Reason*, 123.
22. Bratman, *Intention, Plans, and Practical Reason*, 123.

Bratman sometimes resorts. Moreover, these principles have informed theories of culpability for centuries, and quite obviously, theories of culpability consider some cases of not intending to do *X* to be nonetheless cases of doing *X* intentionally: acting knowingly or acting with *dolus eventualis*, for example. Imagine, for example, that wearing down sneakers were a serious crime. My wearing down my sneakers would be considered intentional (again, acting knowingly or with *dolus eventualis*), in spite of the fact that I do not intend to wear them down, and this would be the case even if my sneakers were not a family heirloom, even if I were not aware that I was wearing them down.

At least for the purposes of showing the inadequacies of the simple view, it is not *necessary* to engage in the sophisticated discussions regarding the individuation of Intentional states that abound in the specialized literature, things such Roderick Chisholm's principles of diffusiveness and of nondivisiveness of intention, Bratman's own principle of intention agglomeration, and maneuvers of this sort.[23] To repeat, I find Bratman's analyses of these highly complicated issues enlightening; I am just emphasizing something of a neglect that morality undergoes in his philosophy, and which, perhaps, contributes to preventing him from seeing another, easier, and perhaps more compelling way of showing the inadequacies of the simple view. As I shall show next, within the context of contemporary philosophy of mind and action, Bratman is perhaps among those few authors who at least recognize an ethical dimension to the discussion of intentions and their relation to human action. First, because, as we shall see in the next chapter, Bratman is interested in the way in which intentions commit us in certain ways, and in the ways in which intentions function within normative systems of rational and doxastic constraints. Second, because though he does not discuss the issue at length, Bratman does admit the following: "An important role played by our scheme for classifying actions as intentional is that of identifying ways of acting for which an agent may be held responsible; our concern is not limited to the description and explanation of action, but extends to the assessment of agents and to the appropriateness of reactive attitudes of indignation and resentment."[24]

Yet, I insist, Bratman's concern with the ways in which intentions affect the blameworthiness of agents for their wrongdoing could be more decisive, for some of his analyses reveal a certain lack of concern for this normative dimension of intentions. As I discussed Harman's view on the relation between intentions and intentional action, I speculated that his

---

23. Roderick Chisholm, *Person and Object* (LaSalle, IL: Open Court, 1976), 73ff; Bratman, *Intention, Plans, and Practical Reason*, 133ff.
24. Bratman, *Intention, Plans, and Practical Reason*, 124. Note the confusion between culpability and responsibility alluded to in chapter 1.

views seemed to me to allow for a third way of acting that is neither intentional nor unintentional. In Bratman's case, I do not need to speculate, since as he discusses some problems associated with the description and analysis of some spontaneous actions, Bratman suggests, "Many such spontaneous actions might best be characterized as actions that, although they are under the agent's voluntary control and are purposive, still are not intentional (even though they are not unintentional either)."[25]

Now, this additional way of doing things (neither intentionally nor unintentionally) enjoys considerable support from contemporary philosophers. Paul K. Moser and Alfred Mele, as they discuss Harman's discussion of the sniper, tell us: "Since the sniper does not unknowingly, inadvertently, or accidentally alert the enemy, it is natural to insist that he does not *unintentionally* alert the enemy. Such insistence does not entail, however, that the sniper *intentionally* alerts the enemy. There is a middle ground between A-ing intentionally and A-ing unintentionally."[26] Remarks of this tenor are typically made by contemporary philosophers without, for example, any reference to Plato's discussion of a border-land between *hekousisos* and *akousios*. As I mentioned then, the main problem with suggesting that the distinction between intentional and unintentional action is not dichotomous is that one should also take into account how the additional ways of acting might affect the ways in which we blame people for what they do. In the remaining of this chapter I wish to discuss contemporary theses to the effect that the distinction between the intentional and the unintentional does not exhaust the possible ways of acting. And I shall argue that the lack of concern for the moral implications of these descriptions creates problems for these views.

Analysis's "Problem 16" and the Tension between Normativity and Description

Some twenty-five years ago, *Analysis* challenged its readers with one of its famous problems. For my purposes in this book, this problem is of singular importance, insofar as it highlights quite poignantly the normative and the descriptive senses of expressions of the tenor of "he did it (un)intentionally." The problem is the following:

> If Brown in an ordinary game of dice hopes to throw a six and does so, we
> do not say that he threw the six intentionally. On the other hand if Brown

25. Bratman, *Intention, Plans, and Practical Reason*, 126.
26. Paul K. Moser and Alfred Mele, "Intentional Action," in Mele, *The Philosophy of Action*, 230–31.

puts one live cartridge into a six-chambered revolver, spins the chamber as he aims at Smith and pulls the trigger hoping to kill Smith, we would say if he succeeded that he had killed Smith intentionally. How can this be so, since in both cases the probability of the desired result is the same?[27]

I shall delay until the end of this section my solution to the problem—though I suspect and hope that the solution I shall defend should be by now no longer be a tale of suspense. First I wish to discuss E. J. Lowe's solution to the problem, published under the title "Neither Intentional nor Unintentional," and in which, not surprisingly, Lowe argues that there are ways of doing things which are neither intentional nor unintentional.

In a remarkably ingenious answer (to a remarkably ingenious problem), Lowe puts forward a thesis which assumes that intentional and unintentional do not exhaust the realm of ways in which human actions can be done. For Lowe, there is not merely *one* further way of acting, but *two*. These two additional ways of acting he dubs "not intentional" and "not unintentional." One can surmise that these two, added to intentional and unintentional action, would exhaust the ways of doing things. Lowe does not explicitly say that he is presenting four different ways of acting, only that he is analyzing four "closely related forms of proposition."[28] It is safe, however, to assume that he is talking about ways of acting. After all, he analyzes these four forms of propositions in order to discover which are the right labels to apply to Brown's and Smith's *actions*. Let me, then, paraphrase Lowe's thesis and provide definitions of each of these types of acting.

(A) Intentional action: A did Y, knowing that X would certainly result, and X resulted.

(B) Not intentional action: A did Y, not knowing that X would certainly result, and X resulted.

(C) Unintentional action: A did Y, not knowing that X might possibly result, and X resulted.

(D) Not unintentional action: A did Y, knowing that X might possibly result, and X resulted.

Things seem straightforward enough. Problems with Lowe's thesis start when we realize that though here he presents four ways of acting, elsewhere, in a further elaboration of his theory that the categories of intentional and unintentional action are not exhaustive, he tells us that "ordinary usage suggests that there is a gap between 'A did x intentionally'

27. Ronald J. Butler, "Report on Analysis' Problem No. 16,"*Analysis* 38 (1978): 113–18.
28. E. J. Lowe, "Neither Intentional nor Unintentional," *Analysis* 38 (1978): 117.

and 'A did x unintentionally', a gap which is filled by a *third* alternative, 'A did x neither intentionally nor unintentionally'."[29]

In "Neither Intentional nor Unintentional" Lowe presents four ways of acting (or four forms of propositions), but in his "An Analysis of Intentionality," he tells us that there are only three types of actions (or forms of propositions), these three types are:

(A') Intentional action
(B') Unintentional action
(C') Neither intentional nor unintentional action

A resolution to Lowe's apparent contradiction lies in an intricate maze of logical relationships among the four types of action (or forms of propositions). The four ways of acting initially described can be arranged in pairs, giving rise to six possible combinations. The following three pairs contain two mutually exclusive ways of acting:

(E) "Intentional" and "not intentional" actions (A and B)
(F) "Unintentional" and "not unintentional" actions (C and D)
(G) "Intentional" and "unintentional" actions (A and C)

The remaining three pairs contain ways of acting that are not mutually exclusive:

(H) "Intentional" and "not unintentional" actions (A and D)
(I) "Not intentional" and "unintentional" (B and C)
(J) "Not intentional" and "not unintentional" (B and D)

Given the logical relations between some of these propositions, however, it is clear that a proposition asserting that a given action is "intentional" necessarily entails the proposition that the action is "not unintentional," and a proposition asserting that an action is "unintentional" entails the proposition that the action is "not intentional." And now it is easier to see that there are indeed only three ways of acting, and that there is no contradiction in Lowe's thesis, for there are, in the end, just three ways of acting:

(K) Intentionally (and *therefore* not unintentionally)
(L) Unintentionally (and *therefore* not intentionally)
(M) Not intentionally and not unintentionally (neither intentionally nor unintentionally)

---

29. E. J. Lowe, "An Analysis of Intentionality," *Philosophical Quarterly* 30 (1980): 297 (emphasis added).

However ingenious, Lowe's solution nonetheless seems unnecessarily complicated; I discuss it in order to show, precisely, how the explanation of things which are not so complicated can take complicated paths. In any case, there is one description that applies equally to what Jones did and to what Smith did: M (which is logically equivalent to C', to J, and to the conjunction of B and D) properly describes the ways in which Brown acted on each occasion. Brown acted not intentionally and not unintentionally both when he rolled the die and when he killed Smith. "The two cases," Lowe tells us "are thus formally quite parallel."[30] Lowe's view, then, is that it is a mistake, visible in the very formulation of the problem, to refer to Brown's action as unintentional, and to refer to Smith's action as intentional.

Up to this point, there is a certain air of futility in Lowe's views as to the various classes of intentional and unintentional actions, for even if he is right in that intentional and unintentional do not exhaust the ways in which we can act, he has yet to solve *Analysis*'s problem. After all, the complicated web of relationships between different ways of acting, even if correct, does not explain why the overwhelming appeal of referring to Brown's rolling a six as an instance of unintentional action, and to Brown's killing Smith as an instance of intentional action. Just telling us that it is a mistake to refer to Brown's actions as either intentional or unintentional does not explain why it is that we overwhelmingly tend to refer to the rolling of a six as unintentional and to the killing of Smith as intentional.

Lowe does directly address this issue, which is a good thing, although his views are highly problematic. He tells us that what explains why we describe these two formally identical cases differently is the result of "the distinctive moral features of the two cases."[31] Lowe, moreover, provides a simple argument explaining when "not intentional" actions are blameworthy and when they are not: "A harmful act which is *not intentional* is not blameworthy if it is also *unintentional*: but certainly is blameworthy if, as Brown's act was, it is also *not unintentional*."[32] Lowe's suggestion regarding the normative import of the distinctions that he draws is, however, problematic. What Lowe suggests is that

(N) Not intentional and unintentional action (I) is blameless
(O) Not intentional and not unintentional action (J) is blameworthy

The first problem with Lowe's proposal is that it ignores the crucial gradational nature of the impact that Intentional states have for the appor-

30. Lowe, "Neither Intentional nor Unintentional," 118.
31. Lowe, "Neither Intentional nor Unintentional," 118.
32. Lowe, "Neither Intentional nor Unintentional," 118.

tioning of blame, a problem that could give rise to abuses of the sort to which Pascal, for example, argued the doctrine of double effect gives rise. But there are more concrete problems in that Lowe's suggestion runs counter to commonsense morality. For example, most car drivers are aware of the possibility that they may injure innocent bystanders in the course of their driving. It is easy to conceive of cases in which a driver, without fault, will actually injure some bystander; suppose further that a driver on a freeway, who complies with each and every ordinance and law regarding motor vehicles, suddenly faces a suicidal bystander who jumps in front of the car. This case would fit neatly under Lowe's description of action O, an action that is both not intentional and not unintentional (for the driver does not know that it is certain that someone will be injured, though she knows that it is possible that someone may be injured). In such cases Lowe would be forced to hold that this driver's action is blameworthy, but blaming her contradicts, again, moral intuitions (and legal institutions). This is just one example (easily multipliable) that shows that conditions Lowe lays down for a "not intentional" action being nevertheless blameworthy are flawed.

Now, the conditions Lowe lays down for a not intentional action being blameless are also flawed. Let me illustrate this in the following way. On the top of the page where the report on *Analysis' Problem No. 16* begins we find the following notice:

APOLOGY
The Editor apologizes for the title of a recent article, 'Lies, damned lies, and Miss Anscombe', which he now acknowledges was liable to be construed as offensive.[33]

The Editor of *Analysis* did not intend to offend Miss Anscombe. To publish an article with an offensive title was, let us assume, unintentional; had the editor noticed before publishing the article that its title could be offensive, the editor surely would have changed it. Later he realized this, and that is why he, later, apologized. If we analyze this case from the perspective of Lowe's framework, we realize that it is an instance of N, "not intentional" action that is also unintentional, and therefore blameless. The Editor of *Analysis* is correct in supposing that his action deserves (some small amount of) blame (the Editor's apology strikes me as a sufficient response to his blameworthy action). Lowe's scheme, however, cannot explain why the Editor apologizes, insofar as Lowe denies that actions of this sort are blameworthy.

---

33. *Analysis* 38, no. 3 (1978): 113.

Consider another example. Linda, who is a traffic controller at a busy airport, becomes distracted for a few minutes, thus causing a few planes to crash, and bringing about the death of many innocent passengers. This is another instance of N, an instance of an action which is "not intentional" and "unintentional," therefore, Lowe holds, we cannot blame Linda's action.

These examples suffice to show the inadequacies of Lowe's foray into issues regarding culpability. These examples make explicit the following general shortcoming: Lowe's system entails that all *negligent* acts are blameless, insofar as all actions committed negligently are always in Lowe's scheme "not intentional" and "unintentional." This is too high a price to pay for solving *Analysis*'s problem.

Another Look at the Distinction between Responsibility and Culpability

Given the shortcomings of Lowe's approach, let us consider another alternative. In his "Non-Intentional Action," David Chan, like Lowe, tries to show that there exists an intermediate category between intentional and unintentional action. Like Lowe and Bratman, Chan is concerned with the normative implications of the distinction between intentional and intentional action, though I think that as in Lowe's and Bratman's cases, Chan's ingenious ensuing thesis faces difficulties. In Chan's case, moreover, the problems associated with his posited third category of action are compounded by the sort of overcrowded ontology we have discussed in previous chapters, and by the usual confusion between responsibility and culpability.

Chan's first move is to claim that "the presence or absence of intention is not always decisive [in solving the question of responsibility]."[34] But it seems to me that he is thinking about culpability, not about responsibility, at least in the senses in which I am using these terms in this book, sketched already in chapter 1, for he adds: "interest in responsibility arises with the need to *apportion* blame."[35] But, to repeat, the main concern of theories of responsibility is what makes someone an agent in the first place, that is, when can agents be held accountable for what they do; the main concern of theories of culpability is, based on considerations having to do with Intentional states, how to apportion blame differently to wrongdoers who

---

34. David K. Chan, "Non-Intentional Action," *American Philosophical Quarterly* 32 (1995): 139.
35. Chan, "Non-Intentional Action," 139–40 (emphasis added).

are already assumed to be responsible. Chan equivocates between culpability and responsibility, because he also tells us that "[w]e may hold a person responsible for what he accidentally brings about, for what he does that are not actions at all, and even for what someone else does. For instance, a leader is responsible for his subordinates' actions under certain unexceptionable circumstances. Or a ship-captain who accidentally spills oil is responsible even if the occurrence is outside of his control."[36] And in this passage, Chan seems to be interested in issues of what makes persons responsible rather than in the apportioning blame.

Now, the issue of whether or not we can blame agents for what they accidentally bring about is not a simple one. In a colloquial, nontechnical way of speaking we must agree that it is indeed possible to blame agents for the evil outcomes they accidentally bring about. This colloquial sense of "accident" differs from the technical sense of *casus* which we have analyzed, insofar as *casus* contains only nonblameworthy instances.[37] Now, as we have seen, traditionally "accidents" have been distinguished from unintentional blameworthy action. In the technical sense, it is, by definition, impossible to blame agents for what they accidentally bring about, for to accidentally bring about an evil outcome entails that the agent is not to be blamed. And, similarly, it seems counterintuitive that we could blame someone for what someone else does, unless, of course, what someone else does is part of a larger description of the events according to which what someone else does is part of something the blamed agent did. For example, Bob and Susan plan to kill Mel, Susan's coworker, Bob gives Susan a gun and the plan is that Susan will kill him as they leave their workplace. Bob could, of course, be blamed for Mel's death even if he was asleep while Susan fired on Mel.

It is important to point out, however, that the two examples Chan provides are in no way related to the problem of apportioning blame. After all, in these cases the agents (the leader, the ship captain) are punished because whatever happened has been previously described as a *crime*. But, moreover, Chan's examples are instances of a rather peculiar type of crime: those known in the Anglo-American legal tradition as "strict liability offenses," which we discussed in chapter 1, and which are cases in which, quite poignantly, the Intentional states of the agents are, in a sense, irrelevant.[38] The vast majority of crimes, however, are not strict liability offenses.

---

36. Chan, "Non-Intentional Action," 139.
37. See chapter 2.
38. For more on strict liability offenses, see, in addition to the article by R. A. Duff cited in chapter 1, Douglas N. Husak, "Varieties of Strict Liability," *Canadian Journal of Law and Jurisprudence* 8, no. 2 (1995): 189–225.

Problems of culpability arise when, once we are in the presence of a crime (or other evil outcome), we wonder how the different Intentional states the agent had while bringing the evil outcome about might affect the degree of condemnation that we think the agent deserves. Both the ship captain and the leader might be *responsible* because they are agents, and the analysis of Intentional states the agent had when she acts plays an indirect, and at any rate a different, role in the determination of agency than such analysis plays in the gradation of blame.

Given the way Chan equivocates between culpability and responsibility, it should come as no surprise that Chan believes that he has shown that the close relationship between Intentional states and *apportioning* blame is not so close after all, for he has only analyzed examples in which differences concerning the agents' state of mind accompanying the action are irrelevant by default (insofar as our legal system proscribes so). Chan's examples merely show that having this or that Intentional state is not a necessary condition for holding someone responsible, but in no way has he shown that analyses of Intentional states are not necessary for apportioning blame. Chan's own examples can be modified to show this difference.

Think of Chan's example of the leader being responsible for his subordinate's actions. Suppose that we have two leaders, both of whom are *responsible* for the wrongdoing of their subordinates. First of all, it is not clear at all that this is an example of being responsible for someone else's action, for one imagines that when the leader accepted the post, he was informed of the conditions of the post, that is, of the fact that in the event one subordinate did something wrong, he would be held accountable. But imagine that one of the leaders might have actually led one of his subordinates to bring about an evil outcome, or that he rejoiced once it happened, whereas the other leader was completely unaware that the subordinate was engaged in this particular form of wrongdoing. We would probably not be too upset to learn that the law allows no difference in the punishment for the two leaders; being a leader means, among other things, being responsible for what your subordinates do, we might say. But that in no way entails that we would not make a moral distinction between the two leaders, even if we are willing to forgo the force of that moral intuition in some cases. But it seems to me that Chan focuses excessively on what legal systems say that, and ignores the important philosophical discussion of the relevance that Intentional states have for apportioning blame. Quite clearly a legal system can stipulate all sorts of things, but what is at stake is the philosophical justifications of those stipulations.

Chan makes use of another argument in his attempt to show that there exists no close relationship between intentionality and the apportioning of blame. He tells us, "there are cases where an agent is not blameworthy for wrong actions he does intentionally. A person may not be blamed for intentional actions that he is coerced or blackmailed into doing."[39] Yet, the fact that there are intentional actions that cause harm and are not blame-worthy is no great discovery—and coerced behavior does not exhaust all possibilities. We have already analyzed a classification of defenses in crimi-nal law that divides them into two groups: excuses and justifications. Blackmail and coercion when used as defenses are typically construed as excuses, whereas self-defense and necessity defense are paradigmatic cases of justification. And an agent can be justified, and therefore not blamed, for intentionally bringing about an evil outcome. Consider justifications: when an agent kills in self-defense, the paradigmatic case of justification, he clearly intends to kill the aggressor; the person acting in self-defense needs to act with "justificatory *intent*."[40]

Chan is right in that one could be justified or excused for things that one does intendedly, but this is trivially true. It should be clear that merely to provide examples of intended action for which one is not blamed at all is clearly not sufficient to separate the analysis of Intentional states from the issues of culpability. Chan thinks differently; after presenting the exam-ples of the leader and the ship captain, by way of conclusion he tells us: "We do not suffer a great conceptual loss in decoupling intentionality from responsibility. As our examples show, we in fact gain by leaving room for both intentional action for which the agent is not morally responsible, and non-action for which he is held responsible."[41] This "gain" that Chan alludes to is hard to pin down. There are, no doubt, intended actions for which one is not blamed, but, ceteris paribus, if an action is wrong, and the agent commits the action intendedly, she will not be blamed less severely than if she had acted unintendedly. Chan has not shown this normative principle to be false.

Inspired by his alleged decoupling of intentionality and responsibility, Chan puts forward a thesis according to which, in addition to intentional and unintentional action, there exists "a further category of actions that are neither intentional nor unintentional."[42] This is how Chan defines these three categories of actions:

> Intentional action: the action of bringing about an event for the reason the agent had for bringing about the event, or, equivalently the appropriate causa-tion of the event brought about in acting by the agent's intention to so act.
>
> Unintentional action: the action of bringing about an unintended event in the course of performing an intentional action.

---

39. Chan, "Non-Intentional Action," 140.
40. For more on justificatory intent, see Fletcher, *Rethinking Criminal Law*, 555ff.
41. Chan, "Non-Intentional Action," 140.
42. Chan, "Non-Intentional Action," 139.

> Non-intentional action: the action of bringing about an unintended event but not in the course of performing an intentional action; i.e., an action in which the agent is not acting for a reason when performing.[43]

As I have already pointed out, the main problem with suggesting that the distinction between intentional and unintentional action is not dichotomous (or otherwise exhaustive) is that we need to know how the additional description of ways of acting is to be blamed. Arguably, Chan's intentional, unintentional, and nonintentional scheme does exhaust the realm of human action, but he has not presented an account of how severely we should blame actions committed nonintentionally—a problem similar to the one Lowe faces.

One of Chan's examples of nonintentional action is that of mannerisms. Consider John, who has the "mannerism" of swinging his arms as he walks. Further imagine John entering a room whose walls are covered with extremely sensitive buttons which control a railroad terminal's functioning. "Nonintentionally," John activates some of these buttons as he swings his arms back and forth, and thus causes the death of many people. This act will be blamed according to our already existing modes of culpability, that is, it will be either reckless or negligent homicide, both of which are subtypes of *unintentional* action. John's action here is less blameworthy than if he had intended to cause the trains to derail, and more than if this would have been a true accident. Presumably it was not an accident in the technical sense, insofar as we think John should have been more careful (thus, John was at least negligent). What Chan fails to tell us is how blameworthy are his nonintentional actions. We are left to guess. Guessing what the lack of a normative correlate for nonintentional action would be is not easy. I think that there is really no normative correlate to nonintentional actions, because in the final analysis Chan has not really provided us with a third way of doing things.

Anyone attempting to challenge the exhaustive nature of the distinction between intentional and unintentional action must make sure that one of the classes is not defined as the complement of the other. For, if this is so, then some of the "additional" classes of action can be redefined as subtypes of other more primitive classes. Yet, for any class whatsoever, there exists a complementary class. Now, what is the class complementary to Chan's class of intentional actions? If it could be shown that his other two classes are in fact subtypes of this class, which is the complement of the class of intentional action, the relevance of Chan's thesis will suffer. After all, then one could say that what Chan calls "unintentional" and what he calls "nonintentional" are simply subtypes of that more general class of

---

43. Chan, "Non-Intentional Action," 148.

actions that together with intentional actions do exhaust all possibilities. The complement of Chan's class of intentional action should be something along these lines:

> The action of bringing about an event not for the reason the agent had for bringing about the event.

What name should we give to this class which is the complement of Chan's class of intentional actions? In this context, and given that Chan has already used "unintentional action" and "nonintentional action," let us call it "not intentional."[44] Now, if either the extension of "unintentional action" or that of "nonintentional action" were identical to that of "not intentional action," Chan's purpose would be defeated. For if one or the other is coextensional with "not intentional action," then the other one would turn out to be an empty class, insofar as "not intentional action" is the complement of "intentional action." This does not seem to be the case. But if the extensions of "unintentional action" and of "nonintentional action" are included in the extension of "not intentional action," as I wish to show, then Chan would not have succeeded in getting rid of the exhaustiveness of the pair formed by intentional action and its complement.

In Chan's view, both unintentional action and nonintentional action are cases in which an agent brings about *unintended events*. Unintentional and nonintentional actions differ merely with respect to whether or not these unintended events are brought about in the course of performing an intentional action. In the case of unintentional action, unintended events are brought about while the agent does something intentionally; by contrast, in the case of nonintentional action the agent brings about unintended events but not while doing something intentionally. The overcrowded ontology of acts and consequences reappears once more, via Chan's distinction between actions and events-that-actions-bring-about. Regrettably, Chan nowhere tells us what an unintended event is (or, for that matter, what an intended event is). These are obviously crucial definitions, and thus Chan's silence on these matters constitutes a startling disservice to his own project. By analyzing the nature of events or outcomes, the logical shortcomings of Chan's thesis should become apparent.

Let us summarize Chan's thesis. According to him there are three types of actions: (a) intentional, (b) unintentional, and (c) nonintentional. But also according to Chan, there are only two types of "events" as Chan calls

---

44. Of course, the thesis herein defended is that the class complementary to that of intentional actions is the class of unintentional actions, and that the pair is mutually exclusive and jointly exhaustive.

them (or consequences, as I, following Austin and Bentham, would call them): (a) intended, and (b) unintended.

Among the many puzzling aspects of this peculiar state of affairs, I want to focus upon the most obvious one: there exist no "nonintentional" consequences, and therefore, nonintended actions bring about only unintended consequences. Consider again Chan's example of nonintentional action: mannerisms. Let us imagine Lisa tugging her ear nonintentionally in the course of giving a lecture on theory of action. Imagine she does this many times during the lecture, so much so that she bruises her earlobe. The bruise is the consequence of her nonintentional action, yet it is for all that still an unintended consequence of such an action and not a nonintended outcome: Chan does not allow for nonintended consequences. Intentional actions can be accompanied by intended consequences, and unintentional action can be accompanied by unintended consequences; the consequences that would be associated with nonintentional action should be, one would have imagined, nonintended consequences. But Chan is emphatic in denying this: the consequences of nonintentional actions are unintentional, rather than nonintentional, as one would have expected. It seems, then, that all nonintentional actions should be treated as unintentional, at least regarding their consequences. This is a perplexing consequence of a theory that allegedly has made visible the inadequacy of the intentional/unintentional dichotomy.

As it turns out, Chan's thesis does preserve an exhaustive relationship between intentional action and *something*, in this case that something is what I have called "not intentional actions." It must be remembered, though, that the only reason I had for calling this class of actions "not intentional" is that I am discussing Chan's thesis, and he already uses "unintentional," in his own peculiar way. I agree with Chan in referring to his intentional actions as intentional actions. But I would much prefer to change the names of both his "unintentional action," and his "nonintentional action," to something else that would reveal that they are subtypes of the general category of "not-intentional action," which in turn I would simply call "unintentional action."[45] That there are subtypes of unintentional and of intentional action in no way challenges the exhaustiveness of the distinction. The fact, for example, that there are different types of unintentional action and different types of intentional action in no way affects the thesis that actions are either intentional or unintentional.

---

45. That there are subtypes of unintentional and of intentional action in no way challenges my view that the distinction between the two categories is dichotomous. The evolution of the criminal law has been marked by a proliferation of modes of culpability, i.e., of subtypes of intentional and unintentional action. See chapter 3.

At this point, a question necessarily arises: why use these complicated and misleading names? What I mean by complicated and misleading names is this: Chan's "intentional" and my own "not intentional" are indeed exhaustive, Chan's "unintentional" and "nonintentional" are included in my "not intentional," but why should not we look for better names? It should by now be clear that Chan has chosen these terms to refer to his three classes of actions in order to emphasize that he has eliminated a certain exhaustiveness between intentional and unintentional action. He has not, though. This hardly manageable alliteration of intentional, unintentional, nonintentional, and not intentional, is surrounded by a halo of futility reminiscent of Lowe's own alliterations. Regardless of how we refer to the different classes of action, there remains an unassailable dichotomy dividing the whole realm of human action.[46] Chan's attempt, to undermine the exhaustive nature of the distinction between intentional and unintentional action, like Lowe's, fails. I wish to examine one more such attempt.

Intentionality, Epistemology, and Normativity

Michael Gorr and Terrence Horgan put forward a thesis not explicitly or exclusively aimed at showing the existence of a third category of action called "nonintentional"—such as is clearly the case in Chan's theory—but that, nevertheless, recognizes the existence of such a category. Gorr and Horgan's thesis constitutes, albeit indirectly, another attempt to undermine the dichotomous nature of the distinction between intentional and unintentional action. Gorr and Horgan's thesis, perhaps more than any of the other ones discussed in this chapter, ignores the normative implications of the distinction between intentional and unintentional action. In contrast to Chan, moreover, Gorr and Horgan do not provide a definition of "nonintentional actions," they only provide definitions of "intentional action" and "unintentional action":

> (I) P's A-ing at t is intentional under the description 'A-ing' if and only if (i) this event is an act and (ii) P knows at t, of this act, that it is an A-ing by him.

---

46. In his "Are There Unintentional Actions?" *Philosophical Review* 72 (1963): 377–81, J. W. Meiland puts forward the view that there exist no unintentional actions. His thesis, more than a frontal attack on the dichotomous nature of the distinction between intentional and unintentional action, is an attack on the very existence of one of the classes of actions forming the pair, that of unintentional actions. His strategy, however, resembles Chan's in that he allegedly shows that there are no unintentional actions while nevertheless maintaining a dichotomy between intended and unintended *results*, which he calls "intrinsic" and "extrinsic" respectively.

(UI) *P*'s *A*-ing at *t* is unintentional under the description '*A*-ing' if and only if (i) this event is an act, and (ii) *P* does not believe, at *t*, of this act, either that it is an *A*-ing by him or that there is a significant chance that it is an *A*-ing by him.[47]

Gorr and Horgan's definitions of "intentional" and "unintentional" action reveal quite clearly the huge importance which epistemological considerations acquire in the context of their thesis. The first clause of both (I) and (UI) is identical (that the event be an act), so the only way to distinguish among them is by analyzing the epistemological differences contained in the second clauses. The nature of the first clause of both (I) and (UI) makes it easy to convert these into definitions of intentional and unintentional *action*, instead of "intentional" and "unintentional" *simpliciter*. If instead of saying ". . . is intentional . . ." in (I), or ". . . is unintentional . . ." in (UI), we say ". . . is an intentional action . . ." and ". . . is an unintentional action . . ." respectively, we can dispense with the first requirement in both cases, and call attention to the criterion distinguishing a type of action from the other.[48] Let us, however, quote another passage in which they leave no doubt regarding the role that epistemology plays in their distinction between intentional and unintentional action: "to call an act described as being of a certain type 'intentional' is to indicate simply that the agent realized (at the time) that he was performing an act of that type, while to call an act described as being of a certain type 'unintentional' is to indicate simply that the agent did not believe (at that time) that he was performing an act of that type."[49] And so, Gorr and Horgan are aware of "an obvious asymmetry between (I) and (UI) in that the former requires that the agent *know* that his act possesses certain properties whereas the latter requires not simply that he *not know* this but that he not even believe that there is a *significant chance* that this is so."[50]

This asymmetry supports their view that the distinction between intentional and unintentional action is not exhaustive, and that those actions which fall beyond the scope of application of this distinction are "nonintentional." To be sure, it is easy to construct a definition of "nonintentional" in accordance with Gorr and Horgan's theory, and using their own terminology:

---

47. Michael Gorr and Terence Horgan, "Intentional and Unintentional Action," *Philosophical Studies* 41 (1982): 255.
48. I do not wish to suggest that Gorr and Horgan's definitions are infelicitous in this respect. They may have reasons not to include action in the left side of their biconditionals. Whether or not these are good reasons is not important for my purposes. I propose to include "action" in the way explained to emphasize my point.
49. Gorr and Horgan, "Intentional and Unintentional Action," 254.
50. Gorr and Horgan, "Intentional and Unintentional Action," 255.

(NI) P's A-ing at t is non-intentional under the description 'A-ing' if and only if (i) this event is an act, (ii) P believes, at t, of this act, either that it is an A-ing by him or that there is a significant chance that it is an A-ing by him, and (iii) P does not know, at t, of this act, that it is an A-ing by him.

Gorr and Horgan's distinction, then, between intentional and unintentional action is not exhaustive, and exhaustiveness can only be achieved once we add to these two types of action a third type of action: nonintentional actions. What is not clear, however (it is as unclear as it was in Lowe's and Chan's cases), is why we should not simply revise the criteria that gave rise to the distinction in the first place, instead of complicating the matter by introducing new and problematic categories. But, again, as was also the case with Chan, the very name that is used to refer to the class of actions found in this "border-land" between intentional and unintentional actions is highly misleading. In Chan's case it was misleading because it suggested that he had eliminated a dichotomy, which in fact he had not. In addition to this, in Gorr and Horgan's case it is also misleading because it is the very name that they use when dealing with misguided attempts to classify *nonactions* as either intentional or unintentional. Consider their example: "A manifestation of the patellar reflex, for example, is not properly describable as either intentional or unintentional—it is simply non-intentional."[51] It is not at all clear why one should use "non-intentional" both to refer to those cases of nonaction—in which the distinction between intentional and unintentional simply does not obtain—and to some cases of action. Gorr and Horgan's description of nonintentional actions is surprising: "there will be conceivable cases (albeit bizarre ones) in which an agent will be said to have performed an act under a given description even though it will not be proper to say that his act is *either* intentional *or* unintentional under that description."[52]

Given Gorr and Horgan's definitions of (I) and (UI), it is not hard to see that there are cases of actions better described as (NI). All actions in which the agent *believes* she is behaving in certain way but does not *know* that she is so behaving would be nonintentional, and it is rather obvious that there are countless actions of this sort; arguably the *majority* of our actions are of this sort. In fact, the cases of nonintentional actions will all be epistemologically complex scenarios; Gorr and Horgan have thus added to the traditional difficulties inherent in distinguishing intentional from unintentional those difficulties inherent to the epistemic considerations regarding the nature of knowledge. There is nothing "bizarre"

---

51. Gorr and Horgan, "Intentional and Unintentional Action," 255.
52. Gorr and Horgan, "Intentional and Unintentional Action," 256.

about there being cases in which an agent believes but does not know that she is behaving in certain way. Consider one of Gorr and Horgan's cases: "Suppose, for example, that an assassin plots to kill the king by placing dynamite under his throne and detonating it from some safe distance. Unfortunately (for him) he has (and realizes he has) only an unreliable detonator which works just less than half the time. Nonetheless he pushes the plunger, the dynamite explodes (although he is far enough away that he cannot tell whether it does) and the king is killed."[53] Gorr and Horgan recognize that it is clearly wrong to suggest that the assassin killed the king unintentionally, but, of course, that does not entail that the assassin killed the king intentionally: this, they claim, is an example of nonintentional action. As I have already noted, from the normative perspective, to call a harmful act intentional is, ceteris paribus, to suggest that it should not be blamed less severely than if we would call the act unintentional. Now, what shall we do with nonintentional actions? Clearly, Gorr and Horgan have not provided an answer to this question (neither has Chan). And Gorr and Horgan do not seem interested in providing a constructive answer; they seem indifferent to the normative role of the distinction between intentional and unintentional action.

The closest Gorr and Horgan get to elucidating the normative dimension of the distinction between these types of action is to claim that cases like the assassin's are "cases in the middle range" and that therefore they "are best classified as non-intentional."[54] So nonintentional actions are in the "middle range" between intentional and unintentional, which may be taken to suggest that the judgment of blame passed upon the agent committing an action nonintentionally should be more lenient than the one passed on her in the case of intentional action and sterner than the one passed on her in the case of unintentional action. Yet, this contradicts our most basic intuitions regarding praise and blame, and begs for an explanation.

I see no reason not to consider the assassin's behavior a case of murder; and I know of no legal system in which the assassin of Gorr and Horgan's example would not be guilty of murder. *Par excellence,* the bringing about of the death of a human being constitutes murder only if such a death is caused intentionally. Yet for Gorr and Horgan the assassin did not commit murder (since his action is not intentional).Their thesis contradicts not only deep-seated moral intuitions, but also basic tenets of all civilized legal systems (which, arguably, are informed by our moral intuitions). Requiring that the agent *knows* that she will succeed in bringing about the event she aims to bring about is too stringent a requirement, for then actions would

53. Gorr and Horgan, "Intentional and Unintentional Action," 257.
54. Gorr and Horgan, "Intentional and Unintentional Action," 257.

only be properly said to be intentional in very few cases: those accompanied by epistemological certainty. And with such a requirement in place, it will turn out that most of what we call intentional is in fact nonintentional, for it is extremely uncommon that, say, a criminal knows (in the sense of justified true belief) the consequences of his action.

The assassin, moreover, *does know*, with incorrigible certainty, that he is attempting to kill the king, in spite of the fact that he does not know whether or not he will succeed. If we are strict in the application of Gorr and Horgan's epistemological criterion, we end up with two relevant descriptions of the assassin's action, and each of them calls for a different and independent degree of condemnation:

(1) The assassin nonintentionally killed the king, although
(2) The assassin intentionally attempted to kill the king (and succeeded).[55]

If the assassin were caught, and if he were to be judged according to Gorr and Horgan's guidelines, he could be convicted for (1) attempted murder and for (2) nonintentionally causing the death of the king (and how much he should be blamed for this is not clear).

What is particularly perplexing is that the assassin not only intentionally attempted to murder the king, but he used appropriate means to achieving such a goal, and actually accomplished his goal, yet the killing of the king would not be, in Gorr and Horgan's estimation, intentional. Perhaps in more formal terms the perplexity I am alluding to is more visible. An agent may want to do X, in order to bring about the outcome Y; X itself is an appropriate means to attain Y; X is performed intentionally and Y is attained. Yet, for Gorr and Horgan, Y is not necessarily an intended consequence; it could very well not be, provided that the agent does not *know* that X will cause Y.

Let us tinker with Gorr and Horgan's example. Imagine another example identical to theirs in every respect, except that in this new case the detonator is reliable and the assassin knows this. There is no justification for treating (blaming) the assassin of their example differently from the one who knows (assuming it is possible *to know* something like this) that the dynamite will indeed explode. But, apparently, it is Gorr and Horgan's

---

55. Traditionally, of course, the only actions that could properly be attempted are intended actions. It is not possible to intend to accidentally spill ink, because the moment you start intending to do it, it stops being accidental. Now, given Gorr and Horgan's thesis, this is no longer so obvious. It is possible that certain of Gorr and Horgan's nonintentional actions may be accidental, since we have to deal with highly complex issues concerning the relationship between consciousness, self-awareness, and knowledge.

view that the blameworthiness of the action in which the assassin uses an unreliable detonator is different than the blameworthiness of the action in which the assassin uses a perfectly reliable detonator. What this difference is and why there is a difference at all are questions that beg for answers. Moreover, prima facie, the thesis that there is a difference in these two cases gets little support from our moral intuitions, let alone from our legal institutions.

The exaggerated coupling of intentionality with epistemic considerations is inadequate, since it creates more problems than it solves. Gorr and Horgan's "not believing" is far too stringent a requirement for unintentional action. For it is common to find ourselves embracing unjustified or false beliefs. Consider Marianne, a slightly paranoid individual, who (wrongly) believes that her driving creates a "significant chance" that people will be injured, and has similar beliefs with most of her other activities. Most of her actions, then, will be nonintentional, and therefore, whenever she causes harm she should be blamed more severely than a nonparanoid person: Gorr and Horgan are forced to punish Marianne for her paranoia. As can be seen, Gorr and Horgan's "knowing" is also far too stringent a requirement for intentional action. For the requirements of knowledge (justification and truth) are not easily met, and then only a minuscule number of actions would ever be intentional. This twofold stringency has obvious consequences. Gorr and Horgan have to cope with the existence of a third class of action with rather lax membership criteria and whose very existence stands in opposition to moral intuitions.

In conclusion, the presence or the absence of some Intentional states when people act is crucial in determining how blameworthy people's acts are. I have discussed here the ways in which contemporary analyses of the distinction between intentional and unintentional action tend not to take into account the normative implications of this distinction. While I agree with Bratman and Harman, among others, in rejecting the simple view, I believe that this rejection needs to be accompanied by an analysis of the normative implications of the distinction between intentional and unintentional action. Moreover, such normative analysis in fact provides us with an easier, much more straightforward way of showing that the simple view is flawed.

The thesis that the simple view is flawed is entirely different from the thesis that the distinction between intentional and unintentional action is not exhaustive. The first thesis is correct; the second thesis is incorrect (at least to the extent that the additional forms of acting are not given a normative assessment). The two theses can be easily conflated because by disassociating intentional action from intended action one opens the floodgates for all sorts of multifarious criteria explaining the distinction between the intentional and the unintentional. To the extent that whether or not a person has an intention constitutes an exhaustive distinction, defenders of the simple view are forced to assume as well (whether they know it or not) that the distinction between intentional and unintentional action is exhaustive as well, insofar as the latter distinction tracks the former. I have argued that the distinction between intentional and unintentional action is exhaustive without appealing to the argument inherent to the simple view.

My main strategy in trying to show that the distinction between intentional and unintentional action is exhaustive has been to emphasize the important normative roles that the distinction plays in the way we apportion blame. Some of the contemporary attempts to show that the distinction between intentional and unintentional action is not exhaustive face serious difficulties when we analyze their normative implications. Some of these difficulties rely on my claiming that this or that consequence of this or that theory contradicts our moral intuitions. Although the sorts of intuitions to which I have appealed strike me as truly deep-seated and compelling, part of the work sustaining my appeal to intuitions is done by paying attention to the history of culpability presented in the previous chapters. Intuitions of the sort of those I have appealed to in this chapter inform, and have informed for centuries, the theories of culpability found in philosophical treatises and in legal enactments. Still, something needs to be said as to why certain Intentional states, above all intentions, have the normative force that I claim they have (and why some of the normative implications of the nonexhaustiveness theses discussed in this chapter are problematic). This I shall endeavor to do in the next chapter.

[6]

The Normative Force
of Intentions

In the previous chapter I attempted to clarify some aspects of the relationship between intentions and action. One of my main goals was to discuss ways in which the analysis of intentions should be decoupled from the analysis of intentional action, that is, that theses like the "simple view" exaggerate the connection between intentions and *intentional* action. Nonetheless, intentions are really closely linked to action; indeed, no other Intentional state is as closely linked to action as are intentions. Explaining this tight connection between intentions and action goes a long way toward allowing me to explain the unique normative force of intentions.

At the outset I need to analyze the peculiar structure of the Intentional state of intending, insofar as the very existence of a bona fide Intentional state of intending has been doubted in the specialized literature, and even those authors who believe that this Intentional state exists nevertheless recognize that positing its existence is a rather complicated philosophical move. Consider what Davidson says in this regard:

> Someone may intend to build a squirrel house without having decided to do it, deliberated about it, formed an intention to do it, or reasoned about it. And despite his intention, he may never build a squirrel house, try to build a squirrel house, or do anything whatever with the intention of getting a squirrel house built. Pure intending of this kind, intending that may occur without practical reasoning, action, or consequences, poses a problem if we want to give an account of the concept of intention that does not invoke unanalyzed episodes of attitudes like willing, mysterious acts of the will, or kinds of causation foreign to science.[1]

Davidson's passage makes reference to a rather large set of problems regarding the analysis of intentions. I would like to dispel, right off the bat,

---

1. Davidson, *Essays*, 83.

two of Davidson's fears. First, the fear that to posit the existence of intentions as a unique Intentional state, different from related Intentional conative states like desires (broadly construed) or pro-attitudes, and furthermore, not analyzable in terms of these other Intentional states, is to present a disguised form of volitionalism. This fear is made even more pressing given the maneuvers by contemporary volitional theorists such as Moore's in which volitions and intentions are equated.[2] A considerable amount of this dispelling is carried out simply by referring back to my discussion of volitional theories of action, and in particular to my denial of the thesis that for each token action that we carry out we need to postulate a token Intentional state, call it what you will, which has as its conditions of satisfaction that very action (and further, that the action is itself taken to be mere bodily movements). According to my view, intentions are indeed closely related to action, but not in the strong way in which volitional theorists connect token volitions (even if they are presented as token intentions) to token actions, and this constitutes, I think, a rather crisp contrast between the view defended here and volitionalism. Intentions, as I understand them, and in opposition to the way in which volitionalist theorists understand volitions, have actions as conditions of satisfaction, but I take killings, kickings, and embracings to be actions in the same sense in which some bodily movements are actions. Furthermore, as we shall see below, though intentions are not reducible to beliefs and desires, they do include beliefs and desires. Thus, intentions need not have the same fate as volitions.

Second, while it is indeed *possible* that a person would form an intention to build a squirrel house without ever *doing* anything about it, nonetheless this is not *likely* at all. Paradigmatically, when someone intends *X*, she will act in ways that will at least tend to bring *X* about, and this fact is one of the essential elements of intending, and one which is quite important in distinguishing intentions from related Intentional states. Imagine that I communicate to my students my intention to tidy up my office. Month after month, indeed semester after semester, students visit me and see that I have done nothing of the sort: my office is ever messier. Regularly they would ask me, "What about your intention to tidy up your office?" to which I would reply, "It is still there (so far only in the form of a pure intention)." Nothing has prevented me from carrying on with my intention, I simply have not. After some time (months, years perhaps) my students would be justified in believing that either I have not had the intention to clean my office at all (that I have been lying or confused as to what it is to have an intention) or that if I do have the intention, not doing

---

2 . See the discussion of Moore in chapter 4.

anything about it renders me somehow irrational. While pure intendings, understood as intendings that do not give rise to any action, not even to the attempt to act, are possible, they are not very common.

In order to explain the complicated relationship between intentions and action, I shall in what follows pay close attention to Searle's analysis of intentions, insofar as it makes explicit the uniqueness of intentions without appealing to anything mysterious or foreign to science. Searle's framework and his recent work will allow me to suggest a way in which the very logical structure of intentions explains their normative force. Later in the chapter, I shall follow Bratman's insightful work on the connection between intentions and rationality, attempting to show that intentions are not only uniquely related to action, but also uniquely related to rationality. The ways in which intentions are related to action and to rationality explain the normative force of intentions in specifying the way in which we blame people for their wrongdoing; they explain why, throughout history, intentions have figured so prominently in theories of culpability. I shall conclude the chapter with Christine Korsgaard's recent discussion of personal identity, attempting to draw some parallels between the role that intentions have in constituting our selfhoods and the role that they play in theories of culpability.

Intentions and the Belief/Desire Analysis of Intentional States

A popular and elegant approach to the analysis of Intentional states is to attempt to explain many of them in terms of two very basic, primitive intentional states: beliefs and desires. While in the context of the analysis of intentions this approach tends to be reductionist, that is, its proponents frequently suggest that intentions are simply aggregates of beliefs and desires, which in turn are seen as genuine primitive Intentional states, the way in which Searle deploys this approach to the analysis of intentions reveals other of its shortcomings. In particular, Searle shows how this approach fails to account for *intentions.*

The first thing that we need to note is that, in this context, we are to understand beliefs and desires very broadly: following Searle, we could assume that "belief" includes "feeling certain, having a hunch, supposing and many other degrees of conviction" and "desire" includes "wanting, wishing, lusting and hankering after, and many other degrees of desire."[3] With these two concepts in place and with some rudiments of basic modal

---

3. Searle, *Intentionality*, 29.

logic, we could investigate the results of applying the belief/desire model to the analysis of several Intentional states. For example, the analysis of "fearing that p" should look roughly like this:

> (1) Fear (p) → Bel (◊p) and Des (~p)
> (if one fears that p, then one believes that p is possible, and one desires not p).

The analysis of "expecting that p" goes like this:

> (2) Expect (p) ↔ Bel (Fut p)
> (if one expects that p, then one believes that p will happen, and believing that p will happen is to expect that p).

The analysis of "being sorry that p" would be:

> (3) Sorry (p) → Bel (p) and Des (~p)
> (if one is sorry that p, then one believes that p though one desires that not p).[4]

In spite of the belief/desire model's charm, Searle is keenly interested in investigating its shortcomings, and for good reasons. The system seems too coarse to be capable of distinguishing between similar (yet clearly different) Intentional states. Searle points out that

> being annoyed that p, being sad that p, and being sorry that p are all cases of:
> (4) Bel (p) and Des (~p)
> but they are clearly not the same states.[5]

Nuances of many other intentional states elude the model as well. Consider, for example, being terrified that p. This is not captured by what would at first glance seem like the obvious analysis:

> (5) Terror (p) ↔ Bel (◊p) and Strong Des (~p),

for, as Searle points out, one could believe that an atomic war could occur, very much hope that it does not occur, and yet not be terrified at all that it might occur.[6] Being terrified includes a certain raw feeling not cap-

---

4. Searle, *Intentionality*, 31–32.
5. Searle, *Intentionality*, 36.
6. Searle, *Intentionality*, 31.

tured by any combination of belief and desires, whatever their contents.

The main problem Searle sees with the belief/desire model is not its general coarseness, but, specifically, its inability to yield a plausible account of intentions. He tells us "perhaps the hardest case of all is intention," and regarding the plausible candidate for an analysis of intention:

(6) Intend (I do A) → Bel (◊ I do A) and Des (I do A),

he, rightly, tell us that it constitutes "only a very partial analysis." The crucial missing element is "the special causal role of intentions in producing our behavior."[7] In spite of the fact that, as we noted in chapter 1, Searle warns that "intendings and intentions are just one form of Intentionality among others, they have no special status," intentions are nevertheless special. The event that includes the conditions of satisfaction of my intention "has to come about 'in the right way.'"[8] So here we get the first glimpse of the uniqueness of intentions. They are unlike other Intentional states in that their conditions of satisfaction are somehow special. In order to grasp what exactly is special about intentions, we need first to refer back to that central concept of Intentionality explained in chapter 1: conditions of satisfaction. We need to show how in the case of intentions the conditions of satisfaction must "come about in the right way" (an expression that, for our purposes, can be equated with the expressions "intentional causation" and "causal self-referentiality").

In the case of intentional action, Intentional causation is a form of self-reference. In Searle's own words, "it is part of the content of the Intentional state . . . [of intending] that its conditions of satisfaction . . . require that it cause the rest of its conditions of satisfaction."[9] Thus, "if I raise my arm, then my intention in action has as its conditions of satisfaction that that very intention must cause my arm to go up."[10] And, thus, in order that, for example, Mary's intention to become rich be satisfied, to be carried out, she must become rich in a special way. She must become rich as a result of *her intending to become rich.* One difference between mere desires and intentions should then be clear. If Mary merely desires to become rich, then, from the perspective of the satisfaction of her desire, it does not matter at all how she becomes rich. This special way in which the conditions of satisfaction of intentions must be brought about cannot be captured by the belief/desire analysis of intentional states, and that is why Searle rejects it.

---

7. Searle, *Intentionality*, 34.
8. Searle, *Intentionality*, 3, 82.
9. Searle, *Intentionality*, 122.
10. Searle, *Intentionality*, 122.

The intimate connection between intentions and actions thus begins to emerge. Even if Mary does not engage in any action whatsoever, her *desire* to become rich will *eo ipso* be satisfied when she becomes rich. But the conditions of satisfaction of intentions require that the agent *acts* and that her actions bring about the intended state of affairs in a particular way. Searle points out that there is something odd about the fact that while we have "no special names for the conditions of satisfaction of beliefs and desires," "we have a special name such as 'action' and 'act' for the conditions of satisfaction of intentions."[11] This oddity further emphasizes the uniqueness of intentions.

Searle begins a chapter of *Intentionality* entitled "Intention in Action" by examining syntactic similarities between the deep structures of sentences reporting Intentional states in the following ways:

> I believe + I vote for Jones
> I want + I vote for Jones
> I intend + I vote for Jones

These structures are all very similar. Searle points out that the last two sentences can be rewritten as follows:

> I want to vote for Jones
> I intend to vote for Jones.[12]

While Searle is right about the possibility of this rewrite, it is somewhat puzzling that he would put to use these syntactical remarks in order to distinguish between two groups of Intentional states: (a) beliefs, and (b) desires and intentions gathered together. After all, Searle's main goal is to show the uniqueness of intentions, not of beliefs, and this discussion actually groups intentions together with desires. Thus, Searle does not decisively utilize the syntactic analysis of propositions expressing Intentional states in showing how unique intentions really are. What his syntactic analysis shows is that beliefs are unique—hardly what he is interested in showing.

What, then, is the syntactic difference between a desire and an intention? In order to answer this, it is worthwhile to tinker with the modal emphasis of Searle's approach. Granted, the deep structures of propositions expressing intentions and propositions expressing desires could both be transformed along the lines sketched above. But only propositions expressing intentions must be transformed in such a way. What I have in

---

11. Searle, *Intentionality*, 81.
12. Searle, *Intentionality*, 80.

mind follows from the fact that, as even an incomplete analysis of intention shows (see [6] above), one can only intend one's own future actions. It is impossible to intend anything other than one's own actions; that is, one cannot intend that the sun rises, that one's friend recovers from her ailment, and so on.

Unlike sentences expressing desires, which permit both a connection through the infinitive and through any other particle such as "that," sentences expressing intentions *must* include the infinitive. "I desire to vote for Jones," and "I desire that you vote for Jones" are equally sensible. But "I intend that you vote for Jones" is not sensible, and "I intend that I vote for Jones" is just a clumsy way of saying "I intend to vote for Jones." We could desire (hope, wish, etc.) any conceivable thing; but the scope of those things we can intend is limited by rational considerations that are stricter than those for desires (which are rather lax). The fact that we can only intend things we believe are up to us is a way of expressing the causal self-referentiality of intentions.

It should be kept in mind, particularly by those enamored with ordinary language philosophy, that pointing out that someone actually says, "I intend that the sun rise tomorrow" or "I intend that you become a lawyer" is not to present valid counterexamples to this thesis. The interest here does not lie in mere words. My goal in further developing Searle's inquiry into the linguistic analysis of propositions expressing Intentional states is to reveal an independent, nonlinguistic, underlying fact about intentions that its linguistic rendering helps to make explicit. I can only intend or try to do things that I believe are up to me. This is a fact that derives from the causal self-referentiality of intentions, from that very special feature of intentions to which Searle has devoted so much attention. The logic of intentions is whatever it is, independently of the way in which people ordinarily talk about intentions.

The main bases for distinguishing intentions from all other mental phenomena are found in two of the features of intentions presented above: that the agent must believe that it is possible for him to do X, and must have an Intentional state which contains the fact that X be caused by his representation of X. These two features are *sometimes* also found in other mental states. For example, if John wishes to go to the beach, it is plausible to suppose that he thinks that it is possible for him to go, and that the fact that his going to the beach results from his intending to go to the beach is also part of another one of his Intentional states. (This additional intentional state is neither an intention nor a belief, but a *presentation*, in a sense which I will discuss below.) Similar examples can be construed with wanting, aiming, and hoping to go to the beach. But it is also possible for John to wish (or want or hope, etc.) to be able to breathe under water, or to wish (or want or hope, etc.) to be immortal. And in these cases, it is not necessary that the agent believes he is able to accomplish the desired (or wanted, hoped for, etc.) states of affairs. Similarly, one can wish to be a millionaire and be unconcerned with how one ever gets to be a millionaire, if at all: one need not wish (or want or hope, etc.) that one becomes a millionaire as a result of that very wish (or want or hope, etc).

It is not possible, in contrast, for an agent to intend to be immortal, unless he believes it is possible for him to *accomplish* such a goal; unless he believes that through his action he can bring about this state of affairs. It is only in the case of intentions that there is a necessary connection between the represented state of affairs and the possibility of bringing this about through one's action. Intentions (like plans) are *accomplished*, desires are merely *satisfied*. There cannot be a case of intending *X* that does not satisfy this condition. An agent cannot intend that the movie he is about to see be a good movie, though he can certainly hope, wish, expect, want, imagine, and so on, that it will be.

Intention is, then, the only Intentional state *necessarily* tied to the agent's actions, and containing self-referential causality in the way just sketched (and to which I shall come back immediately). (Volitions, of course, are also necessarily tied to action, but as we saw in chapter 4, we are better off avoiding the talk of volitions.) Loosely echoing Ryle's famous discussion of the differences between "knowing that" and "knowing how,"[13] I suggest that we pay attention to the distinction between "intending to" and "intending that," and I wish to further claim that we can only "intend to," and never "intend that." This linguistic analysis is a useful illustration of the underlying difference between intentions and all other Intentional states.

Some Intentional states seem to be of such a kind as to be always or almost always conjoined with "that" and never with "to." For example, belief, doubt, feel, imagine, conceive, think, seem always to be conjoined with "that" in statements of the form "I believe that it will rain," or "I think that it will rain," and so on. This fact reveals that these Intentional states are not as closely related to the agent's actions as are intentions. And an analysis of each of them, along the lines of my analysis of intentions shall make this point clear. Other Intentional states are sometimes conjoined with "that" and sometimes conjoined with "to." For example, wish, expect, desire, hope, regret, can sometimes be conjoined with "that" and sometimes with "to," in statements of the form "I hope that the sun will come out," and "I hope to catch a fish." This fact reveals that these latter Intentional states are sometimes closely connected with action and sometimes they are not.

---

13. Ryle, *Concept of Mind.*

A word is in order about a certain sense of wanting in which it seems to be more amenable to connections with "to" than to connections with "that," a sense that apparently renders wantings rather similar to intendings. Now wantings, but not intendings, also admit the following cases: "I want you to go," or better yet, "I want food," "I want freedom." These are perfectly acceptable uses of "want" which are not applicable to intendings. And finally, just like desires and wishes, wants are not as strictly bound by rational considerations as intentions are. For example "I want to be (nonmetaphorically) invisible" or "I want to travel to the moon" are perfectly fine wants, but "I intend to be invisible" or "I intend to travel to the moon" suggest that I am doing something to that effect. If I am not, when I intend to be invisible, I probably have a mere wish, and not an intention, or else I am somehow irrational. These factors then sufficiently distinguish wants from intendings. Yet, I admit that there are, in everyday language, cases in which "wanting" is used as a synonym of "intending," but the same can be said of other mental states. For example, "I wish to beat you in our next game of chess" is sometimes analogous to "I intend to beat you in our next game of chess," and also to "I desire to beat you in our next game of chess." The particularities of the way in which we use language need not say much about the underlying facts about the logical structure of intentions.

Part of the difficulty in distinguishing intentions very sharply from related conative Intentional states is that frequently intentions overlap with these other Intentional states. Before a squash game, for example, I typically both intend and desire to win; I have a plan, and have intentions as to what strategy I am going to employ, but I also have a general desire to win. And, typically, my desire to win is more intense than my intention to win. Imagine I am playing the match ball, I attempt to hit the ball in certain direction, but, alas, I hit the ball with the rim of the racket, and thus the ball moves in a direction I was not expecting it to go. Luckily for me, my opponent did not expect the ball to move in that direction. I win the game, though not in the way I had intended to win. In cases like these, the fact that I had an intention which went unrealized is overshadowed by the excitement of having my desire realized; I won, and I don't really care about the fact that my last shot (or even several of them) were lucky shots. There are limits to this indifference, for if I were to win because my opponent is drunk, or because he passed out during our match, even my desire to win would, perhaps, fail to be satisfied. One important point to bear in mind in connection to the preceding discussion is that the difference between intentions and desires is not a matter of intensity. Consider what Bratman calls predominant desires: "I have a predominant desire to A if I desire to A strictly more than I desire to perform any option thought by me to be incompatible with my A-ing."[14] Bratman insists that this is not an intention. I agree. The main difference between intentions and desires is that intentions are necessarily linked to my own actions whereas desires need not be so linked. The most intense of desires is not quite an intention; the least intense of intentions is not quite a desire; though, as noted, since desires and intentions frequently overlap, it might at times be difficult to tell them apart. But this difficulty is only an epistemological affair; the logical and ontological differences between intentions and desires remain unaffected by epistemological considerations. It is sometimes difficult to know what exactly we feel for another person, that is, whether we are in love or merely infatuated, but this does not entail that being in love and being infatuated are the same thing.

The peculiar relationship between intentions and actions is captured nicely, I think, by my suggestion that we can only intend *to* and that we cannot intend *that* or try *that* (or promise *that*). A person can hardly try that someone else does this or that, unless, of course, this is just shorthand for saying something along the lines of, "I will try to make sure that John does this or that." I cannot intend that Elizabeth, my wife, is happy, but I could of course intend to make her happy. Moreover, though I can intend to make my wife happy, it is hard to see how I could possibly intend to make, say, Queen Elizabeth II happy. For it is necessary that the person intending to do such and such believes that it is up to him to accomplish such and such. I have no pertinent relationship with Queen Elizabeth II, and thus, I am aware that I am in no position to intend to make her happy. Yet, unlike the case of intentions, since the connection between desires and actions is loose, and since I could wish many things which I do not believe are up to me, I could, with fewer problems, wish to make Queen Elizabeth II happy. It is befitting, then, that intentions are the Intentional state upon which the theories of culpability have been founded throughout history. Other Intentional states enter into theories of culpability as well (cognitive states like awareness, for example), but the basic distinction in our efforts to apportion blame is the distinction between intended and unintended action.

At the very least, then, intentions do contain at least one belief. A person who intends X must believe that X is up to him. While I may intend to win my squash match today, playing against my usual partner, I cannot, on pain of irrationality, intend to win a match against the number one ranked squash player in the world. Yet, believing that something is up to me is compatible with my being uncertain of success; knowing that something is up to me entails that I know that I *can* succeed in doing it, it does

---

14. Bratman, *Intention, Plans, and Practical Reason*, 18.

not entail that I know that I *will* succeed. Yet still, there is a correlation between the possibility of success and rationality; intending to do things that one knows have an extremely low probability of success might be somewhat irrational. Think of Jones who boards a plane from New York to Seattle. About ninety minutes after taking off, he thinks he is above Chicago, where Smith lives. Jones wants to kill him; thus he manages to open an emergency door and to drop a bowling ball from the plane, intending to kill Smith, who is likely to be gardening at the time. Such an intention reveals, I think, a grotesque disconnect with rationality.

Cases such as this give rise to further complications in the already complicated relationship between intentions and intentional action. For if someone admits that Jones can form this intention, however absurd it might be, then it necessarily follows that if he were to succeed in killing Smith (the bowling ball does fall on him as he tends to his garden), Jones's action is intended, but from the normative perspective, it might be difficult to call it intentional and leave it at that. How blameworthy is Jones's killing of Smith? Did he murder Smith? I think that there is a normative difference between they way in which Jones kills Smith in this example and the case in which he would have boarded a plane to Chicago, gone to Smith's house, and shot him with a gun. Thus I do not think that Jones killing Smith in the bowling ball example amounts to murder.

So in addition to the sorts of examples of intentional actions that are not intended and that I discussed in the previous chapter while analyzing the "simple view," we now see that there might exist intended actions that are not intentional. Perhaps, however, the disconnect between Jones's intention and basic standards of rationality is so dramatic that one would insist that Jones merely wished to kill Smith, that he simply could not have intended to kill him. Yet, for all that, it is clearly possible to form far-fetched intentions; and thus it seems somewhat gratuitous to simply declare that far-fetched intentions are just not intentions.

This belief component of intention is surely subtler than the belief mentioned in the admittedly coarse initial analysis of intentions in terms of beliefs and desires that Searle examines. When someone intends X, she believes that X is within the realm of her possibilities, but she need not believe that she will necessarily succeed in carrying out X. There are plenty of examples in the specialized literature illustrating cases of this sort. Davidson presents an eloquent and famous example: "in writing heavily on this page I may be intending to produce ten legible carbon copies. I do not know, or believe with any confidence, that I am succeeding."[15] But while it is not necessary that the intending agent knows or believes with great

---

15. Davidson, *Essays*, 92.

confidence that he is succeeding, or will succeed, it is necessary for him to believe that succeeding is up to him, that if he were to succeed, this would be an action of his. If, in this example, Davidson knew that he had no carbon sheets, he could not possibly intend to make the ten copies.

An intention to do *X*, moreover, also involves a certain desire to do *X*. This desire needs to be understood broadly. If a gunman points a gun to Jones's head, orders him "Kill Smith!" and Jones obeys, Jones kills Smith intendedly; he forms the intention to kill him and then proceeds to carry out his intention. (In light of the discussions in the preceding chapters, this fact alone is not enough to claim that Jones, in the final analysis, is to be blamed for what he did—he might be excused or justified.) While it is true that Jones would have desired much more intensely not to be put in such a predicament in the first place, in the context in which he acted, he had a desire to kill Smith. Similar considerations apply in the context of so-called weakness of the will or *akrasia*.[16] These are cases in which an agent acts against her all-things-considered better judgment. For example, I know that, all things considered, I should refrain from eating sweets, but I nevertheless go ahead and *intendedly* eat sweets. An important distinction must be made between cases in which I am truly physiologically addicted, and cases in which I am not. For if I am not really addicted, it can be plausibly argued that when I go ahead and intendedly eat sweets in spite of my desire to lose weight or to improve my health, I have concluded that the satisfaction that this sweet will give me now trumps my other desires, whether I admit it to myself this bluntly or not. Thus, it is not really true that I, all things considered, prefer not to eat sweets. But if I am really addicted, then this argument is not as plausible; and indeed a central aspect of addictions is precisely that they overpower our better judgment. In either case, however, the agent who displays weakness of the will, even in the case of the fully physiologically addicted agent, intends to do what she does. And in those cases, she has a desire to accomplish what she intends, even if such desires, and indeed such intention, stand in opposition to other desires or intentions.

Cases of *akratic* action are in this respect similar to cases of coercion. Consider again a gunman situation. He puts a gun to your heard and orders you to kill Jones. Suppose that you obey the gunman. Since you have *decided* to obey the gunman, that is, you have deliberated and decided (rightly or wrongly) that you should do as the gunman says in order to save your own life, you have thus formed the intention of killing Jones, and thus you must also desire to succeed in killing Jones, since this is the only way to save your life. Here you have intended to kill Jones, and in a sense you

---

16. For more on *akrasia*, see Donald Davidson, "How is Weakness of the Will Possible?" in Davidson, *Essays*, 21–42, and references contained therein.

have desired to kill him as well, even if such a desire is only the result of coercion, and even if you have a much more intense desire to never have been put in such a predicament. Cases of addiction can be seen as cases in which one is overpowered, not by guns, but by biochemical processes inside our bodies.

While intentions are not reducible to beliefs and desires, they contain beliefs and desires, in the ways just sketched. The remaining element of the analysis of intentions is related, as we would by now expect, to the causal self-referentiality of intentions and their conditions of satisfaction.

Intentions, Causality, and Presentations

An important aspect of the difficult relationship between intentions and actions is known in the specialized literature as the problem of deviant (or wayward) causal chains. Given Intentional causation, there always exists a rather small set (frequently a singleton) of causal chains that would render the bringing about of a certain result a genuine condition of satisfaction of an intention; all other possible causal chains are deemed deviant. For example, let us suppose that Jack intends to kill his neighbor Jill. He has been planning the kill for a while. One day he goes to a store to buy a weapon. While driving on the highway, a careless pedestrian walks just in front of Jack's car, who in vain tries to avoid the collision. The pedestrian dies instantly. Suppose that the pedestrian happened to be Jill. Examples of this tenor abound in the literature. The point of the example, of course, is that Jack intends to kill Jill, he brings about Jill's death, and yet he does not kill Jill intendedly (or, for that matter, intentionally). Running over an unknown pedestrian who happened to be Jill is not the condition of satisfaction of Jack's intention to kill Jill.

Had Jack merely *desired* to kill Jill, running her over accidentally would have been a condition of satisfaction of that desire. Strictly speaking, there are only deviant causal chains in the case of intentions, not in the case of any other conative desires. And this special sort of causality between the Intentional state of intending and its conditions of satisfaction is a further element that helps distinguish intentions and related Intentional states. Searle, along with many contemporary authors, worries about the problem of deviant causal chains. He thinks, moreover, that the solution he gives to this problem is "not entirely satisfactory" and that "something may still be eluding us."[17] Though I am not interested here in attempting a solution to the problem of deviant causal chains, I do wish to specify one aspect regarding the scope of the problem, and why it

---

17. Searle, *Intentionality*, 139.

might be less relevant to the analysis of the Intentional state of intending than typically assumed.

Though in this chapter I have been trying to make explicit the ways in which intentions are more closely linked to actions than the ways in which any other Intentional states relate to action, one should keep in mind that analyzing intentions is one thing and analyzing their conditions of satisfaction is another thing. "Pure intending" does exist, and that is precisely the phenomenon that we are trying to analyze. But here we need to proceed carefully. It will not do, I think, simply to say I could intend *X* without this intention ever prompting me to act. Recall the example of cleaning my office at the outset. I could intend to tidy up my office, though I might never actually get around to engaging in any behavior whatsoever tending to satisfy such intention. Whether or not I try to satisfy (carry out) my intention, whether or not the contents of my intention comes about through a deviant causal chain or does not come about at all, my intention can nonetheless exist.

As I pointed out at the outset, intentions and actions are intimately linked; intentions do constitute a special Intentional state in virtue of the way in which they are linked to actions. But the connection is not so intimate as to render the result of there not being token intentions without there being token intended actions. Intentions can exist without their conditions of satisfaction materializing. What complicates the connection between intentions and actions in Searle's case is that though he speaks generally about "intentions" *simpliciter*, he in fact distinguishes between two types of intentions: (1) prior intentions and (2) intentions-in-action. Prior intentions are "external" to the action, and intentions-in-action are "internal" to the action. Internal here means being "part of" the action. There is a sense, then, in which the connection between intentions-in-actions and actions is more intimate than the connection between prior intentions and action. And thus, the discussion of deviant causal chains can be separated much more easily from the discussion of prior intentions than from the discussion of intentions-in-action.

I have doubts about the cogency and usefulness of the distinction between prior intentions and intentions-in-action, and that is why throughout, even while discussing Searle's own views, I choose to refer just to intentions, and to ignore Searle's distinction between prior intentions and intentions-in-action. Many of my doubts stem from my reading of Brian O'Shaughnessy's "Searle's Theory of Action."[18] Like O'Shaughnessy, I have difficulty accepting that there is anything beyond a mere temporal difference between, as Searle would have it, "intentions which are formed prior to action and those that are not."[19] If anything

---

18. O'Shaughnessy, "Searle's Theory of Action," especially 271–79.
19. O'Shaughnessy, "Searle's Theory of Action," 263.

other than mere temporal considerations holds, it might turn out that Searle would be embracing some form of volitionalism, for intentions-in-action might be just like good old volitions. Furthermore, if anything other than mere temporal considerations holds, then Searle would be also making it harder to distinguish *prior* intentions from desires, for they would not be so closely connected to actions after all. In any event, Searle has tacitly admitted that for some purposes the distinction is immaterial. As he replied to O'Shaughnessy's objections to the distinction between prior intentions and intentions-in-action, Searle posed the following question: "why should we call this interior Intentional content [an intention-in-action] an 'intention'?"[20] His answer deserves to be quoted fully: "At one level, it does not matter. The notion 'intention-in-action' is just a technical term. As long as you recognize the nature of the component, and in particular its causally self-referential conditions of satisfaction, it is not of very great interest what we choose to call it."[21]

I think that without risking oversimplification, I could here ignore the distinction between prior intentions and intentions-in-action. Prior intentions and intentions-in-action are, by Searle's own admission, equally causally self-referential Intentional states; they both require Intentional causation if they are to be effectively satisfied. No matter how closely related intentions and actions are, it must be possible to discuss intentions without discussing actions, and I think this is part of the strength of the way in which I interpret the Intentional approach to intentions. And analyzing intentions and actions separately is also a way of avoiding some of the problems of volitionalism.

Intentions, then, are complex Intentional states, which include beliefs and desires, but which, apparently, cannot be *reduced* to beliefs and desires alone. The causal self-referentiality between intentions and their conditions of satisfaction impedes such reduction. While I believe that such reduction is indeed not possible, I would like to follow Searle (who also believes that the reduction is not possible), in seeing "how far we can get" in the attempt. The obvious move is to include the causal self-referentiality characteristic of intentions as conditions of satisfaction of garden-variety beliefs or desires which in turn are part of the complex Intentional state of intending. Searle suggests the following analysis:

Int (I will do A) $\rightarrow$ There is some intentional state x such that x contains

Bel ($\Diamond$ I will do A) &
Des (I will do A) &
Bel (x will function causally toward the production of I will do A)
& Des (x will cause: I will do A)

---

20. Searle, "Reply to O'Shaughnessy," 297.
21. Searle, "Reply to O'Shaughnessy," 297.

And then Searle asks, "Now does all this add up to intention?" and he answers: "I think not. To construct a counterexample we would need only to construct a case where someone satisfied all of these conditions but still hadn't actually formed an intention to do *A*."[22] I think Searle's answer is cryptic and, as it stands, it might be question-begging as well: the proposed analysis is purportedly an analysis of the Intentional state of intending and the reason why it fails cannot be simply to say that someone could have this Intentional state and still not be intending, without explaining what is it about intending that this purported analysis does not contain. Apparently, the missing bit is not the causal self-referentiality of intentions since this seems to have been included in this analysis. (And to explore the relevance of the locution "forming an intention" as opposed to simply "having an intention" is a nonstarter in this context, for Searle admits the obvious point that sometimes we act without ever having "formed an intention," though in these cases we still have some intention-in-action.)

I think that Searle's views on intentions might contain the elements to explain why this is not a successful reduction of intentions to mere complexes of desires and beliefs. These views are associated with a certain attitudinal aspect of intending, which comes across nicely in Searle's discussion of the similarities between acting and perceiving. "Raising your arm," Searle points out, "like seeing a table, characteristically consists of two components: the experience of raising your arm and the physical movement of the arm." And the Searle continues:

> We can probe the parallel between action and perception further by considering Wittgenstein's question: If I raise my arm, what is left over if I subtract the fact that my arm went up? The question seems to me exactly analogous to the question: If I see the table what is left over if I subtract the table? And in each case the answer is that a certain form of *presentational* Intentionality is left over; what is left over in the case of visual perception is a visual experience, what is left over in the case of action is an experience of acting.[23]

The appeal to the experience of acting is complicated. Searle is emphatic in warning us:

> The term ['experience of acting'] would mislead if it gave the impression that such things were passive experiences or sensations that simply afflict one, or that they were like what some philosophers have called volitions or acts of willing or anything of that sort. They are not acts at all, for we no more *perform* our experience of acting than we *see* our visual experiences. Nor I am claiming that there is any special feeling that belongs to all intentional actions.[24]

---

22. Searle, *Intentionality*, 104.
23. Searle, *Intentionality*, 87 (emphasis added).
24. Searle, *Intentionality*, 88–89.

Two problems seem to arise. First, if the experience of acting is not a feeling or attitude found in all intentional actions, if *ex hypothesi*, it is not a belief or a desire, it is not an action, and it is nothing like a volition, then what is it? Second, whatever the experience of acting turns out to be, it is not clear why the reductionist belief-desire theorist cannot insist that she could somehow include it into the conditions of satisfaction of a desire or a belief. The answer that I suggest applies to both problems is based on an analysis of the notion of a presentation.

Although Searle has himself discussed presentations, and has suggested that when one has a *presentation* of a given states of affairs one is not committed to its conditions of satisfaction, whereas when one has a *representation* of a state of affairs one is committed to its conditions of satisfaction,[25] the best way to explain their relevance here is to go back to Brentano. Brentano, unlike most contemporary philosophers of mind, divided mental phenomena into three groups: "three main classes of mental phenomena must be distinguished, and distinguished according to the different ways in which they refer to their content. . . . In the absence of more appropriate expressions we designate the first by the term 'presentation', the second by the term 'judgement', and the third by the term 'emotion', 'interest', or 'love'."[26] This tripartite classification of mental phenomena is different in important respects from the more familiar one that sees only beliefs (Brentano's judgments) and desires (Brentano's emotions, interest, or love) as primitives. Now, regarding presentations Brentano tell us: "we speak of a presentation whenever something appears to us. When we see something, a color is presented; when we hear something, a sound; when we imagine something, a fantasy image."[27] According to Brentano's theory, it is possible to have an Intentional state of, say, a tree, without forming any belief or desire about the tree. And, moreover, Brentano is emphatic about the fact that presentations, and not beliefs or desires, are the most primitive Intentional state:

> It is clear that presentation deserves the primary place, for it is the simplest of the three phenomena, while judgment and love always include a presentation within them. It is likewise the most independent of the three, since it is the foundation for the others, and, for exactly the same reason, it is the most universal. . . . We can conceive, without contradiction, of a being which has no capacity for judgment or love, equipped with nothing but the capacity for presentation, but we cannot conceive of it the other way around.[28]

---

25. Searle, *Intentionality*, 23ff., 46ff.
26. Franz Brentano, *Psychology from an Empirical Standpoint* (London: Routledge 1995), 197–98.
27. Brentano, *Psychology*, 198.
28. Brentano, *Psychology*, 266–67.

The explanation of the extremely complex relationship between intentions and actions can benefit from considering Brentano's concept of presentations. The causal self-referentiality of intentions is *presented* to the person when the person has an intention. This is part of what it is to have an intention. But the person need not desire nor believe that the causal self-referentiality will obtain. The foundational nature of presentations explains why when we postulate an agent having a presentation of the state of affairs whereby what she intends to do is to be caused by her having that intention, we are not postulating that she has a volition, or a particular feeling.

Presentations explain also why to "reduce" the presentation to a belief or to a desire (or to a combination of beliefs and desires) is not promising. Part of the reason why the belief-desire approach to intentions is reductionist is that this approach does not sufficiently recognize the existence and the uniqueness of presentations. Insofar as intentions contain a presentation of the causal self-referentiality between them and actions, the specific attempt to explain intentions wholly in terms of beliefs and desires is reductionist in that it distorts the nature of intentions.

If the complex relation of causal self-referentiality between intentions and actions were part of the conditions of satisfaction of beliefs or desires, at least one problem facing volitional theories of action would reappear. In chapter 4 I discussed one sensible objection to volitional theories of action. To the extent that volitional theories of action assert that whenever we act we have both an intention for some of the consequences of our action and also a volition for the bodily movements that constitute our action, they seem to fly in the face of our common experience of acting, for we rarely find ourselves willing bodily movements. And then the objection would be deployed to the reductionist account of intending by noting that when we act we rarely find ourselves believing or desiring that such and such self-referential causal relation must obtain.

Yet, the same objection cannot be made when the self-referential causal relation is just part of a presentation. For insofar as presentations have no direction of fit, there is a sense in which they can be in the background, which is not amenable to Intentional states with direction of fit, like beliefs and desires (although beliefs and desires in other ways can be in the background as well). For example, imagine that Bob believes that his parents are going to visit him; in addition to this belief, which has direction of fit, he also has a certain presentation of his parents with no direction of fit— this is the Brentanian sense in which presentations are more fundamental than beliefs and desires. If we were to ask Bob about this presentation, he might even be somewhat unaware that he had it at all, but I do not think he could deny that the presentation was there, in the background at least. Something similar would hold for intentions. Alicia intends to buy a new car; whatever else her intention contains, it contains some sort of general presentation about her buying a car. If one were to suggest to Alicia that she indeed had this presentation, she would not, in the final analysis, deny that such presentation was indeed necessary for her having the intention that she did. Incidentally, proponents of volitional theories of action, too, would benefit from adopting a tripartite classification of Intentional states, for then they would be able to say something along the lines of "every time we act we have a presentation of certain bodily movements," which might even be in the background in the way just sketched, without facing the traditional problems that they have faced with volitions. (I do not think that this move would solve all problems for volitional theorists, for to the extent that the presentation must be about a set of quite specific bodily movements, it remains a problematic notion.)

That we cannot have an intention to do X without having a presentation of the complex connection between the intention to X and doing X is simply part of the logic of intending, just as it is part of the logic of beliefs that we cannot have a belief that such and such is the case without having some presentation of such and such. I wish to stress two points about this claim. First, the claim about this being part of the logic of intending is of special importance. As he considers the famous Wittgensteinian question, "When I raise my arm, what is left over if I subtract the fact that my arm goes up?" Searle points out that this question is interesting "only if we insist on an ontological answer. Given the non-ontological approach to Intentionality suggested here, the answer is quite simple. What is left is an Intentional content."[29] Needless to say, I agree with Searle's insight here, and I have tracked Searle's strategy as one that avoids an ontological approach to Intentionality and blame, bracketing the discussion of the ultimate ontological status of intentions and other Intentional phenomena, and focused on their logical structure. Second, it might be objected that insofar as the logic of intending is not self-evident, it is hard to see how people who ignore it can intend to do things. But this objection misses the fact that we do all sorts of things without understanding their logical structures. As he discussed a related issue of the self-referential nature of intentions, Harman expressed rather eloquently what I would like to say to this kind of objection: "It might be wrongly objected, by the way, that a child can intend to do something before it has the concept of an intention and, therefore, before it can have self-referential intentions. But there is no reason why the child must have a theoretically adequate concept of intention before it can have self referential intentions. Who of us has a theoretically adequate concept of intention?"[30]

---

29. Searle, *Intentionality*, 16.
30. Harman, "Practical Reasoning," 158, n. 5.

That the analysis of the logic of intentions sketched above is not generally known is not an objection to its being on the right track, or to its not being exhibited by intending agents, even if they are unaware of its existence.

We can then summarize the analysis of intentions as follows. An agent intends X when

  (1) The agent believes X is up to him
  (2) The agent desires to bring about X
  (3) The agent has a presentation, in the sense explained, of his intention causing X.

Unlike traditional theories of action, moreover, which depend on the implausible and ontologically expensive thesis that whenever we do X, we have both intentions and other garden-variety Intentional states regarding X itself, and also volitions regarding the bodily movements which are necessary in order to actually do X, this account of intentions depends on no implausible thesis. To be sure, to point out that we hardly ever find ourselves willing merely bodily movements when we act is to present a powerful objection against volitional theories of action. But it is not a promising objection to the account of intentions just presented to say that we hardly ever find ourselves experiencing the presentation of the causal self-referentiality of intentions. For, intending to do X necessarily entails that one has formed a presentation of the ways in which X must be brought about, simply as a result of the very logical structure of intentions. And this presentation would be there even if we do not think about it; upon reflection we would have to admit that the presentation must have been there. This presentation, in connection with the belief that X is up to me and with the desire to do X (in the senses already explained), *constitutes* the experience of acting. Only things that are the Intentional content of the complex Intentional state containing the causally self-referential presentation of X, the desire to X, and the belief that X is up to the agent, and that are brought about by the agent having this complex Intentional state in the appropriate ways are, strictly speaking, intended.

One problem remains. If the peculiar causal self-referentiality of intentions is part of a presentation, and if presentations have no direction of fit, how can there be deviant causal chains? For if the presentation is really without direction of fit, then it does not stipulate any specific way in which X *must* be caused; presentations have no normativity. (Recall that the fact that only intentions can give rise to the problem of deviant causal chains is a way in which intentions can be distinguished from all other Intentional states.) The solution to this problem is that while the presentation, taken in isolation, has no direction of fit, the whole Intentional state of intending, which includes a belief and a desire (which have direction of fit) has direction of fit, and thus gives rise to the problem of deviant causal chains. It might be objected to this solution that then, since desires and other conative Intentional states also involve presentations, the problem of deviant causal chains also arises in connection to these other Intentional states. Yet, while it is true that if I want candy, I necessarily have a presentation of candy, I do not have a presentation of my-having-candy-being-caused-by-my-wanting-it. If I want to work hard on my book in the next few days, and I have a presentation of my working hard on my book being caused by my having this "want," and I believe that working hard on my book is up to me, then I have an intention to work hard on my book (which can, of course, coexist with overlapping desires, as examples such as the one regarding squash matches show).

We can now see how this analysis of intending applies to some of the famous examples of allegedly different forms of intending. Take Bentham's oblique intentions (rather similar to the Model Penal Code's "Knowledge"). An agent obliquely intends (or acts with knowledge regarding) Y when:

(1) The agent believes X is up to him.
(2) The agent desires to bring about X.
(3) The agent has a presentation, in the sense explained, of his intention causing X.
(4) The agent believes (or knows) that bringing X about will also bring Y about.
(5) The agent does not desire Y.

Or take the notion of *dolus eventualis*:

(1) The agent believes X is up to him.
(2) The agent desires to bring about X.
(3) The agent has a presentation, in the sense explained, of his intention causing X.
(4) The agent realizes that bringing X about is likely to bring Y about as well.
(5) While the agent does not desire Y, he does not mind bringing Y about.

While it is easy to understand why, from the normative perspective, bringing Y about as a result of having these sets of Intentional states has been considered intentional action, it also patently obvious that from the purely descriptive perspective, these sets of Intentional states do not amount to bringing about Y intendedly. In spite of the differences, however, the normative similarities between *dolus eventualis* and oblique intention, on the one hand, and bona fide intended action, on the other, are so meaningful that it seems justifiable to treat these modes of culpability as if they were indeed intended, even though they were not, because there seems to be no major difference in the blameworthiness of the agent who brings X about and the one who brings Y about. It seems downright irrational not to admit that the normative distinction between these two ways of doing things is not too important. For cases of oblique intentions, or of *dolus eventualis*, are cases in which agents, while not directly intending the evil outcome, nevertheless have Intentional states that resemble intentions in ways that warrant equating, or almost equating, their normative implications with the normative implications of intentions.

The special connection between intentions and actions is part of the answer as to why intentions are so important in apportioning blame to agents for what they *do*. Intentions typically issue in action, and knowing that someone did a bad thing while intending to do it is to know something about the sort of state in which her mind was, which entails some sort of commitment to doing something bad—a commitment whose strength diminishes considerably if such an intention did not exist. In order to explain these commitments, we need to pay attention to the relationship between intentions and rationality.

Intentions, Rationality, and Commitments

It is probably a commonplace to assert that intentions are closely linked to rationality; some authors actually distinguish practical reasoning from theoretical reasoning along these lines: "practical reason is concerned with what to intend, whereas theoretical reason with what to believe."[31] The occurrence of the word "intend" in the preceding quotation is exact; practical reason is not concerned with what to hope or with what to wish for, but exactly with what to intend. Why?

One of the most useful accounts of the relationship between intentions and rationality is found in Bratman's work. Before discussing this relationship in itself, I wish to discuss what might seem to be a mere terminological issue, but which in the context of my interest in analyzing the Intentional state of intending in itself, is of singular importance. Like Searle, Bratman stresses a temporal distinction between intentions. He urges us to distinguish the present intentions that we have when we act, something akin to Searle's intentions-in-action, apparently not from intentions formed previously to the action (prior intentions), but from inten-

---

31. Harman, "Practical Reasoning," 149. Harman claims, moreover, that this is the traditional way of marking the distinction between practical and theoretical reason.

tions concerning future actions. Just as I have misgivings regarding Searle's distinction between prior intentions and intentions-in-action, I believe that in spite of whatever advantages Bratman's temporal distinction between present and future intentions might have, the distinction faces some difficulties. There are no important differences in the logical structure of the Intentional state of intending attending to whether the Intentional state of intending occurs before I act, while I am acting, whether it contains as conditions of satisfaction things I am doing right now, or things I am doing later on.

What recommends following Bratman in paying special attention to what he calls future-directed intentions is the way in which the focus on this type of intentions allows us to see the connection between intentions and rationality. For, Bratman argues, future-directions *commit* us in special ways. And these commitments expose the huge normative force of intentions, as contrasted with that of related Intentional states. While I believe that there is a sense in which present-directed intentions commit us in similar ways, I believe that Bratman's strategy reveals these commitments in particularly clear ways. Thus I think that Bratman's suggestion that we realize that "the future-directed case is central" is quite valuable.[32]

But this is an important point. What Bratman calls a future-directed intention is just an intention not being carried out at the moment. Any intention that is not what Searle calls an intention-in-action, that is not being satisfied at the moment, would be one of those that Bratman calls future-directed intentions, and will be, too, one of those intentions Searle calls prior intentions. Bratman's future intentions and Searle's prior intentions are the same thing. Recall my example of intending to tidy up my office at the beginning of the chapter. As long as I have not tidied up the office, my intention is both a future intention (in Bratman's sense) insofar as its conditions of satisfaction are something that I am yet to do, and a prior intention (in Searle's sense) insofar as its conditions of satisfaction are something that I am yet to do.

I wholeheartedly agree with Bratman's call for the focus on what he calls future-directed intentions (I will follow his lead in the remaining of this section), but I interpret Bratman's position as an invitation to focus upon the Intentional state of intending, and to separate this analysis, as far as possible, from the analysis of intended action. This way of interpreting Bratman might be somewhat idiosyncratic, but nevertheless I think it is justified. I found support for this interpretation in Bratman's own writings. Bratman, rightly, opposes a certain skepticism about intentions as bona fide Intentional states quite common in the recent specialized literature.

---

32. Bratman, *Intention, Plans, and Practical Reason*, 4.

These four approaches revolve around the following four interconnected theses:

(1) The methodological priority of intention in action,[33]

This is the view that the best way to understand intentions is to understand them as they occur "in action." This view leads to a second skeptical stance.

> (2) The desire-belief theory of intention in action: we understand intentional action, and action done with an intention, in terms of the agent's desires and beliefs, and actions standing in appropriate relations to those desires and beliefs.[34]

Endorsing these two theses naturally leads to the adoption of the last two skeptical tenets:

(3) The strategy of extension,

and, finally,

(4) A reduction of future intention to appropriate desires and beliefs.[35]

Bratman opposes, in the final analysis, the focus upon intentions-in-action and their concomitant reductionist effects. Bratman wishes to focus on the Intentional state of intending, and the way he emphasizes this point, the way in which he distinguishes this enterprise from the usual strategy of analyzing intentional action rather than intentions (indeed "a dominant view in contemporary philosophy of mind and action"),[36] is by calling the Intentional state of intention itself a future-directed intention.[37] Bratman's concern with future-directed intentions is of a piece with my concern with the Intentional state of intending. These preliminaries out of the way, I shall continue talking about intentions *simpliciter*.

What is it, then, about intentions that commit us in the ways that Bratman suggests they commit us? Many of Bratman's most relevant arti-

---

33. Bratman, *Intention, Plans, and Practical Reason*, 5.
34. Bratman, *Intention, Plans, and Practical Reason*, 6.
35. Bratman, *Intention, Plans, and Practical Reason*, 7.
36. Bratman, *Intention, Plans, and Practical Reason*, 7.
37. A list of authors who embrace this sort of skepticism includes, as we saw in chapter 3 and 4, Austin and Bentham, but it includes as well many contemporary authors such as Elizabeth Anscombe, Robert Audi, Wayne Davies, and Alvin Goldman, among many others. See the references in Bratman, *Intention, Plans, and Practical Reason*, 176, nn. 10 and 13.

cles on this subject are gathered together in a collection entitled *Intention, Plans, and Practical Reason,* and the title of the book, coupled with a remark I made in the previous chapter, that for Bratman plans are "intentions writ large," points in the direction of an answer. Our intentions, our plans, are subject to normative constraints that are more demanding than the normative constraints exhibited by other conative Intentional states. Recall, once more, my example of tidying up my office, but now imagine that rather than intending to tidy up my office, I would merely have wished to tidy it up. I don't think that if that were indeed the case, my not having actually tidied it up would be evidence of irrationality or that it would have constituted enough ground for claiming that I must have been lying or confused when I expressed my desire in the first place. Our lives, to some extent, are replete with unfulfilled desires of this sort, though, for reasons that shall become clear momentarily, unfulfilled intentions cannot fill our lives in the same way. This is not to say, to repeat, that there are no rational normative constraints on Intentional states other than intentions. If my desires were, for example, for a fairy godmother to materialize and tidy up my office for me, this would be irrational, and the same is true of absurd cognitive Intentional states, that is, the belief that my fairy godmother will come and clean my office. All I am claiming is that these sorts of rational constraints are typically greater in the case of intentions than in the case of other Intentional states.

Insofar as we are planning agents, Bratman points out, we form intentions, and these intentions help us coordinate our actions.[38] The skeptic about intentions could rebut along lines that Bratman expresses eloquently: "Why do we bother forming intentions concerning the future? Why don't we just cross our bridges when we come to them?"[39] Bratman, no less eloquently, answers: "plans are not merely executed. They are formed, retained, combined, constrained by other plans, filled in, modified, reconsidered, and so on."[40] I would like to add two remarks to Bratman's reply to the skeptic. First, intentions are part of the furniture of our Intentional states; we simply intend to do certain things, and not all of our intentions require that we act—if we tried to only have intentions-in-action, that itself would be a (rather unrealistic) plan, that itself would be an intention, and unless our whole life were to be postulated as one single action, this intention would itself be an intention-in-action. Even if the skeptic were able to show that intentions are reducible to beliefs and desires, she would not be able to deny what seems to me to be a primitive

---

38. Bratman's recent work has focused on collective action. See, e.g., *Faces of Intention* (Cambridge: Cambridge University Press, 1998).
39. Bratman, *Intention, Plans, and Practical Reason,* 7–8.
40. Bratman, *Intention, Plans, and Practical Reason,* 8.

fact about our psychology, if there ever was one: we have intentions that we are not carrying out at the moment. As she prepares a rebuttal to this claim, the skeptic surely will form intentions, some of which she will not carry out at the same time that she forms those intentions. Second, the analysis of the ways in which, and the reasons why, intentions commit us in the ways they do is also valuable, even if all we had were intentions-in-action, because it would still shed light on why theories of culpability have always revolved around this crucial Intentional state.

Bratman distinguishes between two dimensions in the ways that intentions commit us: what he calls the "volitional dimension" of commitment (I would have chosen a different name, perhaps "conative dimension")[41] and the "reasoning-centered" dimension of commitment. The volitional dimension of commitment comes out clearly, again, when we distinguish intentions form desires. "Suppose I desire a milk shake for lunch, recognize that the occasion is here, and am guilty of no irrationality. Still, I might not drink a milk shake; for my desire for a milk shake still needs to be weighed against conflicting desires—say, my desire to lose weight."[42] Intentions are different. "In contrast, suppose that this morning I formed the intention to have a milk shake at lunch, lunchtime arrives, my intention remains, and nothing unexpected happens. In such a case I do not normally need yet again to tote up the pros and cons concerning milkshake drinking. Rather, I will simply proceed to execute (or, anyway, try to execute) my intention to order a milk shake."[43] Intentions are "conduct-controlling," whereas desires and other conative states are merely "potential influencers" of action. Of course, the way in which intentions control conduct is complex in the sense that it would be irrational if my having formed an intention this morning to drink a milk shake for lunch would be literally irrevocable—and Bratman devotes considerable attention to the ways in which this controlling aspect of intentions, together with the reasons why it might be overridden by other considerations, manifest themselves. For my purposes, however, it is enough to point out, with Bratman, that the ways in which intentions control our behavior are much tighter than the ways in which desires and other conative states do.

The reasoning-centered dimension of intentions has two components. The first of these components is closely related to the volitional dimension just described. Forming an intention makes further deliberation somewhat unnecessary. When we form an intention to do *X*, we are, in principle, settled on doing *X*. Of course, if conditions were to change, we would accordingly change our intentions, but in the normal course of events,

---

41. Bratman himself can be seen as a volitionalist.
42. Bratman, *Intention, Plans, and Practical Reason*, 15–16.
43. Bratman, *Intention, Plans, and Practical Reason*, 16.

forming intentions gives rise to some sort of "stability or inertia."[44] The second component relates to the way in which intentions are typically nestled in complicated webs of other intentions and larger plans; intentions are both normatively affected by and they in turn affect other intentions.

It is important to stress that when someone intends, she does not also intend or desire or believe that this initial intention have the normative force that it has; that is, she does not say to herself, "I hope that having formed this intention, then it will more or less settle deliberation," nor does she say to herself, "I hope that this intention coheres with my other plans," and so on. Intending is, as a matter of logic, conduct-controlling, even if it were possible not to be fully aware of this fact. Intending, then, commits us in some ways; if I form the intention to do X, I am committed to do X (although these commitments are defeasible), and I am also committed to not do things which prevent me from doing X.

The way in which intentions, in virtue of their very logical structure, commit us is far from being mysterious, and in fact is rather similar to the way in which promises commit us, although, as we shall see in due course, in a more fundamental way. To promise to do X is to commit oneself to do X, and this is so in spite of the fact that the commitment could perhaps be overridden by other considerations. Making a promise *means* that one is committing oneself to what one is promising to do. The analogy between the way in which intentions and promises give rise to commitments deserves special attention. Perhaps the best way to explore this analogy is to take a look at Searle's recent work on the structure of social reality and on the nature of rationality in action; after all, arguably most of his recent views revolve around the phenomenon of promising. In *Rationality in Action* Searle tells us, "The single most remarkable capacity of human rationality, and the single way in which it differs most from ape rationality, is the human capacity to create and to act on desire-independent reasons for action. The creation of such reasons is always a matter of an agent *committing* himself in various ways."[45] The institution of promising is crucially linked to the remarkable human capacity to create desire-independent reasons. When we obligate ourselves, we impose conditions of satisfaction upon conditions of satisfaction. Searle's own example illustrates what he means by imposing conditions of satisfaction upon conditions of satisfaction:

> Suppose a speaker utters a sentence, for example, 'It is raining', and suppose he intends to make the assertion that it is raining. His intention in action is, in part, to produce the utterance 'it is raining'. That utterance is one of the conditions of satisfaction of his intention. But if he is not just uttering the sen-

---

44. Bratman, *Intention, Plans, and Practical Reason*, 16–17.
45. John R. Searle, *Rationality in Action* (Cambridge, MA: MIT Press, 2001), 167.

tence, but actually *saying that* it is raining, if he actually *means* that it is raining, then he must intend that the utterance have satisfied truth conditions . . . that is, his meaning intention is to impose conditions of satisfaction (i.e. truth conditions) on conditions of satisfaction.[46]

Searle claims that to impose conditions of satisfaction on conditions of satisfaction is, *eo ipso*, a commitment. The speaker is committed to the truth of the claim that it is raining; she is committed to not say things that contradict the view that it is raining, and so forth. This commitment constitutes a desire-independent reason for action. And there is nothing moral about it: "you ought to tell the truth," "you ought not to lie," or "you ought to be consistent in your assertions" are *internal* to the notion of "assertion."[47]

The case of assertions and the commitments that arise from them can of course be extended; Searle further tells us that "all of the standard forms of speech acts with whole propositional contents involve the creation of desire independent reasons for action."[48] That is why Searle tells us that "virtually all speech acts have an element of promising."[49] This seems exaggerated. It is hard to see where in the speech act of asking, say, *What time is it?* the element of promising is to be found. Yet, many, perhaps most, speech acts do include the element of promising. The reason why asserting, requesting, ordering, and so forth are all forms of committing ourselves is because all these speech acts contain elements of promising. Searle is explicit about this: "For a long time philosophers tried to treat promises as a kind of assertion. It would be more accurate to think of assertions as a kind of promise that something is the case."[50] So his example could be extended to cover requests and orders, that is, if I request *X* from you, or if I order you to do *X*, I am, among other things, committed to not preventing you from doing *X*, and so on. Searle admits that there are ways in which we could commit ourselves without the help of any speech act. For example, "one may commit oneself to a policy just by adopting a firm intention to continue with that policy."[51]

Yet, it is precisely the sort of commitments that Searle by and large ignores, that is, the commitments that arise simply from pure intentions,

46. Searle, *Rationality in Action*, 173.
47. Searle, *Rationality in Action*, 173ff. and passim.
48. Searle, *Rationality in Action*, 174.
49. Searle, *Rationality in Action*, 181. In the Spanish version of *Rationality in Action*, which was published earlier than the English version, and which is virtually identical to the latter, it is stated that "all" (not merely "virtually all") speech acts contain an element of promising.
50. Searle, *Rationality in Action*, 181.
51. Searle, *Rationality in Action*, 175.

that are crucially important to me here, not only because I am interested in Intentional states rather than in speech acts, but also because Intentional states are more fundamental than speech acts. One main reason explains why I think commitments that arise from intentions are more fundamental than the commitments that arise from speech acts. As we shall see immediately, echoing Searle himself (in spite of the fact that he ignores commitments that "are not created publicly"[52] via speech acts), the normativity of Intentional states is not the result of human conventions. The importance that the priority of Intentionality over speech acts is at times difficult to appreciate because recently Searle has turned his attention to the ways in which speech acts help create social reality. This difficulty is augmented by the fact that Searle wrote *Speech Acts* in 1969, and *Intentionality* in 1983, and many crucial aspects of Intentionality are explained in terms of speech act theory, and this might suggest that speech acts are more fundamental than intentional states. But it is exactly the other way around, the discussion of intentionality is more fundamental than the discussion of speech acts. The only reason why Searle would appeal to speech acts to explain intentionality is that speech acts were, by the time he wrote *Intentionality*, already a familiar and respected aspects of standard philosophical lore. But Searle's own admission, at the outset of *Intentionality*, is eloquent regarding the preeminence of Intentional mental states over speech acts: "A basic assumption behind my approach to problems of language is that the philosophy of language is a branch of the philosophy of mind. The capacity of speech acts to represent objects and states of affairs in the world is an extension of the more biologically fundamental capacities of the mind (or brain) to relate the organism to the world by way of such mental states as belief and desire, and especially through action and perception."[53]

I agree with Searle's view regarding the priority, biological and otherwise, of Intentional mental states over speech acts, though I wish he had done more to develop his own insight in his recent work on social ontology. In focusing on the normative implications of promising, Searle effectively bucks a venerable trend in the history of philosophy according to which the realm of normativity is significantly, indeed irreconcilably, different from the realm of facts. But, as promises show, we can indeed derive normative statements from purely descriptive statements, as Searle did in his famous "How to Derive 'Ought' From 'Is'":[54] roughly, from

---

52. Searle, *Rationality in Action*, 175.
53. Searle, *Intentionality*, vii.
54. John R. Searle, "How to Derive an 'Ought' from 'Is,'" *Philosophical Review* 73 (1964): 43–58, and see also the excellent collection *The Is/Ought Problem*, ed. W. D. Hudson.

the fact that you promise to *X* it follows that you ought to *X*. But his derivation of an "ought" from an "is" is vulnerable to objections of the following sort. Insofar as the normativity that Searle has been able to derive in this case entirely follows, if it indeed follows, from the constitutive rules of promising, it is not a robust sense of normativity at all. It is, indeed, the same sort of normativity that follows from the constitutive rules of chess, according to which chess players ought to move the bishops diagonally, and this feeble sense of normativity might understandably appear uninteresting to moral philosophers working on the difficult problem of the naturalistic fallacy.

I think these sorts of objections do pose a serious challenge at least as to the scope of what Searle thinks, and what many commentators think,[55] he has accomplished. For Searle admits that he has nowhere discussed the thickly normative considerations as to which factors, and why, should override the normative force of promises. If I know, for example, that by moving a bishop nondiagonally I can prevent a catastrophe, I would of course move it nondiagonally, just as I would break my promise of visiting with you over the weekend if by breaking such a promise I could prevent a major catastrophe. But such a challenge loses a great deal of its appeal when the target is the normativity that follows from the logical structures of nonconventional phenomena. The constitutive rules of chess have changed, and could change even more; the constitutive rules of promising can, perhaps, also change, and indeed the constitutive rules of all conventional phenomena can change, as long as (the relevant groups of) people agree that they should be changed. But the logical structure of intentions cannot change, at least not just merely as a result of our agreeing that they should be different—there might be wholly unconventional biological mutations that give rise to a change in the logical structure of Intentional mental states, but this is an altogether different sense of "change."

To be sure, the commitments that stem from the logical structure of intentions are also defeasible. My intention to work very hard on this book during the next few days would be overridden, for example, if a loved one is in need of my help, or if a great and unexpected opportunity would open up, and so on. Yet, the commitments that follow from the logical structure of intentions are not as defeasible as those that arise in connection to conventional phenomena. For they are not conventional: the rules of games, just as those of legal and sociopolitical institutions, can be changed, and the event that brings about such change could very well be the realization that there is a good reason to override the rule, which from now on

---

55. See the references in Lepore and Van Gulick, *John Searle and his Critics*, 394. Over ten years ago, Lepore and Van Gulick counted fifteen reprints (in different languages) of the article in volumes devoted to ethics.

becomes part of the constitutive rules of such games and institutions. But, in any case, the fact that the commitments of intentions can be overridden does not render the fact that they do give rise to prima facie commitments less interesting. The burden of proof in determining whether someone must or must not do what she is committed to do falls, in principle, on the person arguing that the prima facie commitment is actually overridden; this burden of proof need not be, in actual cases, difficult to carry, though it nonetheless constitutes an important theoretical point.

Intentions and Personal Identity

The connection between the fact that intentions give rise to (prima facie) commitments and the fact that they figure so prominently in theories of culpability should by now have emerged. To do something intendedly reveals that one was committed to doing it; if that thing which one did intendedly is a bad thing, then one is clearly at least not less blameworthy for bringing it about than if one had done it unintendedly. Being committed to bad things, by itself, speaks volumes as to how to assess our doing those bad things. And I think that this information does not require (though by no means does it preclude) a full-blown neo-Aristotelian analysis of other character traits of agents who do bad things. Regardless of whatever character traits one has, that one is committed to a bad thing (in the normatively neutral sense in which since chapter 1 I have stipulated my use of this and similar expressions such as "evil outcomes") makes one, ceteris paribus, no less blameworthy than if one would have done this bad thing without being so committed. The general Aristotelian discussion of character traits is not necessary to explain why intended wrongdoing is, in principle, never less blameworthy than unintended wrongdoing. This normative principle follows solely from the very logic of intentions, and though defeasible, it is not at all as trivial as the sorts of normative claims that follow from the constitutive rules of games and legal and sociopolitical institutions.

Recently, in her prestigious Locke Lectures delivered at Oxford University,[56] Christine Korsgaard started by provocatively claiming that "Human beings are condemned to choice and action." This remark is part of Korsgaard's ambitious project of showing how actions help us constitute our own identity. I think that it is worth briefly touching upon

---

56. Although Korsgaard's lectures are still unpublished, they are nonetheless available from her website: http://www.people.fas.harvard.edu/~korsgaar/#Locke%20Lectures (visited in August of 2003). All my quotations are from the lectures as they appear on Korsgaard's website.

Korsgaard's views, not only because of the eloquence with which they are expressed, but because while our projects are clearly different, they do intersect in a couple of places, and such intersection will shed light on the nature of culpability. One of Korsgaard's main theses is that "we human beings constitute our own personal or practical identities—and at the same time our own agency—through action itself. We make ourselves the authors of our actions, by the way that we act." Though not expressly stated, I see no reason why Korsgaard would disagree with what I take to be the true claim that, first and foremost, it is our intended actions through which we constitute ourselves. Indeed, she points out that: "to call a movement a twitch, or a slip, is at once to deny that it is an action and to assign it to some part of you that is less than the whole: the twitch to your eyebrow, or the slip, more problematically, to your tongue. For a movement to be my action, for it to be expressive of *myself* in the way that an action must be, it must result from my entire nature working as an integrated whole."

Putting aside the mereological aspects of Korsgaard's view, it seems to me that the reason why she would not accept that twitches are actions is that they do not express our selfhood in any meaningful way. If genuine twitches are by default not actions, then, just as they would not be means through which we express our selfhood, they would not give rise to any judgment of blame either. Moreover, the reason why Korsgaard finds slips "more problematic" is, I suspect, that some slips of the tongue (and of other parts of our bodies) can in some cases be actions, though except in contrived cases, unintended actions. We express our selfhood through *some* of our unintended actions as well as through our intended actions, though, of course, less meaningfully. And to continue with the parallels between the two projects, the differential effect that intended and unintended actions have for Korsgaard in expressing our selfhood is of a piece with my own concern with the differential blameworthiness of intended and unintended actions.

After having clarified the exact scope of Korsgaard's claim that we express our selfhood above all through *intended* action, I can discuss the other point at which Korsgaard's project intersects with mine. This second intersection regards the constitutive role played by the logical structure of intentions: intentions constitute, paradigmatically, our selfhood, and intentions constitute, paradigmatically, the grounds for the blameworthiness of our actions. According to Korsgaard, "there is no *you* prior to your choices and actions, because your identity is in a quite literal way *constituted* by your choices and actions." And then Korsgaard adds:

> The identity of a person, of an agent, is not the same as the identity of the human animal on which the person normally supervenes. Human beings differ

from the other animals in an important way. Because we are self-conscious, and choose our actions deliberately, we are each faced with the task of constructing a peculiar, individual kind of identity—personal or practical identity—that the other animals lack. It is this sort of identity that makes sense of our practice of holding people responsible, and of the kinds of personal relationships that depend on that practice.

What distinguishes our identity from that of animals is, in other words, our capacity to act intendedly; our capacity to act intendedly is of course wholly dependent upon our more fundamental capacity to form intentions. And, ultimately, it is these capacities to form intentions and to carry them through that make sense not only of the practice of "holding people responsible," but also of the possibly entirely private mental phenomenon of finding people in different degrees blameworthy for the bad things that they do. What explains why for Korsgaard this identity constitutes our own selfhood and what explains why we never blame agents less sternly for their intended wrongdoing than for their unintended wrongdoing is, in the end, the same thing: the logical connection between intentions, actions, and rationality.

Korsgaard emphasizes the importance of constitutive standards. This is what she has in mind:

> Why shouldn't you build a house that blocks the whole neighborhood's view of the lake? Perhaps because it will displease the neighbors. Now *there* is a consideration that you may set aside, if you are selfish or tough enough to brave the neighbor's displeasure. But because it does not make sense to ask why a house should serve as a shelter, it also does not make sense to ask why the corners should be sealed and the roof should be waterproof and tight. . . . there is no room for doubting that the constitutive standard has normative force.

Simply as a matter of logic, a house *ought* to serve as a shelter. Just as, simply as a matter of logic, intending to do X entails that one *ought* to do X, and, where X is a bad thing, doing X intendedly is never less blameworthy than doing it unintendedly. As I have been careful to admit already in chapter 1, my project is narrow, surely narrower than Korsgaard's, in the sense that I merely wish to discuss one set of factors, among many sets, which affect the way in which we apportion blame to people for the bad things that they do. I am of course willing to accept that someone who does a bad thing X intendedly and who also has a bad character might in the final analysis deserve more blame than someone who does X intendedly but does not have a bad character. But the narrowness of my project allows me to avoid possible objections to my thesis.

Korsgaard's appeal to constitutive *standards* seems to me to be virtually identical to Searle's appeal to constitutive *rules* in order to explain why promising to X gives rise to the claim that one ought to do X. And to that extent she is similarly vulnerable to the charge of triviality, that is, that to focus upon the normativity that follows from constitutive rules is to focus on the normativity of games.

The narrowness of my thesis inoculates it from such a charge of triviality. I have bracketed all sorts of factors that significantly affect the blameworthiness of our actions. The logical structures of Intentional states, in particular those of intentions, do give rise to important normative claims: they form the bases of a theory of culpability. But culpability is but one aspect among many in the final elucidation of the blameworthiness of our actions. I have avoided the thorny discussion of what makes some actions bad in the first place, and I have simply presented an account as to how to deal with one aspect of the rather complex formula that we use to decide on the blameworthiness of actions. And, finally, I have been mostly concerned with the ordinal gradation of blame rather than with the much more complicated project of devising a system that might yield concrete, cardinal gradation of blame. It is in part because of my having avoided the discussions of substantive moral issues that the normative force of the theory of culpability defended here is a good candidate for something like universal appeal. While I believe that the foundations of a theory of culpability are the sets of logical structures of intentions and other Intentional phenomena (and that the normativity that flows from these structures is not at all trivial), I very much doubt that all the phenomena that I have chosen not to discuss here could be resolved by appealing to different sets of constitutive rules without thereby trivializing those other phenomena.

My appeal to Korsgaard's views regarding the role that she believes actions play in constituting our identity serves mostly expository purposes. The correctness of my views regarding Intentionality and blame does not depend on the correctness of her views on action and identity. Accounts, perhaps slightly less ambitious than Korsgaard's, of the role that intentions—and it is intentions in the final analysis—play in constituting some aspects of our selfhood are almost commonplace in the literature. Bratman, for example, states, "very general plans—projects as we might say—structure our lives in a way analogous to the way in which more specific plans for a day structure deliberation and action for that day."[57] Recall, again, that for Bratman plans are "intentions writ large"; it is clear, then, why I claim that for him intentions are crucially important in structuring parts of our selfhood. Or take R. Jay Wallace's line: "actions [intended actions, that is, and ultimately intentions] of morally responsible people are thought to reflect specially on them as agents, opening

---

57. Bratman, *Intention, Plans, and Practical Reason*, 30.

them to a kind of moral appraisal that does more than record a causal connection between them and the consequences of their actions."[58] As Wallace, among others, also discusses, for agents to be the subject of our judgments of praise and blame requires that we see those agents as autonomous beings, with their own conceptions of the good. The role that these agents' actions, and above all their intended actions, play in allowing us to see them in these ways is crucial.

The distinguishing mark of a theory of culpability is that it is concerned with the different condemnations that arise as a consequence of the Intentional states which an agent has when she brings about an evil outcome. The most important mental state that a theory of culpability studies is the intention of the agent. Some reputed philosophers have welcomed, for example, the Model Penal Code's silence regarding the terms "intended action" and "unintended action," arguing that these concepts are just too complicated. Yet, in spite of the fact that the Model Penal Code does avoid the expressions "intended action" and "unintended action," it does not thereby avoid the concepts themselves.

The reasons why intentions figure so prominently in the theory of culpability defended here stem from the essential elements in their logical structure. The sort of skepticism which the thesis that to bring about an evil outcome intendedly is never less blameworthy than to bring it about unintendedly invites is on a par with the sort of skepticism that the claim that the theses that houses ought to serve as shelter, or that in chess, bishops move diagonally invite. But unlike the case of chess, or, in general, cases of games and legal and sociopolitical institutions, the logical structure of intentions is not open to deliberation. The sort of normativity that can be derived from the logical relations between intentions, actions, and rationality is neither trivial nor as easily defeasible as the normativity that arises from the constitutive rules of games and institutions.

The same sorts of logical considerations explain the role that the distinction between being aware or not being aware that one is bringing about a given evil outcome plays in the theory of culpability defended here. For, to continue appealing to the analogy with Korsgaard's views on identity, actions that I *know* I am doing, even if I do not directly intend to do them, speak more meaningfully about my selfhood than actions that I do not intend to do, and that I am not even aware that I am doing. Similarly, when *X* is an evil outcome that we do not intend to bring about, to bring it about knowingly is never less blameworthy than to bring it about unknowingly. Sometimes, although we do not intend to bring about a

---

58. R. Jay Wallace, *Responsibility and the Moral Sentiments* (Cambridge, MA: Harvard University Press, 1996), 52.

given evil outcome, we are practically certain that we will bring it about. Traditionally these sorts of cases have been called oblique, indirect, non-purposive, or conditional intentions. I have argued that they are not intentions at all; intentions are an Intentional state, just as beliefs and desires are Intentional states. What explains why the Intentional states in these cases have been called intentions is that the normative implications of those complex sets of Intentional states are, frequently, extremely similar to the normative implications of bona fide intentions.

Views along the lines that "we *are* what we *do*, what we *choose*, and ultimately what we *intend*" wax poetic, but they are not off the mark. Two important qualifications need to be added to adages of this sort, which will no doubt rob them of much aesthetic value, but which will endow these adages with philosophical accuracy.[59] The doctored adage would read roughly like this: "We are, in part, the sum total of, first and foremost, our intended actions, and to a lesser extent, of some of our unintended actions." The most important way to figure out which of our unintended actions matter in determining who we are, and how much they matter, is to pay attention to the distinction between acting knowingly and acting unknowingly.

---

59. Not only are views of this tenor frequent in the specialized philosophical literature (see the preceding quotations from Wallace, Bratman, and Korsgaard), but they have appeal within popular culture as well. Louis Levy (played by the real-life famous clinical psychologist Martin Bergmann), the wise philosopher who is the protagonist of Cliff Stern's documentary, in Woody Allen's *Crimes and Misdemeanors*, poignantly tells us what, deep down and in the end, is the true meaning of life.

[7]

Intentions and Blame

Most discussions of the normativity of intentions focus on the ways in which intentions interplay with rationality; when someone simultaneously intends to do X and not to do X, she is criticizable on account of her irrationality. We *ought* not intend to X and not to X simultaneously. But, as I have pointed out in the previous chapter, the intimate relationship between intentions and rational constraints gives rise to a different sort of criticism, the criticism encapsulated in the claim that intended wrongdoing is more blameworthy than unintended wrongdoing. A good way of approaching the discussion of the relationship between intentions and normativity is to take a look at Michael Bratman's discussion of the relationship between judgments of agent rationality and judgments of blameworthiness. Bratman begins by noting the similarities between these two types of judgment. "Since in making . . . judgments of agent rationality we are assessing underlying habits and dispositions, these judgments bear a resemblance to judgments of moral praiseworthiness or blameworthiness for some action or intention. This is so because such judgments of praiseworthiness or blameworthiness are also typically based on assessments of the traits that lie behind the action or intention."[1] Immediately, however, Bratman points out "an important difference" between the two types of judgment:

> It is natural to suppose that a person is blameworthy for a failure to live up to some standard only if she at some point had it in her power to change herself so that she would live up to the standard. . . . When we criticize an agent for failing to live up to our standard of agent rationality [in contrast], we need not suppose that she presently has it in her power to change herself so as newly to conform to that standard; nor need we suppose that she ever in the past had it in her power to change herself so as now to live up to the standard.[2]

---

1. Bratman, *Intention, Plans, and Practical Reason*, 51.
2. Bratman, *Intention, Plans, and Practical Reason*, 51–52.

It is in virtue of this difference, Bratman further adds, that "judgments of agent rationality are in this way analogous to legal judgments of strict liability."[3]

It would be a colossal difference between judgments of agent rationality and judgments of blame if judgments of agent rationality were in fact analogous to legal judgments of strict liability, for most certainly judgments of blame, at least those that belong to the theory of culpability defended here, are not at all like judgments of strict liability. Yet, I think that Bratman's analogy between judgments of agent rationality and legal judgments of strict liability faces difficulties. For the fact, if it is a fact, that the principle of alternate possibilities has no purchase within the realm of judgments of agent rationality, does not quite entail that these judgments are like legal judgments of strict liability. After all, agents' deviations of standards of rationality can be more or less pronounced, ranging from the insignificant to the grotesque, and thus we could criticize the grotesque deviations from standards of rationality much more strongly than we would criticize insignificant or minor deviations. When an agent truly *cannot* do otherwise, this fact constitutes a defense even in strict liability offenses (for the so-called voluntary act requirement would not be satisfied in such cases.) So, the fact, if it is a fact, that (normative) judgments of agent rationality are appropriate even when the agent cannot do otherwise should not be explained by analogizing these cases with strict liability offenses.

But there are more differences between judgments of agent rationality and the way in which theories of culpability deal with judgments of blameworthiness. First, theories of culpability focus on rather specific Intentional states, that is, intentions and the cognitive state of being aware of what one is (possibly) doing, whereas, as Bratman points out, judgments of agent rationality can cover all sorts of Intentional states, including "habits and dispositions" and traits of character in general. Second, and closely related, the Intentional states that are of interest to the theory of culpability defended here are internal to the action itself, they do not "lie behind" it; intentions, as I have been arguing, can exist without giving rise to action, but actions seem to be inescapably defined in terms of intentions. Forming intentions and developing character traits can, of course, be evaluated normatively, but culpability, as I understand it, is only concerned with evaluating how intentions affect the blameworthiness of overt actions. Finally, the judgments of blame with which I am interested are importantly different, not only from Bratman's treatment of judgments of agent rationality, but also from the standard treatments of judgments of blame themselves.

---

3. Bratman, *Intention, Plans, and Practical Reason*, 52.

Bratman asserts that the standards of rationality to which we hold agents accountable have the following function: they are "guides for the development of basic habits of thought and action, in our children and in our selves." Thus, Bratman asserts that "the theory of rationality is part of the theory of education."[4] Bratman confesses that to focus on the educational aspect of the impact of judgments of rationality on our educational goals is to take "a broadly pragmatic approach."[5] While I think that Bratman carries out his pragmatic approach in fruitful ways, I think that it is also important to examine these issues from a less pragmatic perspective. We could observe someone else's actions silently, that is, privately, without ever making even the slightest attempt to educate that person, and we could judge that his actions fail to meet some requisite standards of rationality. Bratman's view of the educational role of judgments of agent rationality is reminiscent, of course, of the moral education theory of punishment.[6]

Recall Searle's dictum to which I have referred repeatedly throughout the book (and which I developed further in the previous chapter) according to which the philosophy of mind is more fundamental than the philosophy of language. The importance of this principle, in this context, is that while focusing on the very phenomenon of judging that someone is irrational might be somewhat uninteresting for those overly pragmatic, this focus might allow us to see the phenomenon itself more clearly. But in the case of judgments of blame themselves, the temptation to embrace a pragmatic attitude must be resisted, for it is precisely this sort of pragmatism that contributes to the overwhelmingly common confusion of blame with punishment, as I shall show next.

Blame, Communication, and Punishment

Blaming is something we can do entirely privately, even secretly; to judge that someone should be blamed for what she did is as much an Intentional state as intending to build a squirrel house is an Intentional state, and both sorts of Intentional states can be kept to oneself. Blame is as private as many other mental phenomena; naturally, one may wish to communicate private mental phenomena to others, but, echoing J. E. R. Squires, I think it is clear that "blame is more like holding an

---

4. Bratman, *Intention, Plans, and Practical Reason*, 51.
5. Bratman, *Intention, Plans, and Practical Reason*, 52.
6. See my discussion of this type of justification of punishment, and references in "Punishment, Liberalism, and Communitarianism," *Buffalo Criminal Law Review* 6, no. 1 (2002): 673–90.

opinion than expressing it."[7] Judging that someone deserves blame is one thing; expressing that judgment is another. Moreover, the complex Intentional state of judging that someone deserves blame for his wrongdoing, like the Intentional state of intending, exhibits a complicated relationship with action. Just as intending to *X* typically gives rise to doing *X*, judging that someone is to blame for having done *X* typically gives rise to an action of some sort. But here we find an important difference, for while the actions to which pure intendings typically give rise are quite clearly determined—they are the conditions of satisfaction of those pure intendings—it is not clear what exactly are the actions to which judgments of blame should give rise. It is not even clear if our judgments of blame give rise to our *own* actions, or even to actions at all (a mere happening might be enough). Pure intendings have a very strong tendency to issue in action, in the sense that if they consistently fail to issue in action we believe that either the person having all of these pure intendings is irrational or that these are not intentions after all, but mere desires. The tendency that judgments of blame have to give rise to some sort of action is much weaker. After all, there is nothing irrational or otherwise odd in our judging that this or that person deserves blame for this or that wrongdoing without ever even attempting to do anything about it—we experience this phenomenon on a regular basis.

One standard, but flawed, way in which authors tacitly deal with the tendency of judgments of blame to give rise to some sort of action is to assume that the events to which judgment of blame give rise are instances of punishment, whether it is inflicted by ourselves or by others, or whether the events even are mere happenings or occurrences of so-called divine justice. This facile assumption perhaps explains why there exist so few analyses of the Intentional phenomenon of blaming. But even those rare analyses of blame "in itself," that is, analyses that allegedly discuss the phenomenon of blame independently of the phenomenon of punishment, still do not discuss blame as an Intentional state, but rather blame as a communicative act.[8] This focus on communicative blame is sometimes

7. J. E. R. Squires, "Blame," *Philosophical Quarterly* 18, no. 70 (1968): 56.

8. John Martin Fischer's comprehensive "Recent Work in Moral Responsibility," *Ethics* 110 (1999): 93–139, says precious little about the Intentionality of blaming. Typically, accounts of blame still focus on communicative blame; for example, Elizabeth Beardsley's "Moral Disapproval and Moral Indignation," *Philosophy and Phenomenological Research* 31 (1970): 161–76, and Richard B. Brandt's "A Utilitarian Theory of Excuses," *Philosophical Review* 78 (1969): 337–61, to the extent that they discuss blame, they only discuss the communication of blame. Even Adam Smith, in his *The Theory of Moral Sentiments* (Buffalo, NY: Prometheus, 2000), 94ff.,

expressly stated. For example, while Duff grants that blaming can be a private activity, he still believes that the investigation of this private activity in itself is of limited value for the criminal law. He states:

> My concern . . . is with the proper meaning of moral criticism and blame; more specifically, it is with the activity of criticizing and blaming a person *to her face* for a *past act* of moral wrong-doing. Blame need not involve this activity: it may simply involve forming a private *judgment* on someone's conduct. . . . But to see the connections between moral blame and the criminal process we must attend to the activity of blaming—criticising, rebuking, reproving, condemning—a person to her face for some past action.[9]

Though I do not wish to deny the obvious point that judgments of blame, or for that matter judgments of any type whatsoever, can be communicated, I am more interested in the issues surrounding the structure that these judgment of blame have when they occur in the first place, that is, in the mind, regardless of whether or not this judgment is communicated in any way. And I think that focusing upon private blame can indeed help us to better understand criminal (and other forms of) punishment as well.

Consider Christopher Bennett's interesting, but much more pragmatic, contribution to the discussion of blame.[10] Although he claims to be interested in moral psychology, and one would surmise, in the Intentionality of blame, he actually develops Duff's emphasis on blame as an activity at the expense of blame as an Intentional phenomenon. Early on his article "The Varieties of Retributive Experience," Bennett tells us that he seeks to highlight "the virtues of retributivism" by focusing on "the moral psychology of wrongdoing."[11] Elsewhere he claims that he is interested in "sentiments," and, especially, in "a particular emotional state (albeit one with strong cognitive elements), namely, blame."[12] Moreover, at the outset Bennett also tells us that he will avoid "looking at state punishment"; he will rather look at "our reactions in informal everyday situations" and at "sentiments such as resentment, indignation, remorse, and more fundamentally . . . , blame and guilt."[13]

---

defines blameworthy actions as those that prompt us to punish them. The index of Martha Nussbaum's recent *Upheavals of Thought: The Intelligence of Emotions* (Cambridge: Cambridge University Press, 2001) has an entry for "blame," and it reads: "see punishment, responsibility" (745).

9. R. A. Duff, *Trials and Punishment* (Cambridge: Cambridge University Press, 1986), 40.

10. Christopher Bennett, "The Varieties of Retributive Experience," *Philosophical Quarterly* 52, no. 207 (2002): 145–63.

11. Bennett, "Varieties of Retributive Experience," 146.

12. Bennett, "Varieties of Retributive Experience," 150.

13. Bennett, "Varieties of Retributive Experience," 147.

I welcome Bennett's commendable overture. Bennett, however, does not do justice to it; instead of focusing on the (individual) moral psychology of wrongdoing, Bennett in fact discusses the *social practice* of blaming. While the social practice Bennett describes is in some way related to moral psychology, to present such a description is not to investigate moral psychology. Bennett focuses on a process whereby members of a community blame each other, and communicate this blame with the intention of, sequentially: making wrongdoers suffer, feel guilty, (secularly) repent, and ultimately progress morally. This process, however, renders the practices of blaming and punishing virtually indistinguishable. (It is thus tempting to dub the process "blamishment.") This indistinguishability is evident in the story around which Bennett's article revolves.

The story concerns Bryson and his coworkers. Bryson is bad news. Apart from more serious character and behavioral flaws, Bryson is always late to work. One day, upon arriving to his workplace, late as usual, his coworkers communicate their blame to him, in order to make him feel their disappointment that symbolizes/expresses (Bennett uses these terms interchangeably) his alienation from their community, and which should make Bryson suffer, feel guilty, and so forth. I think that without having to engage in the thorny discussion as to the definition of punishment, it is intuitively clear that Bryson's coworkers are punishing him: they are inflicting unpleasant consequences upon him, from a certain position of authority in which they can condemn his wrongful violation of certain standards of behavior, for something bad (in their eyes) that Bryson did. Thus, to the extent that Bennett focuses on this practice, he is not really discussing blame understood as an Intentional state, but merely its communication in a context in which such communication seems hard to distinguish from punishment.

The value of Bennett's favored strategy of not "looking at state punishment" lies as much in not looking at the *state*, as it does in not looking at *punishment*. Not to "look at" punishment allows us to appreciate the nature of the *individual* psychology of wrongdoing that sometimes culminates in the judgment that someone should be punished. While Bennett's communicative approach does not look at "state punishment," it does not look at the individual moral psychology of wrongdoing either; it looks at a communitarian blame-punishment of sorts (blamishment). In so doing, Bennett offsets the considerable potential that the individual moral psychology of wrongdoing has for shedding light on punishment and its justification.

Blaming and punishing are frequently intimately connected—a certain fit between the severity of punishment inflicted upon wrongdoers and the blameworthiness of their wrongs is an indication of civility and maturity. Blaming and punishing are nonetheless different, and keeping them separate can only contribute to methodological clarity. The shift from punishment to the psychology of blame is recommended by the fact that private, individual blame is theoretically purer than punishment. Whether or not the state punishes depends on political considerations, which are by and large absent in private, individual blaming. Sometimes the state does not punish blameworthy acts because of procedural principles, international law, amnesties, or because of many other pragmatic considerations. Similarly, at the level of individuals, we frequently refuse to punish acts that we find blameworthy, due to a variety of considerations like expediency, strategy, or even laziness. It is unclear whether everyone would, or should, communicate blame in cases such as Bryson's.

Unlike Bennett's communicative blame, blame qua Intentional mental phenomenon is not affected by political principles, or by expediency. We may, consciously or otherwise, sometimes impose barriers on what we allow ourselves to think (should we?), and thus we may refuse to blame, say, those dear to us; but this self-imposed "limitation" is quite different from the political limitations of punishment mentioned above. Aside from self-imposed "limitations," we are free to blame what and as we please.

Bennett claims that sometimes it is not "*our business* to blame a particular wrongdoer."[14] Insofar as "our business" means "our right," and "to blame" refers to "blame as an intentional mental phenomenon," however, it is always our business to blame, just as it is always our business to admire, to regret, and so forth. Of course, we are not free to punish every act we find blameworthy. How and why we privately blame remains, then, while a difficult discussion (as we have seen throughout this book), still a comparatively unpolluted discussion, free from the unavoidable baggage pertaining to the discussion of punishment. It is this comparative purity of the moral psychology of wrongdoing which renders the focus on blaming qua mental phenomenon a promising strategy—a strategy that Bennett claims to adopt, though, sadly, not one he in fact adopts.

Approaches that run together blame with its communication, or blame with punishment, or blame with its communication and with punishment, tend to miss the complexity of the relationship between blame and whatever action blame has a tendency to produce. Bennett, for example, paraphrases John Skorupski's observation to the effect that "fear disposes to flight, anger to attack, grief to mourning," and then concludes that "the same goes for the expression of blame." That is, private blame disposes us to communicate that blame. The behavior that issues from blaming is "withdrawal": "blame or moral condemnation, as an emotional state, issues in behavior that symbolizes the wrongdoer's alienation from the

---

14. Bennett, "Varieties of Retributive Experience," 149.

community."[15] But the relationship between Intentional phenomena and the dispositions to act overtly which they "issue" is a much more complicated affair. As we have seen, not even intentions, which are the Intentional state most closely related to action, *necessarily* issue in action. We can experience anger without being disposed to attack, or experience *paralyzing* fear, and, more pointedly, we frequently blame without being disposed to communicate such blame. Though Bennett does not explain how strongly or frequently mental phenomena dispose us to act overtly in the ways he describes, he insists, in my opinion without sufficient support, that blame, unlike anger, "issues in withdrawal rather than attack."[16]

If blame did not frequently and strongly dispose us to the behavior of expressing-blame-in-order-to-make-wrongdoers-feel-alienated, then Bennett's views would have but a minimal connection to the mental phenomenon of blaming. That is why Bennett sticks to his guns, pronouncing that the behavior to which blame gives rise is "the outward face of . . . blame." This metaphor is as unhelpful as Bennett's verb: "to issue."[17] Though Bennett claims that his point is merely that "insofar as blame is expressed, it issues in the behavior I discuss," and that he insists that "this does not rule out the possibility that blame often remains unspoken,"[18] he still seems to believe that blame always needs to be expressed. For he also suggests that "as with sex, blaming is an activity that superficially appears to consist in one person doing something to another . . . on a deeper understanding, though, they both [sex and blame] involve something that can only properly be done together."[19] Is "unspoken blame" an anomaly, unless "done together"? Blaming can hardly be done together without communicating blame, and blame cannot be both unspoken and communicated. (Bennett's "unspoken blame" simply means "noncommunicative blame," so attempting to defend Bennett by noting the possibility of "nonverbal communicative blame" is a nonstarter.) Quite explicitly, then, Bennett's thesis assumes that blame does give rise to its communication, though he also wishes to salvage the notion of "unspoken blame." Bennett's attempt to "have his cake and eat it too" is, in my opinion, unsuccessful. In fact, neither the long story around which Bennett's article revolves, nor indeed much in his article, sheds significant light on unspoken blame. Bennett is, clearly, overwhelmingly concerned with communicative blame. After all, it is hard to see how "unspoken blame" could be perceived, as sex according to Bennett can, as "someone doing something to another."

---

15. Bennett, "Varieties of Retributive Experience," 151.
16. Bennett, "Varieties of Retributive Experience," 151.
17. Bennett, "Varieties of Retributive Experience," 150 and *passim*.
18. Bennett, "Varieties of Retributive Experience," 152–53.
19. Bennett, "Varieties of Retributive Experience," 153.

Aside from Bennett's problematic handling of the complicated relationship between Intentional states and their tendencies to result in action, in particular regarding the problems pertaining to the relationship between blame and what he calls its "outward face," Bennett's account of communicative blame faces a deeper difficulty. After sketching the nature of communicative blame (making wrongdoers suffer, etc.), Bennett admits: "this sounds slightly too deliberate," and adds: the communication of blame "is not strictly to be understood as an action in which we engage in order to bring about some further effect; rather we engage in it because of our emotional state [of blaming]."[20] But Bennett also claims, however, that "it would be wrong to understand the expression of the emotion of blame as a mere release of pent-up emotion, such as might be taken out on a punch-bag."[21]

The expression of blame involves a "withdrawal which the wrongdoer is very much *intended to recognize*."[22] "The behavior which expresses blame," Bennett continues, "is, after all, an attempt to bring something about, namely, that the offender should recognize that we disapprove of him . . . blame aims at some result."[23] Bennett's thesis, then, is that the communication of blame is not "strictly" done in order to bring something about, though it is "after all" done in order to bring something about. Bennett's claim that "in a complex way, then, blaming behavior is both expressive and purposive" (152) does not wash difficulties away. Clearly, phenomena can be simultaneously expressive and purposive; what they cannot be is simultaneously purposive and nonpurposive. The "complexity" of Bennett's communicative blame remains obscure.

To focus on communicative blame strikes me as a new rendition of the view that Hart attributes to Bentham and Austin, and which he famously called "the economy of threats." This view combines utilitarianism and positivism in such a way that the analysis of blame as an Intentional mental phenomenon is only valuable insofar as such an analysis contributes to alleviate the evils of state punishment. Roughly, the view holds that the value of the analysis of the Intentional states of wrongdoers is simply to ensure that "the threat to punishment announced by the criminal law" would contribute to "the maintenance of law at the least cost in pain."[24] This view, in different ways, continues to be extremely influential, and not only through the vast influence that Bentham and Austin have had.[25] Duff and Bennett

---

20. Bennett, "Varieties of Retributive Experience," 150.
21. Bennett, "Varieties of Retributive Experience," 151.
22. Bennett, "Varieties of Retributive Experience," 152.
23. Bennett, "Varieties of Retributive Experience," 152, 153.
24. Hart, *Punishment and Responsibility*, 40.
25. R. Jay Wallace, in his *Responsibility and the Moral Sentiments*, provides references to many philosophers who embrace versions of the economy of threats thesis (54–55, n. 7).

seem to tacitly accept something like the economy of threats approach—though they do not admit it. After all, we care about the Intentional states of those who do things we consider wrong, even when those things are not punishable by the criminal law, or even punishable at all. But more importantly, I have argued that there exists nontrivial normativity in the very logical structures of intentions; this normativity exists independently of any considerations as to the effects that discussing it might have in regards to the criminal law or any other human endeavor.

The exact nature of blame, understood as the Intentional phenomenon of blaming someone for her wrongdoing, is complicated enough, as I shall show in the next section. But to confuse or to amalgamate the Intentional phenomenon of blame with its communication and/or with punitive practices, as defenders of the economy of threats approach do, further complicates matters (in my opinion unnecessarily). Once actions, that is, the action of communicating blame or the action of punishing, enter the analysis, then the questions "Why do you tell her (or others) that you blame her for what she did?" or "Why do you punish her for what she did?" become relevant. In contrast, the question "Why do you blame her for what she did?" when blame is understood as a private Intentional phenomenon, calls for an answer of an entirely different sort. It is in part because Bennett (and those influenced by the economy of threats approach) unwittingly conflates these sorts of questions that he has (and others have) difficulties in explaining whether blaming is done for a purpose or not.

In what follows I shall present an analysis of blame understood as a private Intentional phenomenon, a phenomenon constituted by cognitive and emotional elements.

The Cognitive Dimension of Blame

A tradition of sorts exists in philosophical circles of following ordinary language in claiming that there are two general types of blame: moral and nonmoral. Lionel Kenner begins his *On Blaming* in the following way: "The first point that I wish to make is that we blame inanimate objects, just as we blame people. We may blame the weather for our ill health, the car's brakes, or the road surface for the accident."[26] As should by now be obvious, I am not interested in this sense of blame; I am only concerned with blaming people, and even more specifically, with blaming people for their wrongdoing.

---

26. Lionel Kenner, "On Blaming," *Mind* 76: 238–49, at 239. Richard B. Brandt, in a similar move, for example, divides blame into moral and nonmoral. See, e.g., his "Blameworthiness and Obligation," in *Essays in Moral Philosophy*, ed. A. I. Melden (Seattle: University of Washington Press, 1958).

Bernard Williams refers to the type of blame with which I am interested as a "'focussed' application of blame" and he opposes it to the purely "diagnostic" sense of blame, whereby the storm is to blame for the damage to the roof.[27] I would like to refer to the sort of blame in which I am interested as moral blame, and to diagnostic blame as nonmoral blame, but not without repeating a point already made in chapter 1, when I first discussed Williams's distinction between these two types of blame. Williams's "focussed" blame can obtain in nonmoral cases, such as the case of a bank robber blaming her idiotic partner for having botched the robbery. While robbing banks is itself immoral, there is a sense in which the bank robber's judgment of blame is not merely diagnostic. She does not simply say "my partner is the cause of our having been caught" in anything like the sense in which "the storm is the cause of the damage to the roof." The first type of statement has strong normative implications, whereas the second is mostly, if not exclusively, descriptive.

By blaming her fellow bank robber, moreover, she assumes that her partner did something wrong. This sense of wrong is slippery in that it is not necessarily a violation of moral norms. The blaming robber might even accept that robbing banks is in general a bad thing, but still blame her partner's failure to carry out their plan. She could reason along the following lines: "I know robbing banks is morally wrong, but we had agreed that we were going ahead with our robbery, that is, we had discounted the general moral injunction against robbing banks and we had concluded that in this case we were justified in robbing the bank." In this context, the idiotic robber was negligent, and for that she deserves blame. Had the idiotic robber actually intended to frustrate the robbery (say, because she underwent a sobering epiphany of moral lucidity as she pointed her gun at the bank manager), her partner should blame her, in principle (and assuming that the blaming robber does not undergo such moral conversion), more sternly, for, in her view, her partner now has *betrayed* her, has done "wrong" intendedly.

I am now dealing with private blame; the blaming robber need not in any way communicate her blame to her idiotic partner. The question I am interested in answering is the following: What are the Intentional states of the blaming robber when she blames her idiotic partner? To answer this question requires presenting a general analysis of the Intentional state of blaming someone else for her wrongdoing. This is the way I wish to go about presenting such analysis. The Intentional state of blaming someone for her wrongdoing involves several Intentional states, which I will present in increasing order of contentiousness. First, blaming contains several

---

27. Williams, *Making Sense of Humanity*, 35–45.

beliefs (in the broad sense of belief explained in the previous chapter). If A blames B for having done *X*, then

(1) A believes that *X* is a bad thing.
(2) A believes that *X* is an action of B.
(3) A believes that B is a moral agent.
(4) A believes that there are no excuses, justifications, or other circumstances that preclude blame.

That the blaming agent must have these beliefs is, I hope, unproblematic. Whether or not the blaming agent is conscious of having these beliefs is somewhat irrelevant; for if she is not conscious of having some of these, upon being asked to introspect, she would have to admit that she had them. Consider (1); as a matter of definition, in order to blame someone for something she did, one must consider that whatever is the source of blame is bad. This sense of "bad" is peculiar along the lines just sketched, but the blaming agent cannot help believing that the thing which gives rise to blame is bad. "I blame you for the great thing you have done" belongs to the world of Monty Python. Now (2) is similarly straightforward, as it also follows definitionally or quasi-definitionally from the very description of the Intentional state of blaming. If I blame you for what you did, then *a fortiori* what you did is your doing, it is your action.

Beliefs (3) and (4) are somewhat more complicated. They make reference to some of the issues which I have carefully avoided throughout the book: When is someone a moral agent?; when are we justified or excused in doing what we do?; and so on. The main principle of the theory of culpability defended here, that intended wrongdoing is never less blameworthy than unintended wrongdoing requires, quite obviously, a ceteris paribus clause. Unintended but inexcusable wrongdoing could be more blameworthy than intended but excusable wrongdoing. But, assuming that there exist two hypothetical cases in which the only difference is the presence or the absence of an intention to do the bad deed, the principle holds. Within the context of the discussion of blame, to keep things simple, I am stipulating (3) that the blamed person is a moral agent, that is, that she is responsible. As we saw in chapter 1, responsibility is a precondition of culpability, and to be responsible means to be a moral agent, namely, to be a candidate for blame. I also stipulate (4) that blame is not precluded by the presence of any excuse, justification or other type of defense. Although the blaming agent might believe that some excuses or other defenses obtain, they would not *completely* preclude blame; in the final analysis, the bad thing that the moral agent did is blameworthy. Again, to say "I blame you for what you did, though you are not really blameworthy" is absurd.

In addition to these beliefs, when A blames B for X, she will have the following Intentional states.

(5) A believes that the world would have been a better place had B not done X.
(6) A believes that the world would be a better place if something would happen to B, something that would somehow offset B's Xing.

These two Intentional states are more complicated than the first four beliefs listed earlier. It might actually look as if (5) follows straightforwardly from those four beliefs, for if someone would have the four beliefs listed earlier, not having the belief listed in (5) would be irrational. To believe that a responsible agent did something bad without excuse or justification somehow entails, other things being equal, that one believes that it would have been preferable if she had not done it. The locution "one believes that it would have been/would be preferable" can be translated into "one prefers" and, in turn "one prefers" can, in the very broad sense of "desire" that I explained in the previous chapter, be translated into "one desires," Thus one might formulate (5) and (6) as desires, along these lines.

(Conative 5) A desires that B had not done X.
(Conative 6) A desires that something happens to B by way of offsetting B's X'ing.

I am not strongly opposed to this rendering of my own versions of (5) and (6), but I still prefer to express them as I did originally, in terms of beliefs. I think that while desires are not as closely linked to action as are intentions, nonetheless they have a sort of connection to action that beliefs need not have. For example, while I might believe that the world would be a better place if we could all live 200 years, I have no desire to live 200 years. In many cases of course, these two renderings coexist and might even be quasi-synonyms: I believe that the world would have been better had the Nazis never seized power, and I desire that they had not seized power. But I believe that the relationship between believing that the world would be better if X and desiring X does not amount to a full-blown bi-conditional.

Beliefs have a way of being in the background that is not quite equally amenable to desires (though Freudians might perhaps disagree).[28] We

---

28. See, e.g., Searle, *Intentionality*, 141–59.

hold innumerable beliefs of which we are not typically conscious; we can, sometimes, recall them "at will": I have just remembered that my fifth-grade teacher was called Marta; no matter how hard I try, however, I cannot remember the name of my fourth-grade teacher—though it might "come back" to me. I believe that "my fifth-grade teacher's name was Marta," and I was not conscious of this belief until a few minutes ago, when I *looked for* an example of a belief of which I was not at the time conscious; moreover, this belief will recede into unconsciousness soon, I imagine. Like this one, there are many beliefs which are in the background of our mind, some of which might eventually move into consciousness just to subsequently recede into the background again. Desires, again contra Freudians, are not typically like this. I still have not recalled the name of my fourth-grade teacher, but I think that if try hard I might remember it (I have no idea what exactly this "trying" entails, but we have all succeeded in trying to remember things). What would the equivalent phenomenon for desires? I am not sure that there exists an equivalent phenomenon. After all, remembering that at some point one had a desire is not to thereby have that desire all over again. I now remember that as a young kid, I had a desire to be a professional table tennis player; I do not thereby now desire to be a professional table tennis player. But, in general, since I am trying to disassociate blame as an Intentional mental phenomenon from whatever actions this phenomenon might give rise to, I prefer to render these two elements in terms of beliefs than in terms of desires.

The belief contained in (5) is deceivingly simple. Consider the following example: Susan, for reasons that are not important here, hates her colleague Bob, and believes that it would be a great world if bad things happened to him; it would be great, for instance, if Bob were to be fired. One day Bob is caught plagiarizing material to use in his own book, and for this he is fired. Susan believes (1) that plagiarism is a bad thing, that Bob engaged in plagiarism, that (2) this was an action of his, that (3) he is a moral agent and that (4) he had no excuse or justification or any other defense available. Does she really need to believe that the world would have been better had Bob not plagiarized? It seems that she cannot believe that it would have been better had he not plagiarized, since she believes it would be great for him to be fired, and it is in virtue of his plagiarism that he is now fired.

Perhaps one could explain the apparent conflict in Susan's desires by noting that desires are not subject to very strong rational constraints; one could, without being irrational, hold diverse desires that conflict with each another. I could, for example, wish to finish writing an article over the weekend, and simultaneously wish to go on a leisure trip over the weekend (to repeat one conclusion from the previous chapter: to *intend* both courses of action is much more problematic). While this sort of answer might be correct as far as it goes, it does not go too far. There is something interesting in Susan's conflicting desires that should not simply be put aside by claiming that our desires can be in conflict without rendering us irrational.

Another way of explaining the conflict between Susan's desires is to insist on the peculiar sense of "bad" used in (1). Just as the bank robber can blame her idiotic partner for botching the robbery, even if she considers robbing banks, *in general,* a bad thing, Susan can, while believing that plagiarism is, *in general,* a bad thing, believe that this particular instance of Bob's plagiarizing is not bad. If Susan does not think that what Bob did is a bad thing then she does not blame him and thus she does not really wish he had not done what he did. But it seems that this is too facile a solution to the problem.

Imagine now that, rather than caught plagiarizing, Bob would have been caught raping another colleague. Only callous wickedness would explain Susan being happy that Bob had raped. No matter how intensely she might have wished to see Bob fired, and even if she is somehow happy that Bob *was caught*, she would have preferred that Bob did not actually *rape* anyone. Susan now believes that the world would be better if Bob were fired and that the world would be better if he would not have done that thing which got him fired—but this does not quite show that her two beliefs are exactly contradictory after all. She believes it is fine that he is fired, but still believes that it would have been better that he had not done such a bad thing.

G. E. Moore's discussion of organic wholes looms in the background of this issue.[29] Susan might believe that the whole Bob-is-caught-plagiarizing-and-is-thereby-fired is preferable to the whole Bob-plagiarizes-and-nothing-bad-happens-to-him, and even to the whole Bob-does-nothing-wrong-and-nothing-bad-happens-to-him; but she probably does not believe that the whole "Bob-is-caught-raping-and-is-thereby-fired" is preferable to the whole "Bob-does-not-rape-and-does-not-get-fired." And, of course, Susan could regret that any part of a whole took place, without rejecting the whole; she might resent the fact that a bad thing, that is, an instance of plagiarism, happened, but still believe that all in all, insofar as this bad thing brought about Bob's dismissal (a great thing), the whole is a good thing.

Consider the following case. Tom is driving recklessly. You have warned him about his driving repeatedly, but your warnings just make him more reckless. He crosses an intersection at such a speed that he cannot avoid

---

29. See, e.g., G. E. Moore, *Principia Ethica* (Cambridge: Cambridge University Press, 1992), 28ff.

running over a pedestrian, who instantly dies. It turns out that the pedestrian was Dr. Evil, the world's greatest malefactor. While you might not believe that the world would be better had Dr. Evil remained alive, you still believe that the world would be better had Tom not acted as he did. While you do not regret that Dr. Evil is dead, you resent that Tom killed him in the way he did. (Cases like these do not constitute an objection to central thesis of the theory of culpability defended here. Had Tom intended to kill Dr. Evil, you might actually praise him, but this does not show that it is false that intended wrongdoing is never less blameworthy than unintended wrongdoing. After all, intendedly (or even knowingly) killing Dr. Evil, the world's greatest malefactor is, *ex hypothesi*, not an instance of wrongdoing, but recklessly killing a pedestrian who happens to be the world's greatest malefactor is an instance of wrongdoing.) Similarly, Susan can both regret that Bob plagiarized but still not regret that he is being fired. I shall come back to the important distinction between regret and resentment below, when I discuss the emotions associated with blame, though I will first say a word about (6).

The connection between (5) and (6) is not as clear as the connection between (1) through (4), on the one hand, and (5) on the other. Let us assume that on a given occasion someone believes all the beliefs contained in (1) through (5), why should you believe that something should now happen to the wrongdoer? And what, in any case, is this mysterious "offsetting"? My answer to the first question is to suggest that the question is actually formulated in the wrong way; the obvious question should be: Why should you *not* believe that it would be a good thing if something happened to the wrongdoer such that the wrong is offset? To *believe* that wrongdoers deserve, in principle, to suffer the consequences of their wrongdoing, not necessarily to do anything about it, seems to me the most psychologically intuitive position to have. Of course, it might be that the way to "offset" the wrong thing that B did, that is, in order to try to make the world be as nice as it was before B did his bad thing, has nothing to do with doing anything to B himself at all. But, given that we cannot simply go back in time, to believe that B should somehow pay, somehow suffer, for what he did, strikes me as the most plausible strategy for offsetting his wrongdoing.

I think few would like to accept that this is a good strategy. Part of the fear of admitting this fact, it seems to me, follows from conflating blame with its communication and with punishment. Many would fear that by accepting that the prima facie intuitively appealing belief that wrongdoers deserve that something bad ("something bad" is purposely meant in loose sense) should happen to them, is to buy wholesale all sorts of allegedly vindictive and problematic theses as to the justification of punishment. In particular, the fear is that accepting that to believe that wrongdoers deserve to somehow "pay" for their wrongdoing is a constitutive element of blame, is to embrace retributivism.

Retributivism is the theoretical alternative to a cluster of numerous and popular justifications of punishment grouped together under the rubric of "consequentialist." Consequentialist justifications of punishment are fundamentally teleological, forward-looking; their goal could be rehabilitation, repentance, incapacitation, deterrence, or combinations of these. In contrast, retributivism is a fundamentally deontological, backward-looking justification of punishment. Admittedly, there are many forms of retributivism (strong, weak, positive, negative, etc.),[30] but Michael Moore's succinct remark captures well its essence, present in all its variants: "Retributivism is a very straightforward theory of punishment; we are justified in punishing because and only because offenders deserve it."[31] R. A. Duff, who embraces a form of "communicative retributivism" radically different from Moore's, nevertheless, like Moore, holds that retributivism's "central slogan is that punishment can be justified only as being deserved."[32]

While I will have something to say about retributivism below, I cannot present a full-blown account of it here.[33] And while I do not think that retributivism is as uncivilized or problematic as it is frequently assumed to be, I would here just like to say that accepting my account of blame does not *entail* a commitment to retributivism at all. It does, I hope, and as I will argue in the last section of the chapter, present a prima facie case for retributivism's plausibility. Just as intended wrongdoing is, ceteris paribus, no less blameworthy than unintended wrongdoing, blameworthy wrongdoing that is punished, ceteris paribus, constitutes a better situation than one in which blameworthy wrongdoing is not punished. I have been at pains to insist that from the fact that one believes this or that about this or that instance of wrongdoing, nothing *necessarily* follows in the realm of action. Indeed, while it is probably a wise policy not to impose upon ourselves any predetermined limits as to what we allow ourselves to *think*—no thought should be forbidden—the same policy in the realm of action is absurd.

---

30. For a comprehensive account of the varieties of retributivism see, e.g., R. A. Duff, *Punishment, Communication, and Community* (Oxford: Oxford University Press, 2001), 1–34.
31. Michael Moore, *Placing Blame*, 91. In addition to Duff's taxonomy of retributivism, Moore presents another valuable one in *Placing Blame*, 83–103. I gloss over whether desert provides merely a necessary condition (negative retributivism) or both a necessary and a sufficient condition for punishment (positive retributivism). I need only note that retributivists of all stripes agree that desert is the crucial rationale for the justification of punishment.
32. R. A. Duff, *Punishment, Communication, and Community*, 3.
33. But see my *Punishment and Retribution* (Aldershot: Ashgate, forthcoming 2005).

In any event, I would like to present two main arguments that seek to show that something along the lines of the belief contained in (6) does in a way flow from accepting (1) through (5).

First, I think it is valuable to look at cases of praise, rather than at cases of blame; cases involving good deeds seem not to present as many difficulties. Imagine that Ruth did something absolutely great, say, after years of efforts, she single-handedly found a cure for AIDS. If we were to tinker with the beliefs contained in (1) through (5) regarding blame and adapt them to relate to the phenomenon of esteem understood as an Intentional mental state ("praise" might seem too difficult to separate from actually communicating the praise and I wish to refer to the counterpart of private blame), we will get something along the following lines. You believe that what Ruth did is a good thing, you believe that what Ruth did is an action of hers, you believe that Ruth is a moral agent, you believe that there are no reasons that take any of the merit from this deed away from Ruth, and you believe that the world is a better place because of what she did. Would you not too believe that something good should happen to Ruth? I think you would. And I think that, formally, esteeming and blaming, understood as private Intentional phenomena, are quite similar.

The second argument is a development of Williams's insightful, though regrettably brief, discussion of the relationship between the logic of blame and the logic of advice. Williams tells us "if 'ought to have' is appropriate afterwards [after the wrongdoing has occurred] in the modality of blame, then (roughly) 'ought to' was appropriate at the time [before the agent does the bad deed] in the modality of advice."[34] Of course, first and foremost, Williams's move emphasizes the connection between blame and rationality. But it also relates to the discussion of the belief contained in (6). Why would you advise someone not to do *X*? Presumably, because you believe that doing *X* is a bad thing to do. What if the person ignores your advice (or never heard it)? You would believe that the world is worse off because of what the person did. Since, you know that you cannot turn back time, you now wish that something would happen in the world in order to bring it back to the state in which it was before the person acted. Again, I think that you would probably believe that this "happening" would be connected to the person who did the bad thing.

Now, on many occasions wrongdoing brings with it its own sort of offsetting consequences. Your friend Mike confides in you about his plan to invest some money in an extraordinarily risky (and immoral) scheme; you advise strongly against it. Mike goes ahead and invests the money, and alas, his money is embezzled; he loses his life-savings. Here you might believe

---

34. Williams, "Internal Reasons and the Obscurity of Blame," in *Making Sense of Humanity*, 40.

that having lost his money is offsetting enough, or even too much. Imagine now your friend John, who tells you that he is so interested in getting a good grade on a term paper that he is going to plagiarize it; you advise strongly against it. John goes ahead and plagiarizes, and he gets caught, which causes him to be expelled from the university. You might think that what has befallen John is offsetting enough (or even that it is excessive). Now, compare what would happen if you change each of these examples in such a way that nothing bad happens to Mike or to John: John makes tons of money, John fooled everyone in his university, and graduated with highest honors. I think that although you believe that Mike's investment strategy is ridiculously risky, you would not believe that the world would become a better place if Mike were to lose his money. If Mike were to ask you about whether you stand by your initial advice in spite of the fact that he is making so much money, you would say that you do, that you still think that this is a risky scheme, but that you are happy for him. You might, to be sure, mildly lament that he got away doing the wrong thing, just like you might be mildly sad about sports teams which "win ugly," even though, if you like the team, your happiness for its victory overshadows the mild disappointment we feel given the way in which the victory was attained. I am not arguing that one *should* be somewhat sad when teams win uglily, just that if we analyze the meaning of winning uglily it includes a preference that the victory would have been different. Sometimes we care so much about the victory that we really do not care much about its ugliness, but it would, by definition, be true that had the victory been beautiful, we would have enjoyed it much more. In many ways, this overlap between the enjoyment of the team's victory and the very mild sadness produced by the way in which the team won is reminiscent of the example I presented above of playing squash. If, on match point, I intend to place the ball in a certain corner, but I accidentally hit the ball with the rim of the racket sending to a different place, but winning anyhow, the desire to win the game overshadows the fact that my intention was not fulfilled.

But if John gets away with his plagiarism, you would think that the world is a worse place because wrongdoing of this sort has not been offset (change the example to John raping or killing someone, rather than merely plagiarizing, if necessary). Some instances of wrongdoing are such that they do justify having the belief contained in (6), and in some cases this belief is not easy to ignore. Indeed, some instances of wrongdoing do give rise to a distinctly *emotional* response. The sight of someone who we believe is an extremely bad person, who constantly does bad things, for which he feels no remorse, and in no way suffers any bad consequence, can make us quite sick. This "feeling sick" need not be a bad thing. Feeling sick about sickening things is almost uninterestingly appropriate.

The Emotional Dimension of Blame

The emotional aspect of blame is rather complex. In principle, if A holds the beliefs contained in (1) through (6), then A feels, almost by definition, a certain sense of regret that X took place; A feels sad that B did X. But I do not think that this is the most characteristic emotion associated to the phenomenon of blaming; one could experience a similar sense of sadness about things which are not the result of human actions. Rather, the most important emotion of blame is a singular feeling of indignation or resentment or outrage (I shall use these terms interchangeably) directed at the agent who, one believes, has done something bad. So, in addition to the beliefs listed in the previous section, blaming someone for her wrongdoing involves also an attitudinal Intentional state, something along the following lines:

> (7) B's having X'ed tends to make A *feel* something negative, that is, a reactive emotion, like outrage, indignation, or resentment.

This is perhaps the most complicated of all the Intentional states that are central to the analysis of blame. For it is not at all clear which exact feeling one feels when one blames, or what the exact role of this feeling might be. A preliminary word of warning regarding the way I approach this component of blaming: just as intention and desires sometimes overlap, the essential emotion of blame typically overlaps with other emotions, rendering the emotion particularly associated with blame at times difficult to distinguish from those other emotions with which it might overlap.

Recall Williams's blaming robber and idiotic robber, again. Let us assume that they succeed in robbing the bank, but suppose that idiotic robber, as they safely drive away in their escape vehicle, begins to negligently jump up and down inside the car in excitement, and as a result bumps into blaming robber, bruising her slightly. From blaming robber's perspective, her having been bruised by her partner satisfies conditions (1) through (6) and yet it is possible that blaming robber would not really feel any substantial emotion like indignation or resentment toward idiotic robber—something more akin to exasperation, or even to pity, perhaps—though, she might believe that her partner is to blame for jumping up and down like that.

The crucial element in the explanation as to how it is possible for blaming robber not to feel any significant amount of indignation or resentment in this case is *not* that the harm is slight. It is, rather, that the Intentional states of idiotic robber as she bruised her are, at most, constitutive of negligence, and negligence is, short of accidentally bringing about an evil outcome, the least blameworthy way of doing things. In principle, very low degrees of blame are accompanied by very tenuous feelings of indignation or resentment. Imagine that idiotic robber's negligent jumping up and down inside the vehicle actually causes the trunk to open, thus allowing the booty to be lost. I would like to argue that even in this case the feelings of indignation and resentment might still be more tenuous than it might initially appear. For blaming robber knows, as in the previous case, that idiotic robber was merely negligent. Of course, now the harm is, from their perspective, significant, and, *for that harm*, blaming robber might feel quite intense *regret*, sadness, and other emotions of the sort; but she would not feel particularly intense *resentment* or *indignation* towards her partner.

Indignation can be quite tenuous even in cases of grave moral harm. We would not resent too much a negligent agent who causes the death of many innocent children—he was, after all, negligent, even if we would feel great sorrow, deep regret, and like emotions, due to the deaths of the innocent children. What constitutes "a wrong" in the first place is a discussion that I have expressly avoided here, and while very serious wrongs might give rise to strong feelings of regret, they do not necessarily give rise to strong feelings of outrage, resentment, or indignation. While the *event* of the death of the innocent children justifiably gives rise to very deep feelings of sorrow, the negligent *action* of killing the children does not provoke similar feelings of indignation. The negligent killing of an innocent human being, as an action, produces, in principle, less intense feelings toward the agent, than the cruelly intended humiliation of a colleague at a social gathering. I am by no means suggesting that the preservation of human life is less important than the prevention of humiliations in social contexts: the death of an innocent human being, qua an *event*, calls for much more regret than the humiliation of a human being, but the *action* of unintendedly killing a human being, qua *action*, is not particularly abhorrent.

The distinction between the set of emotions exemplified in *regretting* (or lamenting, etc.) and the set of emotions exemplified by *resenting* (or feeling indignation, outrage, etc.), is fundamentally the following. The sorts of emotions that accompany blame, namely, indignation, resentment, outrage, and so forth, are *directed to the agent for what she did*; when one blames someone for her wrongdoing, one is outraged that she behaved as she did. Frequently, one also experiences other emotions, that is, sadness, regret, sorrow, about what happened. But the two sets of emotions are different, and they are caused by different phenomena. Only in a sense of resentment quite different from the one I use here can we resent the storm for killing someone; whereas we can easily resent Susan for murdering John. The set of emotions containing regret is related to the death of the person somehow taken in isolation; the set of emotions containing indignation and outrage are caused by the assassination of the person.

Imagine the following case. Linda accidentally kills your dearest friend; he had fallen asleep in Linda's driveway, and she ran her over as she came from work. While you would feel great sorrow for losing your friend, you would not at all feel resentment toward Linda, since, *ex hypothesi*, she killed your friend accidentally, which means that she is blameless. Your friend's death, sad as it is, does not call for indignation or outrage. Emotions like resentment, indignation, and outrage are directed towards an agent. (The agent need not be an individual human being: we are outraged by the policies—the actions—of an entity such as Nazi Germany; had an earthquake, for example, killed the same 12 million innocent people who died at the hands of Nazi criminals, we would be extremely sad, but not *outraged* by the tragedy, unless, of course, in theistic fashion, we resented God for allowing the earthquake.) But, insofar as these emotions are directly linked to the agent, and to the way in which she *acted*, and since there are *ways of acting* (modes of culpability) that are not terribly blameworthy, the emotions that accompany blame need not be terribly intense. The intensity of the emotions associated with blaming tracks the degree of blameworthiness of actions.

Still, I wish to stress the difference between the claim that the emotions constitutive of blame track the blameworthiness of the way in which an agent acted, on the one hand, and the claim that feeling certain emotions and blaming are the same thing, on the other. To be sure, blaming and feeling outrage toward someone for what she did are closely related. Nonetheless, blaming is a more complex phenomenon than merely feeling outrage; while outrage is associated with an agent for his wrongdoing, it need not in every case be accompanied by all the Intentional phenomena contained in (1) through (6) above. In particular, the beliefs contained in (5) and (6), but also that contained in (4), could be absent in cases where one simply *feels* outrage.

The distinction between the sort of agent-centered emotion I am claiming is essential to blame and other less specific emotions is not new. Descartes, for example, clearly distinguished between regret, which he understood generally as "a sort of sadness," from resentment or indignation, which is always connected to wrong*doing*. Feeling resentment or indignation toward someone else for what he has done is similar to feeling remorse or repentance towards oneself. One cannot really feel remorse or repentance except in connection to something one has *done*. I might be sad because I am not able to run fast, though I do not feel any resentment or indignation for this (I believe, rightly or wrongly, that I simply do not possess the sort of body necessary to be a fast runner).

I think, moreover, that some form of the distinction between emotions like regret, which are not directed at an agent, and emotions like resentment, which are directed at an agent, is part and parcel of our folk psychology. A couple of years ago, I watched a news broadcast reporting an assassination carried out by *Euskadi ta Askatasuna* (or ETA, the independentist Basque terrorist group). The report included footage of the press conference by officials of the local Basque government; at some point, one of the officials said something along the lines of "The government of *El Pais Vasco* regrets the death of so and so," at which time he was violently interrupted by an enraptured crowd who yelled, in the midst of all sorts expletives: "You should not merely *regret* [that he is dead], you should *resent* [*ETA* for assassinating him]!"[35] The crowd, surely not consisting of philosophers, objected, quite naturally, to the mere regretting of an *event* without condemning, without resenting, the agent who heinously, *intendedly*, assassinated an innocent person.

The key factor affecting the intensity of the feeling of resentment is the gradational nature of the judgments of blame that form the theory of culpability discussed throughout this book. Intended wrongdoing, in standard cases, gives rise to sterner judgments of blame than unintended wrongdoing does (although in some cases, like the grenade juggler discussed in chapter 1, the judgments of blame remain the same in spite of different Intentional states). While it is important to point out that the intensity of the feelings of indignation associated with blame tracks the blameworthiness of the action itself (and not the harm it produces), this is just the first step in accounting for the complicated relationship between judgments of blame and the feelings of indignation that accompany them. Wallace presents the following example: "you may believe that an especially charming colleague who has cheated and lied to you has done something morally wrong, insofar as he has violated a moral obligation not to cheat or lie for personal advantage, and yet you may have trouble working up any resentment or indignation about his case."[36] Can you really blame your colleague without feeling any resentment or indignation toward him? Wallace, in spite of the fact that he is interested in emphasizing the role that emotions play in blaming, answers this question affirmatively. Given what I have said in the previous paragraphs, it might be a foregone conclusion that I agree with Wallace in answering this question affirmatively. Yet, my reasons for a qualified, proto-affirmative answer to this question are different from Wallace's, and these differences are helpful in highlighting some strengths of my account of the emotional aspect of blame.

Wallace answers this question affirmatively because his account of blame does not actually require that the blaming agent feel any emotion as

---

35. I am, in this context, translating the Spanish *lamentar* as "to regret" and the Spanish *condenar* as "to condemn" or "to resent," to the extent in which these terms capture the essential emotional element of blaming.
36. Wallace, *Responsibility and the Moral Sentiments*, 76.

she blames someone else for his wrongdoing. It merely requires that the agent believes that having such an emotion would be appropriate. In his own words: "an emotional response of this sort [indignation, resentment] is not necessarily required for you to hold your colleague morally blame-worthy . . . it suffices for you to believe that indignation or resentment would be fitting responses on your part, and that they would be fitting because the colleague has done something morally wrong."[37] Surprisingly, then, it turns out that although Wallace claims that "blame is construed essentially in terms of emotions,"[38] the emotions essentially connected to blame need not be experienced at all by blaming agents. For Wallace it would be enough if the emotions are part of the propositional content of some belief(s) of the agent. You might have trouble feeling indignation or resentment towards your colleague, but as long as you admit that having those emotions would be appropriate, then you could be said to be blam-ing him. If I were to follow Wallace's lead, I would have to reformulate (7) along the following lines:

(Wallace's 7) A believes that B having done X justifies feeling resentment or indignation.

While this is not an entirely unacceptable formulation of what goes on when we blame (and while it is not inconsistent with my analysis of blame), I wish to resist this modification of my initial formulation of (7). For I believe that this sort of move renders the connection between blame and its requisite emotions far too weak. Like Wallace, I believe that the emo-tions associated with blaming are not "arbitrary feelings of disapprobation and dislike."[39] Also like Wallace, I would like to disassociate myself from noncognitivist views of emotions and in general from theses that distin-guish too sharply between reason and the emotions. But then, if emotions are connected with beliefs about morality that have full propositional con-tent, it is puzzling that Wallace would so facilely concede that there are times in which we blame someone without feeling any indignation or resentment toward her.

After all, as Wallace has it, whenever we blame someone without feel-ing any of the appropriate emotions toward her (resentment, indignation, etc.), we nonetheless believe that it would be appropriate to feel such absent emotions. But if he admits that it would be appropriate to feel the emotion, it is tempting to suggest that it is inappropriate not to feel it. The sense of "appropriate" operative in Wallace's writings cannot be as tenuous as that in statements like "It is appropriate to wear a tie while teaching,"

---

37. Wallace, *Responsibility and the Moral Sentiments*, 77.
38. Wallace, *Responsibility and the Moral Sentiments*, 77.
39. Wallace, *Responsibility and the Moral Sentiments*, 77.

for it is clearly not inappropriate not to wear a tie while teaching. To the extent that the normative force of the term "appropriate" diminishes, so does the potential value of employing such a term. The talk "appropriateness" for Wallace has to be more normatively robust. Wallace, rightly, I think, claims that: "If you know that a moral obligation that you accept has been breached, and that there are no exonerating circumstances that you are aware of, and you *still* do not believe that the moral response of indignation or resentment would at least be appropriate on your part, then it seems doubtful that you really do hold the colleague . . . as having done something blameworthy in this case."[40] I find Wallace's suggestion quite plausible. But I wonder why Wallace, given his own views on emotions, that is, that they are not arbitrary feelings and that they have propositional content as a result of their intimate connection to our beliefs, stops short of a thesis of the following tenor: If you know that a moral obligation that you accept has been breached, and that there are no exonerating circumstances that you are aware of, and you *still* do not *feel* indignation or resentment, then it seems doubtful that you really do hold the colleague as having done something blameworthy in this case.

A possible reaction to cases of this sort is to suggest that your not feeling a certain emotion that you believe would be appropriate to feel reveals some sort of moral failing (although it might still be seen as a moral failing even if you do not believe that it is an appropriate emotion). And such a reaction seems quite consistent with, perhaps dictated by, the sorts of cognitivist views of emotions that Wallace claims to espouse. If one believes that it is "appropriate" to feel a certain emotion in a certain situation, why is it not also "appropriate" to actually feel the emotion itself? Wallace's humble sense of "appropriate" is also problematic in that there are many other emotions and beliefs which one might also have believed to be "appropriate" when one blames others for their wrongdoing. For example, one might believe that keeping a written log of the most dramatic wrongdoings one has seen is appropriate, or one might believe, more realistically, that informing the wrongdoer of the wrongness of his actions is appropriate, or one might believe that feeling relief in realizing that one does not engage in such forms of wrongdoings is appropriate. While these beliefs range over more actions and emotions than one could possibly believe to be appropriate, they seem to be accidental to blaming itself; whereas there is a sense in which the emotions of indignation and resentment seem to be essential to blaming.

To be sure, emotions like "indignation" and "outrage" can be manipulated in order to advance all sorts of political agendas, conservative and

---

40. Wallace, *Responsibility and the Moral Sentiments,* 77.

progressive alike. Nonetheless, these emotions constitute important aspects of our humanity. If George would rape a helpless child and Arnold were to witness this atrocity without *feeling* any indignation or resentment towards George, our moral sensibilities would be offended doubly: by the rape itself and by the inhumanity of Arnold. Arnold's inhumanity would be negligibly vindicated if we knew that while he did not feel any resentment or indignation towards George for what George did, he believed that feeling such emotions would have been "appropriate." This is why the emotion of indignation has been so central in moral philosophy throughout history. Already in Aristotle we find the insight that not feeling indignation in cases where one should, and feeling indignation in cases where one should not, are quasi-vices. "Righteous indignation is the observance of a mean between Envy and Malice, and these qualities are concerned with pain and pleasure felt at the fortunes of one's neighbours. The righteously indignant man is pained by undeserved good fortune; the jealous man exceeds him and is pained by all the good fortune of others; while the malicious man so far falls short of being pained that he actually feels pleasure."[41] Aristotle reserves the term "indignation" for what others otherwise call virtuous or justified envy. While Descartes' terms are different from Aristotle's, for example, he clearly echoed Aristotle's view when he analyzed these emotions:

> Indignation is a species of hatred or aversion which one naturally has for those who do some evil, whatever its nature. And it is often mingled with envy or with pity, but it has nevertheless an altogether different object. For one is indignant only with those who do good or evil to people who do not deserve it, but one bears envy against those who receive this good, and takes Pity upon those who receive the evil. It is true that it is, in a way, doing evil to possess a good one does not deserve. This may be the reason why Aristotle and his followers, supposing that Envy is always a vice, called that which is not unvirtuous by the name of Indignation.[42]

The point that I wish to emphasize, then, is that while emotions are but one of the many Intentional states present when someone blames, they cannot just be relegated simply to the propositional content of a belief in the way Wallace does. Unlike Wallace, I would suggest that when we blame, we must *feel* the emotion and not simply believe that feeling it would be appropriate.

---

41. Rackham, trans., *Nicomachean Ethics*, by Aristotle, 105. Rackham, compellingly, suggests that "it is difficult not to think that some words have been lost here, such as 'and the righteously indignant man is pained by the undeserved misfortune of others'" (105, n. c).
42. René Descartes, *The Passions of the Soul*, trans. Stephen Voss (Indianapolis, IN: Hackett, 1989), 124.

Yet, Wallace does believe that he gives emotions an important place in his analysis of blaming. After having admitted that in some cases one could blame without feeling indignation or resentment (provided that one believes that those feelings would be appropriate), Wallace poses the following question: "if it is not really necessary to be the subject of reactive emotions for one's stance to count as holding someone morally responsible [to find someone's action blameworthy], then why bring in such emotions at all"?[43] And Wallace believes that this line of questioning misses the fact that without reference to feelings of indignation and resentment we "would not capture what is distinctive" of blaming; without reference to feelings of indignation and resentment "blame would be rendered superficial . . . reduced to a way of describing what an agent has done."[44] But if these feelings of indignation and resentment need not be actually experienced by the blaming agent, it is hard to see how Wallace's own account does justice to the centrality of these emotions in the analysis of blame.

I have chosen to discuss Wallace's account of the emotions associated with blame because I think it is valuable and sophisticated, even if I am right in the foregoing. But, beyond the specifics of my disagreement with Wallace regarding the proper place of emotions in blaming, there are good reasons to insist on the point that the feelings associated with blame must be actually experienced by the blaming agent, and not simply "believed to be appropriate." There is an obvious difference between feeling a certain emotion, on the one hand, and having the experiencing of that emotion as part of the conditions of satisfaction of an Intentional state. It is clearly different to feel, say, gratitude towards one's benefactor, and it is quite another merely to believe that feeling this gratitude would be appropriate.

As Antonio Damasio has put it, there must be a difference between feelings and thoughts.[45] Consider something as mundane as feeling happy. According to Damasio, feeling happy cannot merely be having "happy" thoughts, for then we could not really say we *feel* happy—rather, we would have to say that we *think* happy.[46] A view which reduces feelings to mere thoughts "empties the concept of feeling hopelessly. If feelings were merely clusters of thoughts with certain themes, how could they be distinguished from any other thoughts? How would they retain the functional individuality that justifies their status as a special mind process?"[47] And

---

43. Wallace, *Responsibility and the Moral Sentiments*, 78.
44. Wallace, *Responsibility and the Moral Sentiments*, 78.
45. Antonio Damasio, *Looking for Spinoza: Joy, Sorrow, and the Feeling Brain* (New York: Harcourt, 2003). Damasio distinguishes feelings from emotions. While I think that such distinction is quite useful in other contexts, it is irrelevant for my purposes here, where I use the two terms interchangeably.
46. Damasio, *Looking for Spinoza*, 86–87.
47. Damasio, *Looking for Spinoza*, 86.

recent, fascinating research on neurology, including Damasio's, actually shows that emotions are discrete, observable, testable phenomena that can be distinguished from other types of mental phenomena. Moreover, feelings as such play crucial roles in our homeostatic regulation and in our survival, both at the level of individual organisms and at the level of our species.

I cannot, of course, carry out an analysis of neurology here,[48] but these cutting-edge neurological findings are intimately linked to philosophical issues. Of interest to me is the way in which both neurology and evolutionary psychology support views according to which emotions are terribly important for our well-being.[49] For example, Damasio sensibly suggests that emotions such as "disgust, fear, happiness, sadness, sympathy, and shame aim directly at life regulation by staving off dangers or helping the organism take advantage of an opportunity, or indirectly by facilitating social relations"[50] (this would apply to the sort of indignation I am discussing here as well). Damasio, by way of a thought experiment, asks us to imagine a society in which people were not capable of experiencing emotions such as "sympathy, attachment, embarrassment" (and, I would again add, indignation). The prospects of such scenario are grim. Sensibly, Damasio concludes that:

> in a society deprived of such emotions and feelings, there would have been no spontaneous exhibition of the innate social responses that foreshadow a simple ethical system—no budding altruism, no kindness when kindness is due, no censure when censure is appropriate, no automatic sense of one's own failings. . . . There would not have been a gradual build-up of wisdom regarding social situations, natural responses and a host of contingencies such as the punishment or reward incurred by permitting or inhibiting natural responses. The codification of rules eventually expressed in systems of justice and sociopolitical organizations is hardly conceivable in those circumstances. . . . With the natural system of emotional navigation more or less disabled, there would not have been a ready possibility of fine-tuning the individual to the real world.[51]

I echo Damasio's portrayal, but, like him and many others working in these fields, with the obvious warning that the mere fact that a certain emotion, trait, or activity can be explained in evolutionary terms does not entail that it is morally correct. As Robert Wright points out, "natural

48. See, e.g., Damasio, *Looking for Spinoza*, for a beautifully written account of the main trends in such research.
49. Not only Damasio's work is related to Baruch Spinoza's metaphysics, but also to William James's psychology, and to the discussion of Intentionality in general.
50. Damasio, *Looking for Spinoza*, 39
51. Damasio, *Looking for Spinoza*, 157.

selection's indifference to the suffering of the weak is not something we need emulate."[52] Damasio argues that though anger, for example, is in many occasions a valuable emotion, it is also "a good example of an emotion whose homeostatic value is in decline."[53] To assume that whatever can be explained evolutionarily is morally correct is obviously naïve. Serious scholars in evolutionary psychology are prone to remind us that emotional and rational navigation systems developed in the course of thousands of years, and that many of the vicissitudes our ancestors might have faced are no longer relevant.

Still, taking a look at evolutionary psychology helps in establishing at least who has the burden the proof in the debate. For example, Damasio is probably right that anger is perhaps an outdated emotion: it has great potential for merely destructive behavior, but someone needs to present arguments. What about resentment (in the sense I use it here)? Is it also outdated? Given resentment's connections to rationality and given the role that it prima facie at least plays in anchoring parts of our moral life, I suggest that the burden of proof of its alleged inadequacy falls on those who suggest it is not a valuable emotion. To be sure, a person can blame too much (even if she never communicates such blame); but a no less important point is that a person without the capacity to blame (and thus to experience the emotions associated with blame) is severely morally handicapped.

My analysis of blame, then requires that the blaming agent actually *feels* resentment towards an agent for what she has done. But then how could I agree with Wallace on the fact that it is possible to blame someone without experiencing any *intense* feeling whatsoever?

The elements of my answer have already been presented at the outset; it is a matter of putting them together in order. (1) The emotions that are associated with blaming someone for his wrongdoing, in principle, track the blameworthiness of the wrongdoing. (2) There are different ways of doing wrong, that is, different modes of culpability, different ways of being blameworthy. (3) Some of these modes of culpability give rise to low degrees of blameworthiness (unconscious *culpa* or negligence, for example), and thus you could have instances of blaming properly accompanied by very tenuous feelings of indignation and resentment. (4) Wrongdoing, almost by definition, gives rise to a certain feeling of regret, but that is not the essential feeling associated with blaming, for we similarly regret harms brought about accidentally, and also harms brought about by hurricanes. If someone brings about the death of many innocent

---

52. Robert Wright, *The Moral Animal: Why We Are the Way We Are; The New Science of Evolutionary Biology* (New York: Vintage Books, 1994), 102 and *passim*.
53. Damasio, *Looking for Spinoza*, 139.

human beings accidentally, we do not blame him, and correspondingly, we do not feel indignation or resentment toward him. Why should we feel indignation toward him? For what? He did not intend or know what he was doing, and it is absurd to expect that he should have cared more about what he was doing, he was careful enough (these are the conditions that explain when someone does something accidentally). What is there to resent? We, of course, can regret the deaths. So (5) even great harms, that is, very regrettable harms can be accompanied by very little blame, and thus by very tenuous feelings of resentment or indignation. And great or very regrettable harms can also be accompanied by very little blame (in cases of negligent behavior) and very tenuous feelings or resentment or indignation. Following Williams, finally, I have urged that (6) although the sense of "wrong" in "wrongdoing" is a normative notion, it is not a thick moral notion on a par with sin or with serious moral evil—hence my developing Williams's example of the bank robbing. Blaming robber can blame idiotic robber even if she believes that robbing banks is, in general, immoral.

The combination of these elements explains how it is possible to blame someone for having done wrong while at the same time experiencing feelings of resentment or indignation so tenuous as to be negligible. I do not think that having a soft spot for a charming colleague should be the most useful sort of example that shows how this is possible. For, to the extent that you your colleague's charms prevent you from feeling resentment toward him for having done wrong, those same charms prevent you also from blaming him. Rather, the sort of situation that I think could exemplify blaming some wrongdoer at the time that one only feels negligible indignation and resentment towards him are cases in which he did wrong in an extremely blameless way (that is, negligently), and in which the wrong he did is such as to be wrong only within a rather specific context. To botch a bank robbery is a wrong only within the very *ad hoc* and narrow perspective of bank robbers. We, while not bank robbers, can observe the tribulations of blaming robber and idiotic robber, understand why blaming robber blames idiotic robber, and believe that idiotic robber's action is indeed blameworthy. And yet, as a combination of the peculiar sense in which botching bank robberies is a wrong and the very low form of blameworthiness in which idiotic robber botched the robbery (I am assuming that by calling her idiotic, it is clear that she botched the robbery negligently), we may have no significant feeling of indignation toward her.

Epilogue: Blame and Retribution

I have left pending the discussion of Wallace's claim that to the extent that an account of blaming leaves out the emotions of resentment or indignation such an account would be reductionist, providing merely a description of what someone does. Wallace assumes that merely to describe a phenomenon when that phenomenon has normative dimensions is reductionist. Yet, throughout the book I have been at pains to emphasize that a mere description of a phenomenon that has normative aspects need not be at all reductionist. For example, that intentions are the way they are entails that they have the normative force that they have; I have merely described intentions, though my description includes reference to some normative elements found in the very logical structure of intentions.

Similarly, I have described the way in which we blame each other in virtue of our wrongdoing. Such description includes reference to normative aspects of blame. In principle, we blame more severely intended wrongdoing than unintended wrongdoing. This is simply the logic of blame. I do not think that the normativity that follows from the logical structure of intending and of blaming constitutes the whole story regarding the innumerable thorny normative discussions that I have expressly avoided throughout this book. But it surely is part of the story, and a part that has been, as we saw on the earlier chapters of the book, systematically misunderstood.

Moreover, part of the strength of the merely descriptive approach that I have endorsed throughout the book is that insofar as the conclusions I have presented are correct, they enjoy a sort of prima facie plausibility once we move beyond the level of mere analysis of Intentional phenomena. For example, it is a fact of human psychology that when we believe someone did something wrong, we believe that, ceteris paribus, the world would have been better had he not done it, and it is a fact of human psychology that we believe that, given that retroactive action is impossible, the world would be better if something would happen which would offset the occurrence of the wrongdoing. These facts constitute *some* evidence in favor of preventing people from doing similar things in the future and in favor of doing something to the wrongdoer to offset the detrimental state of affairs his wrongdoing brought about.

I have stated above that I do not think that retributivism within the context of the discussion of the justification of punishment is just a façade for barbaric behavior. And though I have not discussed retributivism in any detail (since that would take me far afield), I would like to stress that the view of blame defended here in no way *entails* retributivism (though it does not preclude it, and it might loosely support it).

Punishment is an action, whether it is carried out by the state or by religious authorities, or by parents, someone inflicts it, someone does the punishing. Retributivism is a justification of this action. The account of blame I have presented is not a justification, nor does it stand in any need of justification. Of course, were someone to suggest that given the psychological facts about blame presented here, we should always act in such a way as to offset previous wrongs, she would then need a justification for such an extension of the merely descriptive view of Intentional phenomena presented here. Naturally, were someone to suggest that the psychological facts about blame presented here should be ignored when the time to do something about wrongdoing comes, she would also need a justification.

Second, I have avoided discussing what exactly, if anything at all, offsets wrongdoing. Insofar as punishment is not a purely mental phenomenon, retributive justifications of punishment might have a more difficult time avoiding such a discussion. Moreover, my account of (6), that is, of the belief that something must happen such that it offsets the wrongdoer's wrongdoing, is general enough in the sense that it does not entail that what would offsets the wrongdoer's wrongdoing is necessarily punishment. The requirement might be satisfied if immediately after raping Carol, Bob is hit by lightning and is left paralyzed. One might think that he got what he deserved by way of divine, or, if one is an atheist, by way of poetic, justice.

I do not think that the prima facie plausibility that the sorts of psychological facts about the interplay between intentions and judgments of blame necessarily point in the direction of some sort of full-blown retributivist agenda. For example, I believe that cheating, in games or in personal relations, is a bad thing, and when I see someone cheating, I hold the beliefs from (1) to (6) and, depending on the case, I also experience, in varying degrees of intensity, the sorts of emotions contained in (7). And yet, I need not in every case insist on punishing the cheater; the normative implications of the psychological phenomena that constitute blame can in some cases be overridden by other considerations. But even if these normative implications can indeed be overridden by other considerations, this would not alter the fact that these psychological facts are important. I have not discussed what to do to those we blame, that is, whether we should communicate the blame, punish them, and so on, but if my account of what goes on in our minds when we blame is on the right track, any thesis which would, without convincing argument, systematically diverge from the normative implications of intentions and judgments of blame presented here would indeed be in need of special justification.

Bibliography

American Law Institute. *The Model Penal Code and Commentaries: Official Draft and Revised Comments*. Philadelphia: American Law Institute, 1985.

Andenaes, Johannes. "Comparing Study Draft of Proposed New Federal Criminal Code to European Penal Codes." *Working Papers of the National Commission on Reform of Federal Criminal Laws* 3: 1455.

Anscombe, G. E. M. *Intention*. Oxford: Basil Blackwell, 1957.

Aquinas, Thomas. *Summa Theologiae*. London: Blackfriars, Eyre and Spottiswoode, 1974.

———. *Summa Theologiae*. Toronto: Burnes Oates & Washbourne, n.d.

Arendt, Hannah. *Eichmann in Jerusalem: A Report on the Banality of Evil*. New York: Penguin Books, 1977.

Aulisio, Mark. "In Defense of the Intention/Foresight Distinction." *American Philosophical Quarterly* 32 (1995): 341–54.

Austin, J. L. "A Plea for Excuses." *Proceedings of the Aristotelian Society* (1957).

———. *Philosophical Papers*. London: Oxford University Press, 1970.

Austin, John. *Lectures on Jurisprudence: Or the Philosophy of the Positive Law*. London, John Murray, 1861.

Bearsdley, Elizabeth. "Moral Disapproval and Moral Indignation." *Philosophy and Phenomenological Research* 31 (1970): 161–76.

Beauchamp, Thomas L., ed. *Intending Death: The Ethics of Assisted Suicide and Euthanasia*. Englewood Cliffs, NJ: Prentice Hall, 1996.

Bedau, H. A. "Classification-Based Sentencing: Some Conceptual and Ethical Problems." In *Criminal Justice*, edited by J. Roland Pennock. Nomos: Yearbook of the American Society for Political and Legal Philosophy XXVII. New York: NYU Press, 1985.

Bennett, Christopher. "The Varieties of Retributive Experience." *Philosophical Quarterly* 52, no. 207 (2002): 145–63.

Bentham, Jeremy. *The Principles of Morals and Legislation*. New York: Haffner Press, 1948.

Brandt, Richard B. "A Utilitarian Theory of Excuses." *Philosophical Review* 78 (1969): 337–61.

———. "Blameworthiness and Obligation." In *Essays in Moral Philosophy*, edited by A. I. Melden. Seattle: University of Washington Press, 1958.

Bratman, Michael E. *Faces of Intention*. Cambridge: Cambridge University Press, 1998.

———. *Intention, Plans, and Practical Reason*. Cambridge, MA: Harvard University Press, 1987.

Brentano, Franz. *Psychology from an Empirical Standpoint*. London: Routledge, 1995.

Brink, David O. *Moral Realism and the Foundations of Ethics*. Cambridge: Cambridge University Press, 1989.

Bury, R. G., trans. *The Laws*, by Plato. Cambridge, MA: Harvard University Press, 1926.

Butler, Ronald J. "Report on Analysis' Problem No. 16." *Analysis* (1978) 38: 113–18.

Canals, José, and Henry Dahl. "The Standard Penal Code for Latin America." *American Journal of Law* 17 (1990): 236–301.

Chan, David K. "Non-Intentional Action." *American Philosophical Quarterly* 32 (1995).

Charles, David. *Aristotle's Philosophy of Action*. Ithaca, NY: Cornell University Press, 1984.

Child, James W. "Donald Davidson and Section 2.01 of the Model Penal Code." *Criminal Justice Ethics* (1992): 31.

Chisholm, Roderick. *Person and Object*. LaSalle, IL: Open Court, 1976.

Cleveland, Timothy. "Is Davidson a Volitionist in Spite of Himself?" *Southwestern Journal of Philosophy* (1991): 181–93

———. "Trying Without Willing." *Australasian Journal of Philosophy* (1992): 324–42

Código Penal Tipo Para Latinoamérica. Santiago de Chile: Editorial Jurídica de Chile, 1973.

Cohen, A., ed. *The Soncino Chumash: The Five Books of Moses with Haphtaroth*. London: Soncino, 1956.

Compassion in Dying v. Washington, United States Court of Appeals for the Ninth Circuit (1996), 79 F3.d 79024.

Cooney, William. "Affirmative Action and the Doctrine of Double Effect." *Journal of Applied Philosophy* (1989): 201–4.

Council on Ethical and Judicial Affairs, American Medical Association. "Decisions Near the End of Life." *Journal of the American Medical Association* 276 (1992): 2229–33.

Dahl, Henry. "The Influence and Application of the Standard Penal Code for Latin America." *American Journal of Criminal Law* 17 (1990): 235–62.

Damasio, Antonio. *Looking for Spinoza: Joy, Sorrow, and the Feeling Brain*. New York: Harcourt, 2003.

Damaska, Mirjan. "Comparing Study Draft of Proposed New Federal Criminal Code to European Penal Codes." *Working Papers of the National Commission on Reform of Federal Criminal Laws* 3: 1487.

Daube, David. *Roman Law: Linguistic, Social and Philosophical Aspects*. Edinburgh: Edinburgh University Press, 1969.

———. *Studies in Biblical Law*. New York: Ktav Publishing House, 1969.

Davidson, Donald. *Essays on Actions and Events*. Oxford: Oxford University Press, 1980.

————. "On Saying That." *Synthese* 19: 130–46.

Davies, Michael. "Harm and Retribution." *Philosophy and Public Affairs* (1986).

Davis, Lawrence. *Theory of Action*. Englewood Cliffs, NJ: Prentice Hall, 1979.

Descartes, René. *The Passions of the Soul*. Translated by Stephen Voss. Indianapolis, IN: Hackett, 1989, 124.

Duff, R. A. *Intention, Agency and Criminal Liability: Philosophy of Action and the Criminal Law*. Oxford: Basil Blackwell, 1990.

————. *Punishment, Communication, and Community*. Oxford: Oxford University Press, 2001.

————. "Strict Liability, Legal Presumptions, and the Presumption of Innocence." In *Appraising Strict Liability*, edited by Andrew P. Simester. Oxford: Oxford University Press, 2005, forthcoming.

————. *Trials and Punishment*. Cambridge: Cambridge University Press, 1986.

Dworkin, Gerald. "Intention, Foreseeability, and Responsibility." In *Responsibility, Character, and the Emotions*, edited by Ferdinand Schoeman. Cambridge: Cambridge University Press, 1992.

Eser, Albin, and George P. Fletcher, eds. *Justification and Excuse: Comparative Criminal Law Theory*. Freiburg: Max Planck Institute, 1987.

Feinberg, Joel. *Doing and Deserving: Essays in the Theory of Responsibility*. Princeton: Princeton University Press, 1970.

Firth, Roderick. "Ethical Absolutism and the Ideal Observer." *Philosophy and Phenomenological Research* 12 (1952): 317–45.

Fischer, John Martin. "Recent Work in Moral Responsibility." *Ethics* 110 (1999): 93–139.

Fletcher, George P. *Rethinking Criminal Law*. Boston: Little, Brown and Company, 1978.

Gagarin, Michael. *Drakon and Early Athenian Homicide Law*. New Haven, CT: Yale University Press, 1981.

Gewirth, Alan. *Reason and Morality*. Chicago: University of Chicago Press, 1978.

Goldman, Alvin. "The Volitional Theory Revisited." In *Action Theory*, edited by Myles Brand and Douglas Walton. Dordrecht: Reidel, 1975.

Gorr, Michael. "Willing, Trying and Doing." *Australasian Journal of Philosophy* (1979): 237–49.

Gorr, Michael, and Terence Horgan. "Intentional and Unintentional Action." *Philosophical Studies* 41 (1982).

Harman, Gilbert. "Practical Reasoning." In Mele, *The Philosophy of Action*.

Hart, H. L. A. *Punishment and Responsibility: Essays in the Philosophy of Law*. Oxford: Clarendon Press, 1968.

————. *The Concept of Law*. 2nd ed. Oxford: Oxford University Press, 1997.

Holmes, Oliver Wendell. *The Common Law*. Boston: Little, Brown, 1881.

Horder, Jeremy. "Criminal Culpability: The Possibility of a General Theory." *Law and Philosophy* 12: 193–215.

Hornsby, Jennifer. *Actions*. London/Boston: Routledge & Kegan Paul, 1980.

Hudson, W. D., ed. *The Is/Ought Question: A Collection of Papers on the Central Problem of Moral Philosophy*. London: MacMillan, 1963.

Humberstone, I. L. "Direction of Fit." *Mind* 101 (1992): 59–83.

Husak, Douglas. *Philosophy of Criminal Law*. Totowa, NJ: Rowman and Littlefield, 1987.

———. "Review of White's *Misleading Cases*." *Ethics* (1993).

———. "Varieties of Strict Liability." *The Canadian Journal of Law and Jurisprudence* 8, no. 2 (1995): 189–225.

Irwin, Terence, trans. *Nicomachean Ethics*, by Aristotle. Indianapolis: Hackett, 1985.

Kant, Immanuel. *The Metaphysics of Morals*. Translated by Mary McGregor. Cambridge: Cambridge University Press, 1991.

Katz, Leo. *Bad Acts and Guilty Minds*. Chicago: Chicago University Press, 1987.

Kelly, J. M. *A Short History of Western Legal Thought*. Oxford: Clarendon Press, 1992.

Kenner, Lionel. "On Blaming." *Mind* 76: 238–49.

Lacey, Nicola. *State Punishment: Political Principles and Community Values*. London: Routledge, 1988.

LePore, Ernest, and Robert Van Gulick, eds. *John Searle and His Critics*. Oxford: Blackwell, 1991.

Locke, John. *An Essay Concerning Human Understanding*. Oxford: Oxford University Press, 1951.

Lowe, E. J. "An Analysis of Intentionality." *Philosophical Quarterly* 30 (1980).

———. "Neither Intentional nor Unintentional." *Analysis* 38 (1978).

MacDowell, Douglas M., trans. *Against Meidias*, by Demosthenes. Oxford: Clarendon Press, 1990.

Meiland, J. W. "Are There Unintentional Actions?" *Philosophical Review* 72 (1963): 377–81.

Mele, Alfred R., ed. *The Philosophy of Action*. Oxford: Oxford University Press, 1997.

Mill, John Stuart. *Utilitarianism*. Indianapolis, IN: Hackett Publishing Company, 1979.

Mitias, Michael. "Is Retributivism Inconsistent with lex talionis?" *Rivista Internazionale di Filosofia del Diritto* 60 (1983): 211–30.

Mommsem, Theodor. *Romisches Strafrecht*. Graz: Akademische Druck, 1955.

Mommsem, Theodor, and Paulus Krueger, trans. *Corpus Iuris Civilis*. Berlin: Apud Weimannos, 1928.

Moore, G. E. *Principia Ethica*. Cambridge: Cambridge University Press, 1992.

Moore, Michael. *Act and Crime*. Oxford: Oxford University Press, 1993.

———. "Moral Reality." *University of Wisconsin Law Review* (1982): 1061–156.

———. "Moral Reality Revisited." *Michigan Law Review* 90 (1992): 2424–533.

———. *Placing Blame*. Oxford: Clarendon Press, 1997.

Moser, Paul K. and Alfred Mele. "Intentional Action." In Mele, *The Philosophy of Action*.

Mueller, Gerhard O. W. "The German Draft Criminal Code 1960—An Evaluation in Terms of American Criminal Law." *University of Illinois Law Forum* 25 (1961).

Murphy, Jeffrie G. and Jean Hampton. *Forgiveness and Mercy*. Cambridge: Cambridge University Press, 1988.

Nussbaum, Martha. *Upheavals of Thought: The Intelligence of Emotions*. Cambridge: Cambridge University Press, 2001.

O'Shaughnessy, Brian. "Searle's Theory of Action." In LePore and Van Gulick, *John Searle and his Critics*.

————. "Trying (As the Mental 'Pineal Gland')." *Journal of Philosophy* 70: 365–86.

————. *The Will*. Oxford: Oxford University Press, 1980.

Pascal, Blaise. *The Provincial Letters: Moral Teachings of the Jesuit Fathers Opposed to the Church of Rome and Latin Vulgate*. Toronto: William Briggs, 1893.

Plato. *Plato: The Collected Dialogues*. Translated by Hugh Tredennick. Princeton: Princeton University Press, 1961.

Primorac, Igor. "On Retributivism and the Lex Talionis." *Rivista Internazionale di Filosofia del Diritto* 61 (1984): 83–94.

Pringsheim, Fritz. "The Inner Relationship Between English and Roman Law." *Cambridge Law Journal* 5 (1935): 347–65.

Putnam, Hilary. *Reason, Truth and History*. Cambridge: Cambridge University Press, 1981.

Rackham, H., trans. *Nicomachean Ethics*, by Aristotle. Cambridge, MA: Harvard University Press, 1926.

Rawls, John. *A Theory of Justice*. 2nd ed. Cambridge, MA.: Harvard University Press, 1999.

Rein, Wilhelm. *Das Kriminalrecht der Romer von Romulus bis auf Justinian*. Aalen: Scientia, 1962.

Robinson, Paul H. *Structure and Function in the Criminal Law*. Oxford: Clarendon Press, 1997.

Ryle, Gilbert. *The Concept of Mind*. Chicago: University of Chicago Press, 1949.

Saunders, Trevor. *Plato's Penal Code: Tradition, Controversy, and Reform in Greek Penology*. Oxford: Oxford University Press, 1994.

Sayre-McCord, George, ed. *Essays on Moral Realism*. Ithaca, NY: Cornell University Press, 1988.

Schofield, C. I., ed. *Oxford New International Version Schofield Study Bible*. New York: Oxford University Press, 1984.

Schofield, Malcolm. "Aristotelian Mistakes." *Proceedings of the Cambridge Philological Society* 19 (1973): 66–70.

Searle, John R. "How to Derive an 'Ought' from 'Is.'" *Philosophical Review* 73 (1964): 43–58.

————. *Intentionality: An Essay in the Philosophy of Mind*. Cambridge: Cambridge University Press, 1983.

————. *Rationality in Action*. Cambridge: MA: MIT Press, 2001.

————. "Reply to O'Shaughnessy." In LePore and Van Gulick, *John Searle and His Critics*.

Searle, John R., Barry Smith, Leo Zaibert, and Josef Moural. "Rationality in Action: An Exchange." *Philosophical Explorations* 4, no. 2 (2001): 66–94.

Shanker, Stuart G. "The Nature of Willing." In *Wittgenstein's Intentions*. New York: Garland, 1993.

Sher, George. *Desert*. Princeton, Princeton University Press, 1987.

Sidgwick, Henry. *The Methods of Ethics*. London: MacMillan, 1907.

Simester, A. P. "On the So-Called Requirement for Voluntary Action." *Buffalo Criminal Law Review* 1, no. 2: 403–31.

Simons, Kenneth W. "Rethinking Mental States." *Boston University Law Review* (1992): 463–554.

Smith, A. T. H. "On *Actus Reus* and *Mens Rea*." In *Reshaping the Criminal Law: Essays in Honour of Glanville Williams*, edited by P. R. Glazebrook. London: Stevens and Sons, 1978.

Smith, Adam. *The Theory of Moral Sentiments*. Buffalo, NY: Prometheus, 2000.

Smith, Barry, ed. *John Searle*. Contemporary Philosophy in Focus. Cambridge: Cambridge University Press, 2003.

Sorabji, Richard. *Necessity, Cause, and Blame: Perspectives in Aristotle's Theory*. Ithaca, NY: Cornell University Press, 1980.

Squires, J. E. R. "Blame." *The Philosophical Quarterly* 18, no. 70 (1968): 56.

Stalley, R. F. *An Introduction to Plato's Laws*. Oxford: Basil Blackwell, 1983.

———. "Austin's Account of Action." *Journal of the History of Philosophy*, 1980.

Strauss, Leo. *The Argument and the Action of Plato's Laws*. Chicago: University of Chicago Press, 1975.

Taylor, A. E., trans. *The Laws of Plato*. London: J. M. Dent and Sons, 1934.

Thomson, Judith Jarvis. "Killing, Letting Die, and the Trolley Problem." *The Monist* (1976): 204–17.

Usher, Stephen, trans. *On the Crown*, by Demosthenes. Warminster: Aris & Phillips, 1993.

Van Caenengem, R. C. *The Birth of the Common Law*. Cambridge: Cambridge University Press, 1973.

Vince, J. H, trans. *Demosthenes*. Cambridge, MA: Harvard University Press, 1935.

Vinogradoff, Paul. *Outlines of Historical Jurisprudence*. Oxford: Oxford University Press, 1922.

———. *Roman Law in Medieval Europe*. Cambridge: Speculum Historiale, 1968.

Wallace, R. Jay. *Responsibility and the Moral Sentiments*. Cambridge, MA: Harvard University Press, 1996.

Welzel, Hans. *Das Deutsche Strafrecht*. 11th. ed. Berlin: Gruyter, 1988.

White, Alan R. *The Grounds of Liability*. Clarendon Press, Oxford, 1985.

Williams, Bernard. *Making Sense of Humanity and Other Philosophical Papers 1982–1993*. Cambridge: Cambridge University Press, 2003.

Williams, Glanville. *The Mental Element in Crime*. Jerusalem: Magnes Press, 1965.

Wittgenstein, Ludwig. *The Blue and Brown Books*. New York: Harper & Row, 1960.

———. *Philosophical Investigations*. Translated by G. E. M. Anscombe. New York: MacMillan, 1953.

———. *Remarks on the Philosophy of Psychology*. Translated by G. E. M. Anscombe. Chicago: University of Chicago Press, 1980.

Woozley, A. D. "Plato on Killing in Anger." *Philosophical Quarterly* (1972): 303–17.

Wright, Robert. *The Moral Animal: Why We Are the Way We Are; The New Science of Evolutionary Biology*. New York: Vintage Books, 1994.

Zaibert, Leo. "Collective Intentions and Collective Intentionality." *American Journal of Sociology and Economics*, 60, no. 1 (2003): 209–32. Reprinted in *Searle and the Institutions of Social Reality*, ed. Lawrence Moss and David Koepsell, 209–32. Oxford: Blackwell, 2003.

———. "Intentionality, Voluntariness, and Culpability: A Historical-Philosophical Analysis." *Buffalo Criminal Law Review* 1, no. 2: 459–501.

———. "Intentions, Promises and Obligations." In Barry Smith, *John Searle*, 53–84.

———. "Normative Insufficiency of Gewirth's Principle of Generic Consistency." *Apuntes Filosoficos* 4 (1994): 195–210.

———. "On Deference and the Spirit of the Laws." *Archiv für Rechts- und Sozialphilosophie* 82 (1996): 460–71.

———. "Philosophical Analysis and the Criminal Law." *Buffalo Criminal Law Review* 4, no. 1 (2001): 100–39.

———. "Process Teleology: John Dewey's Reconstructed Virtue Ethics." *Revista Venezolana de Filosofia* (1996): 143–63.

———. "Punishment, Justifications, and Institutions." *Studies in Law, Politics, and Society* (2003): 51–83.

———. "Punishment, Liberalism, and Communitarianism." *Buffalo Criminal Law Review* 6, no. 1 (2002): 673–90.

———. *Punishment and Retribution.* Aldershot: Ashgate, forthcoming 2005.

Zaibert, Leo, and Jorge J. E. Gracia. "Philosophy of Law in Latin America." In *The Philosophy of Law: An Encyclopedia*, ed. Christopher B. Gray. New York: Garland Publishing, 1999.

Zeyl, Donald J., trans. *Plato's Gorgias.* Indianapolis, IN: Hackett, 1987.

Index

action
  intentional, 24, 51, 102, 177
  and intentionality, 7
  and intentions, 2–3, 17–18, 32,
      149, 179, 180–81, 184, 186,
      188–89, 191–92, 193, 200
  and nonaction, relation to
      voluntary and involuntary, 149
  and personal identity, 209–211
  volitional theory of, 2, 97, 111–12,
      114–22, 196
acts of will, 111, 117
acts of willing, 115–16
  and infinite regress, 121–22
  problems of, 121
actus reus, 109–110, 134
adikia, 61, 62, 71
akousion, 109
akousios, 2, 44–45, 46–47, 49–50, 62,
      102
akrasia, 190
Analysis, 159, 162, 163
Andenaes, Johannes, 107
Anglo-American legal tradition,
      62–63
  influences on, 82
Anscombe, G. E. M., 7, 114
Aquinas, Thomas, 67, 86, 109
  and doctrine of double effect, 67,
      68, 70, 72–76, 90
  false dichotomy in, 70

on foreseeing vs. intending, 70, 73,
      76
  on "intended accidentally," 71–72,
      73
  and intended/unintended
      distinction, 70
  Summa Theologiae, 68, 69
Arendt, Hannah, 20–21
Aristotle, 23, 33, 38, 44, 67–68, 71,
      72, 84, 90, 92, 109, 110, 240
  on action, 52
  and ignorance, 55, 58
  intended/unintended, 54,
      55–57, 58
  nonintended, 55
  under compulsion, 54
  adikia in, 58
  on *akousios*, 2, 53, 54, 57, 58
  on *atychema*, 58
  on choice, 57
  on *hamatema*, 58
  on *hekousios*, 52, 53, 54, 57, 58
  Nicomachean Ethics, 52, 53, 58, 63
  theory of culpability, 57–60
  virtue ethics, 52
Arnauld, Antoine, 77
assisted suicide, and doctrine of
      double effect, 80
atychema, 61, 71, 93
Augustine, Saint, 71, 73
Aulisio, Mark, 79